INTERVIEWING
A Forensic Guide to Interrogation

INTERVIEWING
A Forensic Guide to Interrogation
A Second Edition

By

CHARLES L. YESCHKE

CHARLES C THOMAS • PUBLISHER
Springfield • Illinois • U.S.A.

Published and Distributed Throughout the World by

CHARLES C THOMAS • PUBLISHER
2600 South First Street
Springfield, Illinois 62794-9265

© *1993 by* CHARLES C THOMAS • PUBLISHER

ISBN 0-398-05867-9

Library of Congress Catalog Card Number: 93-16911

First Edition, 1989
Second Edition, 1993

With THOMAS BOOKS *careful attention is given to all details of manufacturing
and design. It is the Publisher's desire to present books that are satisfactory as to
their physical qualities and artistic possibilities and appropriate for their particular
use.* THOMAS BOOKS *will be true to those laws of quality that assure a good
name and good will.*

Printed in the United States of America
SC-R-3

Library of Congress Cataloging-in-Publication Data

Yeschke, Charles L.
    Interviewing : a forensic guide to interrogation / by Charles L.
Yeschke. — A 2nd ed.
        p.   cm.
    Includes bibliographical references and index.
    ISBN 0-398-05867-9
    1. Interviewing in law enforcement.   2. Police questioning — United
States.
HV8073.Y47   1993
363.2'54 — dc20   93-16911
                                                                            CIP

This presentation is dedicated to Louis L. Yeschke, my father, a beat cop in Pittsburgh, Pennsylvania for most of his thirty-year career, a detective for a while. From time to time he took me with him to visit his patrol area where he pointed out some who were down and out. I watched as he dealt with them in a warm, friendly way. Although not a perfect human being, he tried to live the motto: "There, but for the Grace of God, go I." He represents those who have served, those who have cared.

INTRODUCTION

Interviewing is a complex topic formed from many creative ideas. This presentation is intended to assist in training the world's best investigators as they serve their communities. With self-appreciation, vision, and purpose, interviewers can commit themselves to such service, empowered, contributing to the advancement of democracy.

CONTENTS

INTERVIEWING
A Forensic Guide to Interrogation

Chapter One

INTERVIEWING V. INTERROGATING

While the roles of interviewer and interrogator are still looked upon as synonymous,[58] they are distinctly different in many ways. Through both, truthful information is sought; however, the motive, unique directives used, and the potential use of the final results of each are major differences.

Interviewing, darting to an aim with compassion, a means by which to collect testimonial evidence. Simply stated, an interview is a dynamic human interaction having the purpose of collecting truthful data to be used for mature decision making and just action-taking. An interrogation is a face-to-face meeting with the distinct task of gaining an admission or confession in a real or apparent violation of law, policy, regulation or other restriction.

Interviewing is defined as: the task of gathering information;[28] "a process of dyadic communication with a predetermined and serious purpose designed to interchange behavior and involves the asking and answering of questions";[67 p.5] "a specialized pattern of verbal interaction initiated for a specific purpose, and focused on some specific content area, with consequent elimination of extraneous material"[35 p.16] an interviewer-interviewee interaction with the purposes of identifying the interviewee's problem and gathering information upon which a solution to that problem can be based.[10 p.5] " ... a craft that can be learned, polished, and improved through practice";[25 p.271] "a face-to-face discussion between two people, directed towards some specific purpose."[133 p.319]

> Interviewing is very much like piano playing, a fair degree of skill can be acquired with the necessity of formal instruction. But there is a world of difference in craftsmanship, in technique, and in finesse between the amateur who plays "by ear" and the accomplished concert pianist. The self-instructed player mechanically reproduces on the keyboard certain melodies that have been committed to memory; the artist, by skillfully blending mastery of musical theory, countless hours of practice, and personal interpretation, cre-

3

ates an effect that is technically precise, pleasing to the audience, and expressive to the pianist's inner feelings."[43]p.1

Some authors state: "Interrogation is essentially an interview between the interrogator and the person being interrogated. The basic purpose of an interrogation is the securing of an admission of guilt from a person who has committed a crime." Among the "host of other purposes" of interrogation, they continue: "to eliminate suspects to the commission of the crime"; "to determine full facts and circumstances of a crime"; as well as "to determine the full details concerning the crime."[3]p.22-24

They continue: "Interrogation of all available suspects will rapidly reveal the individuals who could not have committed the crime, and will point the strong finger of suspicion at the most likely suspects."[3]p.30 " ... one elementary and very basic fact concerning interrogation . . . interrogation is no more or less than a process and a technique with a very narrow and well-defined purpose, the securing of a confession of guilt from a guilty person with reference to the commission of a crime."[3] pp.39-40

If the above holds true, there is a real problem in accusing "all" victims, witnesses, or suspects. Such treatment is abusive and unnecessary. There is no need to interrogate "all." Fundamentally, I agree when they state: "The basic purpose of an interrogation is the securing of an admission of guilt from a person who has committed a crime."[3]p.24 However, if all suspects are interrogated as though involved in delinquent or criminal action, such treatment is abusive and intimidating to most people concerned. Such action is self-defeating in the long run.

Others distinguish interviewing and interrogating: "Effective Interviewing and interrogating is an art."[58]p.9 They suggest: "Let's agree on the definition that an interview is a meeting between two or more persons to talk about a specific matter. This would encompass interrogation, that is, the art and mechanics of questioning for the purpose of exploring or resolving issues. The concept of Interviewing is associated with a more informal atmosphere." They continue, "In this book, both terms (Interviewing and interrogating) will be used interchangeably."[58]p.21

In contrast, I consider interviewing and interrogating separate and distinct in many significant ways. I don't deem it appropriate to use the terms interviewing and interrogating interchangeably. Further, interrogating each suspect as though culpable or delinquent is nonsense, leading to negative results. Falsely accusing innocent people of delinquency is not justified and leads many victims, witnesses, and suspects to consider some investigators to be abusive, insensitive, rude, impolite, and authoritarian.

I believe forensic interviewing can be a science, a study of verbal and nonverbal communication in specific human interactions dealing with uncovering truthful facts, information and phenomena through inquiry of victims, witnesses and suspects, while forensic interrogations deal with gaining admissions or confessions from subjects. The central objective of both concern specific topics as applied to questions pertaining to, connected with, or used in courts of law, public discussion and debate.[42]

I view Forensic Interviewing as Polyphasic, based upon my applied observational experience. The flow chart, following, and its related process can assist interviewers to guard against mistakes and increase the possibility of having correct conditions necessary for repeated success. There is implied, through the process discussed, a greater possibility of interview control.

As an interviewer, you are either a student of or a specialist in gathering truthful testimonial evidence. Such students become more aware, more observant, and more interested in comprehending dynamics of interview interactions. They attempt to gain greater insight into interview phenomena to more concisely define and classify processes of interview situations to be better able to establish hypotheses and predict future outcomes of investigative inquiries.

The general topic of science, now considered, brings attention to its relationship to forensic interviewing.

A scientific study is generally held to mean one conducted precisely, systematically and quantitatively.[69] It is a complex activity which is intellectual, practical, and social, satisfying the demands by most scientists for understanding and controlling the natural world. Those aspects interlock and help characterize the enterprise of science.[40,60]

Science is organized knowledge obtained and added to by means of scientific method, which is a set of rules for thinking and a way of looking at the world. It is organized common sense, a method of asking questions about the universe.[21] In their early stages, most sciences are primarily observational, and there are a few quite highly developed sciences which, by their nature, remain so.

In observational sciences, such as astronomy and geology, repetition of a situation at will is intrinsically impossible, and their possible precision is limited to precision of description. The subject matter of an individual science is something in the world of phenomena, having to do with any facts, circumstances or experiences apparent to the senses that can be scientifically described or appraised.[65] "... the most important instrument in science must always be the mind of man.[27] People are as much proper objects of scientific study as the rest of the material world.[15]

> *Man is the measure of all things.*
>
> — *Protagoras, c 481–411 BC*
> *(quoted by Plato, in Theaetelus)*

Thus, observational scientists at their best have one tool: the human mind. One great value of high-quality observational scientists is that they can go into a new region or field, and in one relatively short period of continuous study, be it for a day or a month or a year, come up with a sound interpretation of natural conditions, involving the history of its past, and predictions as to its future ... sound interpretive methods epitomize brilliant scientific intellects.[27]

One potent method of checking correctness or truth is repetition. An investigator's experience indicates objects and situations which repeat themselves. By establishing conditions necessary for repetition, scientists/interviewers verify previous description or observation by finding whether the same results are obtained as before, thus guarding against possible previous mistakes and increasing presumptive probability of having correctly stated conditions necessary for repetition. Possibility of repetition implies possibility of control, although such control may be ideal rather than actual.[60]

The scientific method involves mainly inductive logic, which requires repeated observations of an experiment or of an event. From observing many different examples, scientists can draw a general conclusion.[27] Scientists also use deductive logic, reasoning from known scientific principles or rules to draw a conclusion relating to a specific case. Accuracy of a conclusion reached by deductive logic depends upon accuracy of principles and rules used.[65]

1. The first step in the scientific method is the recognition of a problem. A science can develop when we want to know, are curious about, and/or want to understand an obstacle or a difficulty. Recognition of problems remains a superior intellectual expression of human brains.
2. The second step of the scientific method involves accurate observations and measurements of things involved in the problem.

3. In the third step, data are organized and analyzed. Similarities and dissimilarities are noted. Data are arranged in some meaningful order and classified. From classifications, generalizations can be made as to common properties of different groups of data.

4. An hypothesis or hypotheses are formulated which are tentative solutions or interpretations of phenomena, seeming reasonable in light of available information.

Steps 2, 3 and 4 are often collectively known as induction, that is, reasoning from the particular to the general.

5. Assuming the proposed hypothesis is valid, the scientist then considers what other situations must follow. That is, reasoning out the consequences of this tentative solution. If such and such is true, then such and such must also occur and be true. This is reasoning from the general to the particular, and is known as deduction.

6. The final step in this procedure of the scientific method is verification of deductions; that is, if such and such should occur, does it occur? If it does occur, we get bolder and frame a theory. If the theory becomes firmly established, we frame a law. Scientific laws are only manmade generalities not binding on nature, but hold only for situations under which they were formulated. They are neither sacred nor true.[27]

Applied scientists are job-holding realists. The successful forensic interviewer has undoubtedly been a very heavy component of, and jolts from, serendipity, exhaustively explored intuitions, persistently pursued hunches and fortunate conclusions.[27] Scientists derive some value from intuition, ingenuity, and success in solving intractable problems. Serendipitous discoveries have some significance scientifically and the incompleteness of science is a fact of scientific life.[74] It is difficult to tell in what order I actually use steps of the scientific method. The human mind probably does not actually solve problems in a systematic fashion.[65]

Forensic Truth

Forensic interviewing at times seems to be unwanted, and sometimes considered an unwarranted penetration into the secrets of another. It has been thought to invade privacy, unconstitutionally deprive fifth amendment rights, and delve into the conscience, and invade the area of free will. I try to remember, however, that reality indicates that the evaluation of any truth or deception is a human diagnostic process. In other words, a forensic interviewer is in the role of a Diogenes, Aquinas, or Peirce all searching for truth.

I recommend interviewers fulfill the canon of science, practice right conduct and be professionally competent. The science, moral theology, has a body of well-developed principles which deal with the right to inquire. Is your right to inquire justified? Secondly, are the means used to achieve the end illicit or unjustifiable?

With regard to the right to inquire, interviewers may sometimes assume that once any permission form is signed, they have established that right. But, does my desire to persistently encourage the interviewee to, initially, reveal evidence or, subsequently, confess sometimes border on the use of illicit means to an end? There is no absolute civil duty for anyone to comply, and may legitimately appeal to the doctrine of self-incrimination, the moment such encouragement begins. However, in a democratic society it is important to balance off the rights of all. The right to inquire is established when "a notable good is to be achieved or a notable harm prevented, by someone charged with this duty, or having a legitimate concern therewith, and where inquiry without law is illicit, so there is no right without limitation upon rights in general."[85]

Legal Factors to Consider

Rejection of a confession, as evidence at trial, is one penalty for noncompliance of certain basic legal requirements. A confession must be voluntary before it will be acceptable as evidence. Seeking a confession of interviewees is inappropriate, at least initially. Hence, first and foremost, seek to uncover the truth, and a confession may follow.

To avoid nullification of my efforts, I try to use proper procedures in arranging for the interrogation of a subject, as well as using proper procedures during the interrogation itself. Before a confession is acceptable as evidence it must be voluntary.

Legally, interrogation may be defined as the asking of a question, making a verbal comment, displaying an object, or the presentation of police reports. Those actions may be calling for a response that may be of an incriminating nature. In addition to direct questioning, the subtle use of the other above mentioned actions are considered "function equivalents" by the Supreme Court as held in Brewer v. Williams, 430 US. 387, 97 S.

CT 1232 (1977). They can be considered a form of questioning, but an exception can be found in Rhode Island v. Innes, 446 US. 291, 100 S. Ct. 1682 (1980).

The Supreme Court of the United States, 1979, Dunaway v. New York, 442 US. 200, 99 S. Ct. 2248, held that a confession obtained after a "pickup" without probable cause (i.e., reasonable grounds) to make an actual arrest could not be used as evidence.

If you are a law enforcement officer, make it clear that a suspect is not under arrest, if that is the situation, and is free to leave if desired. If the inquiry is held in an official location, such as a station house, be sure interviewees realize they are not being detained or in custody, if such be the case. Voluntary response is vital in these matters. Make no promises or threats while questioning a suspect.

As a defense against admissibility of confessions in court, attorneys are using the argument that psychological coercion was used to obtain some confessions. That argument is subsequently explored in this presentation.

Beyond the voluntariness test of confessions, the Supreme Court of the United States ruled in 1966, in Miranda v. Arizona, 384 US. 436 86 S. Ct. 1602, that before a person in police custody or otherwise deprived of freedom "in any significant way" could be interrogated, the following warnings must be given:

1. That he has a right to remain silent, and that he need not answer any questions;
2. That if he does answer questions, his answers can be used as evidence against him;
3. That he has a right to consult with a lawyer before or during the questioning of him by the police; and
4. That if he cannot afford to hire a lawyer one will be provided for him without costs.

The Fifth Circuit Court of Appeals expressed the view (pp. 881–882) in Harryman v. Estelle, 616 F. 2d 870 (5th Cir. 1980) that Miranda applies only to "Investigative custodial questioning aimed at eliciting evidence of a crime." Subjects in custody must understand what they are being told. You are not permitted to talk them out of not wanting to talk once they decide not to do so. If any subjects want a lawyer at any time, you are not permitted to talk them out of that desire. All of this is to ensure subjects in custody know they have the right to remain silent.

After receiving required warnings, and expressing willingness to answer questions, the subject in custody may legally answer your questions. But, keep in mind that it is totally unnecessary to embellish or add new warnings because you may be apprehensive of the consequences associated with Miranda. In California v. Prysock, July 1981, the Supreme Court of the United States stated that there is no requirement "that the content of the Miranda warnings be a virtual incantation of the precise language contained in Miranda." "Quite the contrary" said the court, "Miranda itself indicated no talismanic incantation was required to satisfy its strictures." Thus, use advisement, not admonishment, in presenting Miranda.

A dictionary definition of a talisman is anything whose presence exercises a remarkable or powerful influence on human feelings or actions. Incantation is defined as the chanting or uttering of words; repetitious wordiness.

In 1976 the Supreme Court held that the focus of suspicion was not the test of when the Miranda warnings are to be given to a suspect. It held that the warnings were required only in police custodial situations. At that time the Supreme Court removed the misconception that the warnings are to be given to anyone upon whom suspicion is "focused," as held in Beckwith v. United States, 425 US. 341, 96 S. Ct. 1612. Police custody is the test, not focus.[34]

In the case of Orozco v. Texas, 394 US. 324, 89 S. Ct. 1095 (1969) "custody" and deprivation of freedom in any significant way is illustrated and the key factors are the time of the interrogation, the number of officers involved, and the apparent formal arrest of the subject. As far as non-custodial interrogation within a police facility is concerned, the Supreme Court of the United States, in 1977, held that "a non-custodial" situation is not converted to one in which Miranda applies simply because a reviewing court concludes that, even in the absence of any formal arrest or restraint of freedom of movement, the questioning took place in a "coercive environment." In that case, Oregon v. Mathiason, 429 US. 492, 97 S. Ct. 711, the court considered the circumstances of the interrogation when it provided the opinion:

> Any interview of one suspected of a crime by a police officer will have coercive aspects to it, simply by virtue of the fact that the police officer is part of a law enforcement system which may ultimately cause the suspect to be charged with a crime. But police officers are not required to administer Miranda warnings to everyone whom they question. Nor is the requirement of warnings to be imposed simply because the questioning takes place in the station house, or

because the questioned person is one whom the police suspect. Miranda warnings are required only where there has been such a restriction on a person's freedom as to render him "in custody." It was that sort of coercive environment to which Miranda by its terms was made applicable, and to which it is limited.

If suspects, not in custody, freely consent to be interviewed or interrogated, there is no requirement they be given Miranda Warnings. If an interviewee starts a confession, let it continue without interruption to the conclusion of the confession. Later, warnings are to be given to avoid any court holding custody began at the conclusion of the confession.

A custodial subject can waive constitutional rights. Those rights are often reduced to writing and signed, but oral waivers will suffice. Remember not to overdo on the explanation of Miranda.

I consider it important to be fair and practical when interrogating anyone, in particular a custodial subjects (see Intensity Levels 4–6, Polyphasic Flow Chart). It is vital to avoid saying or doing anything that might cause an innocent person to confess. Because reviewing and encouraging are major efforts when seeking the truth as reflected in a confession, legal tactics and techniques which can be used may include the following tactics for interrogation:

1. Exhibit confidence of the interrogatee's responsibility.
2. Use circumstantial evidence to convince the interrogatee to be truthful.
3. Use the interrogatee's behavior symptoms as examples of deception indicators.
4. Empathize with the interrogatee to assist rationalization and face saving.
5. Reduce and minimize the significance of the matter under investigation.
6. Use nonjudgmental acceptance when communicating with the interrogatee.
7. Point out the futility of not telling the truth.

Trickery and deceit are often used in the interrogation situation. The Supreme Court gave tacit recognition to that fact and to its necessity in Frazier v. Cupp, 394 US. 731, 89 S. Ct. 1420 (1969). The court held:

> The fact that the police misrepresented the statements that (the suspected accomplice) had made is, while relevant, insufficient in our view to make this otherwise voluntary confession inadmissible. These cases must be decided by viewing the "totality of the circumstances . . .

If you are not a police officer, then the Miranda decision does not affect you unless you are a moonlighting officer or acting in cooperation with police as a police agent. It is important to realize, however, that regardless of your role as an investigator, if you compel someone to confess, you are causing an involuntary act which cannot be legal evidence. Even though private security investigators, generally, do not have to administer the Miranda warnings as reflected in City of Grand Rapids v. Impens, 32 Cr. L. 2308 (Michigan Supreme Court, December 1982) and other cases, they, nonetheless, should not abuse subjects.

I recommend not using coercion, intimidation, threats, promises, or duress which might compel some individuals to confess; such action is not legal or acceptable. Duress as an action by a person which compels another to do what would otherwise not be done. Further, nasty intimidation reaps resentment, not truthful cooperation. Such tactics are self-defeating and inappropriate; they are not promoted in this writing directly or indirectly.

Although the real world objective of forensic interviewing is often the swift and sure punishment of wrong-doers, there is no reason to treat interviewees in an abusive way. I have found civilized and compassionate treatment of victims, witnesses, and suspects necessary to reaching truthful cooperation; treating them as having some value as human beings is essential to success.

With aforementioned distinctions, the method used to basically train forensic interviewers and interrogators is primarily the same. Mastering skills of interviewing is the secret to the success of both. Learning interviewing is an on-going task. There is no easy way, nor is there a point at which you can say you have learned everything there is to know about it. To stop striving for self-improvement is to regress.

Chapter Two

INTERVIEW PARTICIPANT STRESS

C urrent scientific research demonstrates the significant connection between psychological stress and the onset of devastating physical and emotional illness. The more mental stress people experience the higher their chance of developing various illnesses. For example, the law enforcement profession is considered to be the most emotionally dangerous job in the world.[87]

It can be assumed that interviewer selection is based upon overall temperamental sturdiness reflected in present history characterized by resilient and stable adjustment to major problems of life. Expect your adjustment to conditions of various investigative experiences to be sound, especially if your motivation is high. Obviously, there is no way to predict interviewer reactions in all situations, particularly when functioning under constant stresses of danger to life and limb, inevitable disappointments and frustrations. It is easy to underestimate inertia and irritations experienced if interviewers are slighted depressed or uncontrollably angry.[54p.282]

Because some interviewers never know when danger may appear, they may sustain a heightened state of physical and mental alertness and tension. Even when the average citizen is assertive to voice an opinion, it may cause automatic preparation to defend yourself. Many times, even though you are expected to remain calm and listen, your body cannot vent the pent-up pressure caused by stress. Danger? Maybe. Who, or what, is danger to you? Well, do you really know? It depends on the circumstances and your sensitivity to the stressors affecting you. Be prepared!? It is prudent to be prepared; but readiness is an ingredient of that chemical killer.

Even a disapproving interviewee glance or tone of voice may be judgmental enough to cause autonomic readiness for fight or flight wherein chemical changes significantly alter the function of your total body. Even nurses and social workers face the chemical killer silently building up internal tension to spark possible explosive reaction and destructiveness.

Your pressure-cooker circumstances in life's challenging arena demands an outlet for destructive tension and anxiety. Otherwise, there may be a wearing down process of your body and mind to total disabling or death. With no outlet, tension is turned inward in a disastrous way. Outward use of force or violence is prohibited unless legal and is rigidly controlled. Illegal use of force is entirely out of place in professional settings. Traditionally vented tensions must now meet civil rights regulations. Because you cannot retreat or explode, pressure may work beneath the surface deep within you causing destructive chemical reactions and potential crisis.

Even well-trained psychiatrists and clinical psychologists fall to the pressure of the chemical killer. Investigators face the nagging uncertainty of decision-making dealing with the gravest of human decisions. What you do in a matter of seconds in life's arena is frequently challenged in a judgmental, unaccepting way by those who have unpressured time to intellectualize. It is vital to learn not to be forced into handling too many things in too short a time; polyphasic thoughts cause distress deterring effectiveness.

Under- and overstimulation of your body's autonomic system routinely adds to distress, particularly when there appears no way to vent related built-up pressures of tension and anxiety. When self-image and self-esteem are at stake and basic human needs require fulfillment, there are pressures. Many interviewers routinely face the worst of mankind where terrible traumatic sights, sounds, and decisions cause distress.

In considering stress and its relationship to interview situations, imagine a typical human being as having a core, an innermost compartment, with three surrounding layers. The core consists of personal or private world. The intimate compartment, or layer wraps around the private compartment, or core, as the skin of an orange wraps around inner sections of an orange. The intimate compartment entails married life, close friends, loved ones. The social layer wraps around both the intimate and personal layers. It involves friends, relatives, neighbors, and working associates. The fourth, outermost, compartment is the professional layer encircling the other three compartments. It consists of work associates, professional affiliations, and so forth.

Developing a strong, healthy self-esteem, private core, enables healthy associations and communications within each layer of your compartmented life. Your personal code of behavior determines self-disclosure and how you interact with the world in your intimate, social, and professional layers. Imagine that with weak or inadequate self-image, hooks are attached to each layered compartment restricting growth of those layers. Because the hooks cause personal pain, emotional imbalance and derangement influence related lack of cooperation. A sense of core inferiority sends out a hook named I'm not okay. In contrast, a healthy self-image sends out positive stimulators or prodders to surrounding layers as the basis of personal growth and healthy interaction with other human beings.

Those layers formed around the center core may be likened to a floating mine in an ocean with one or more protruding detonators. Detonators have varying sensitivities to pressure, contact, and so forth. Your responsibility is to deal with and disarm those sensitive mines so they do not explode.

Picture yourself as a type of floating mine. If you have a hair trigger disposition or predisposition you may become easily angered and abusively coercive. If so, expect to have major difficulties with your work product. It may seem appropriate to characterize yourself as a wooden mine sweeper capable of making contact with floating mines, interviewees, so as not to agitate in rough, abrasive ways, causing them to blow up, vent tension, possibly causing your inquiry damage. Deal with interviewee triggering devices so as not to be gruff, rough, insensitive, or unkind.

A stress situation may build tension. Presupposing individuals' desire to do well, maintain an outward poise, and perform intelligent resourcefulness in spite of external distractions, there is a tendency of mounting internal excitement to break into socially undesirable behavior. When desire for prestige, importance, is blocked by a stress situation, behavior may deviate from the wanted norm, expressing itself in aggressiveness, bombast, outward display of anger, nervousness, manic tendencies, incoherent speech, artificial and rigidly patterned behavior, hesitation and inhibition, forced suavity, and freezing.[77]

Bombast is high-sounding but unimportant or silly language; pompous speech. Regarding forced suavity: suave is being graciously smooth, polite when dealing with people easily and tactfully. Manic behavior suggests extreme emotional agitation in which self-control is lost, or, when there is an outburst of wild, uncontrolled feelings and general abnormal excitability.[70]

In terms of finite analysis there are as many stress situations as differ-

ent stress stimuli. In broad perspective, there are two fundamental types:
(a) those thwarting exercise of higher intellectual processes of recall and
judgment, together with their effective verbal expression; (b) those inter-
fering with smooth performance of complicated sensorimotor coordina-
tion's. A person may handle himself well under verbal cross-examination,
but become very rattled when stress-distractions accompany a motor
performance test. The reverse situation also holds true.[77] There are
times to use emotional stress situations to develop needed information
but not as a general rule.[35]

With an intent to work over interviewees, you probably create an
interview atmosphere in which you quickly snap from one of friendly
interest to one of cold disdain. That atmosphere intent is to rattle,
confuse, and observe them under fire. Doing so is self-destructive, routinely
causing defensiveness and resistant or hostility to your inquiry. Nothing
is gained enduring such treatment; hence, why comply. Neither take
sadistic delight in putting other people on the spot nor be so "softhearted"
you cannot put on a convincing demonstration of mild displeasure when
circumstances demand.

Dr. Hans Selye[61] has stated, "Our greatest source of human derangement is stress." Interviewees continuously release themselves of real or
imagined tension; they habitually attempt to leave the stress of the real
world in one way or another.

Selye has considered stress a general calling to arms of the body's
defense forces. He has indicated it is not known what substance causes
stress there are many theories but no solid facts. Selye has advised: "Earn
your neighbor's love" to avoid stress and help cope.[61] Alfred Adler
advises: Neighborly love is the only cure for neuroses or delinquency.[90]
When under stress, certain things happen, according to Selye—"The
endocrines, such as the pituitary located just under the brain, will
produce a hormone which in turn stimulates the adrenal glands." That
stimulation puts your body in readiness to defend itself.

Selye suggests the secret is not to avoid stress, but to "establish a way of
life;" it's important to learn how to live, how to behave in various
situations. He ascribes to the practice of "altruistic egotism" which revolves
about the need you have to look out for yourself first—invest in goodwill
and friendship as well. "If you are desired, considered worthy, if you are
necessary, you are safe," he suggests.[61]

There are two types of stress, according to Selye. There is the pleasant
or healthy kind ("eustress"), and the unpleasant or unhealthy kind

("distress"). Both create radiating excitement and they are both at the foundation of the secreting of hormones. He advises: "The most frequent causes of distress in man are psychological—that is to say, lack of adaptability, not having a code of behavior."[61]

It is beneficial to reduce interviewee tension or at least assist in controlling it to some degree. If there is a high degree of tension, interviewees will neither think clearly nor communicate well.[20 p.41] Tension's foundation is in awareness of some type of danger; real or imagined. The less judgmental and the more accepting you are the more their tensions subside.

When interviewees sense being evaluated by your set of values they may become defensive. Because defensiveness curtails the information flow, I suggest maintaining a universal set of values as well as your personal set of values. Neatly "tuck" personal values away, out of sight, as you interview while exhibiting universal values. Anticipate the respondent's values, needs and assumptions.[52]

Conversation, a dominant outlet for emotions, is beneficial to developing a dialogue which may reveal information. A limited degree of basic tension may channel positive interviewee emotions toward answering necessary questions. If interviewees are somewhat restricted from releasing tensions by moving about and playing with things such as paper clips, they are more likely to release tension through verbal expression.

In highly stressful situations, interviewees need to verbalize thoughts, releasing built-up emotion. It is important to be patient to "hear out" interviewees to permit a discharge of high energy force of emotion stored.[53] Feeling release, "expect them to think more clearly to respond more constructively. With no release permitted, their thinking may be restricted, confused and misleading.[53]

Interview participants may express stress through anxiety and heightened muscle tension while actively struggling to avoid becoming known by another human being. Self-disclosure avoidance can be the basis of stress.[6 p.543] Participants often resist revealing their inner core.

Thus, under great stress, participants are rarely imaginative or aware. Particularly in the face of danger, individuals do not intellectually think clearly.[35] Where there is excessive stress, creative thinking is lost.[6 p.493, 71, 52 p.43] Being overzealous, not considerate, you may cause interviewees to "run for cover" away from the danger they sense.[53] The more tension created, the less clear thinking is available.[20]

There are times, however, to feign loss of temper. At all times be in control of yourself and not really lose your temper. If not in control, you are at a distinct disadvantage, you cannot think clearly in a calculated way when truly angry. To feign anger you appear to lose your temper by what you say and do, but really you are using a tactic to your advantage psychologically. Only if highly skilled should you try that tactic; it is not recommended for the inexperienced. Your decision to use stress-provoking tactics to jar interviewees by using feigned anger is not generally recommended.

Having patience, you may allow time for interviewees to display innermost tension.[71] Tenseness is of particular importance and can be reflected in terms of changes in speech, bodily movements, changes of tone of voice and blocking of thought patterns.[72p.130] Insight into people permits an awareness of tension patterns and motives. Through a relaxation of tension there is typically a change of perception indicating that a problem can be viewed in more than one way—more realistic.[6p.567] Signs of extreme tension, distress are sweating, trembling, stuttering, biting lips, groaning, and digging fingernails into flesh. Additionally, untimely nervous laughing fits are often such a sign.[6p.67]

Tension and emotional strain can cause poised, confident, mature interviewees to be reduced to twitching, stuttering wrecks rapidly approaching nervous collapse.[6p.70] Those normally serious, mature, and competent may appear flustered, upset, immature, and incompetent when faced with a tense, distressful situation.[6p.582] Thus, tension in the voice should be noted as a sign of emotional concern over inquiry issues.[71] General physiological changes, such as burping, sweating, crying, etc., are signs of participant emotional turmoil.

Those changes include excessive coughing and restlessness.[71] Thus, tension develops and lasts as long as the interviewer lacks an understanding of interviewee needs.[6p.78] Because feelings of tension are unpleasant, interviewees are motivated to resolve indecisions to relieve tensions.[35] Hence, evaluate their anxieties and barriers as conflicting with truthful compliance.[6p.247] I believe inner tension is reflected through attempts to hide, disguise, or cover over truth. Deception is often the cause of inner tensions and related autonomic responses.

Signs of anxiety or being out of balance include changes in speech patterns, hesitation in speech, selective inattention, and voice tremors. Anxiety, tension, distress have disjunctive power in interviews and separates participants rather than promotes compliance. Participant anger often follows and is the basis for hostile words and actions expressed and displayed in varying degrees depending upon the type of interview situation.[72 p. 124–128]

A good stress interviewer has knowledge of the full range of both normal and abnormal stress behavior. Experience can assist interviewers to recognize "signs of anxiety such as motor restlessness, dilation of the pupils, perspiring of the forehead and hands, changes in vocal patterns, flushing, inappropriate smiling, increases in gesturing, increased smoking, inattention, blocking of speech, annoyance, and anger."[72 p. 170]

If your strategic, canny maneuvers lack spontaneity and are clearly full of guile, interviewees become defensive.[6 p. 492] Participant defensiveness because of inner fear may produce behavior that is incredibly cruel, horribly destructive, immature, regressive, antisocial, hurtful. Defensiveness causes loss of control. Repugnant or emotionally painful situations are excluded from conscious thoughts because they cause a reliving of feelings and wishes difficult to accept.[52 p. 40] It follows that some past interviewee action caused because of defensiveness may be avoided when you inquire of it in the present here and now.

Interviews are welcomed by interviewees who know they will be judged favorably. They will probably be relaxed and not defensive, a little nervous or anxious perhaps, but certainly not defensive, and hostile.[54 p. 227] Such a relaxed state is common among truthful, compliant interviewees.

It is striking to note how sensitively interviewees react to your mood, approach, attitude, and expectations. When things are right, an atmosphere is created which eliminates or reduces emotional strain. Thus, it is astonishing how interviewee frankness is established when the stress of a situation is reduced; the communication is less arduous and more intimate.[54 p. 226] Using a casual relaxing interview following a high-tension traumatic situation may produce information otherwise not obtainable.[54 p. 142]

Anger can mask tension and anxiety; if legitimate, it continues in truthful individuals for a moderate time only. If kept alive as a shield by the deceptive it may not be broken by logical appeal even when given time to subside. Interviewee crying as a defensive shield can mean several things ... effort to gain sympathy, fear of detection, diversion from issue.[71]

Even though interviewees use recognizable, subtle, elusive ways to oppose your inquiry, be versatile, restrain yourself from outright criticism. Interviewees may enter into meandering of thought to rest mental processes to reduce stress and test the degree of your patience.[53] Train to personally handle stress to control your reaction.[20] Interviews are complicated by appearance, voice, manner or identification which may provoke uneasiness and seem threatening.[23 p. 30]

Successful interviewers comprehend emotional stress in interview situations and how ambivalent feelings affect the flow of communication. In addition, they sense being under the strain of being judged, not only for the quality of their work by peers, but also by each interviewee.[54 p. 227] By examining their own behavior nondefensively, proficient interviewer's learn a great deal through experience to guide them so as not to feel threatened.[5 p. 156]

Interviewee Traumatic Neurosis

At various times, interviewees suffer temporary traumatic neurosis involving fear and anxiety causing them to become unrealistic, exhibiting irrational nonadult responses. Danger signals sensed may stimulate long-existing predisposition to neurosis. Displaying firm and fair authority helps calm respondents. However, some traumatic neurosis could lead to a psychotic state based upon anxieties.[72 p. 213]

Neurosis is reported to result from faulty and inappropriate childhood learning. The seeds of behavioral or emotional disorder usually lie, according to experts, in the approach-avoidance behavior sequence as it leads to suppression and repression, resulting in anxiety. Experts report "the more conflicts that are rendered inaccessible to verbal awareness, the more extensive the impairment."[72 p. 145]

I am convinced that the mentally ill, or those with behavior disorders, differ from the normal population, not in kind or quality of their basic behavior, but in degree or quantity of particular variety of responses. Such behavior is learned.[72 p. 238]

Authorities report self-alienation is being estranged from your real self. I'm persuaded the real self, personal core, of some people becomes a stranger, feared and distrusted. Estrangement, alienation from a person's real self, is at the root of the neurotic personality. Self-alienation is a sickness which is so widely shared that few recognize it.[6 p. 540]

When depressed emotionally, interviewees may exhibit low self-esteem, self-blame, confusion and indecisiveness, and pessimism . . . also fatigue. When sensing symptoms of interviewee depression, I express a positive attitude of understanding. Positiveness may brighten their outlook. Experts express genuine optimism in the treatment of depression; therefore, be confident that your personal optimism is valuable and strengthening to interviewees.[72 p. 175] Hysterical personalities use repression as a major defense mechanism to block out large areas of information and awareness of facts.[72 p. 197]

Severe self-preoccupation characterizes the schizophrenic personality; when children grow up experiencing communication patterns containing a great many double-binds, they are likely to exhibit schizophrenic behavior.[72 p. 158] Double-bind messages are pairs of messages, related but incongruent, contradicting each other. Schizophrenics respond with a kind of cowering silence, while their eyes dart around the room looking for escape, or they might retreat, shaken and silent. Hence, response by that severe personality may not be productive to your information gathering.[6 p. 584]

Many interviewees do not like themselves, maintaining the attitude of I'm not okay—you're okay. They often do not trust themselves to make meaningful decisions. After making "mistakes" in life acting upon some decision, they may feel guilty and alone. Hence, part of your responsibility is to assist them in reducing guilt feelings, allowing them to lead a more constructive life in the future, even though they have done some foolish thing. When interviewees think little of their personal worth, when their self-esteem suffers from some "uncontrollable" action, give them a more positive estimation of themselves, provide forgiveness.

Interviewees need to feel accepted; although, condoning or approval of criminal acts is not suggested or recommended! Provide a feeling of acceptance and forgiveness to encourage toward self-forgiveness and greater compliance.

Having a weak-sister approach to interviewing is not what I am promoting. On the contrary, there is a strength in gentleness, patience, and kindness which leads to confidence. There is no reason you should feel embarrassed or in violation of your personal code of conduct when using methods promoting nonjudgmental acceptance. You need not fear lessening your status by treating interviewees with kindness and empathy.

Chapter Three

UNIVERSALITY OF MANKIND

"Human nature is the character of human conduct as reflected through qualities that are psychological and social—internal and external." " . . . human beings behave in a particular situation, not as a simple matter of cause and effect, but because of heredity, birth, and modified experience."[22] No matter what an interviewee's reaction, it is an attempt to keep a mental steadiness, equilibrium. All interviewees need a sense of balance, a feeling of being in control.[68]

Every bit of human behavior, be it professional activities or in personal life, is couched within a philosophical context, based upon principles of being, knowledge, or conduct. Human conduct or human nature has rules of action, such as cultural values followed by interviewees throughout life while struggling to fulfill multiple and interacting needs. Attitudes flavor striving.

Complications develop while seeking out goals to satisfy needs. Two types of behavior are used to meet barriers in ingenious attempts: either solving the problem or becoming frustrated. Frustration in human affairs evokes emotional reactions of aggression, regression, fixation, and assorted defense mechanisms.

A noted psychiatrist was asked: "As individuals, do we ever achieve absolute satisfaction with life; do we ever reach the point when there are no worries at all on our minds?" His answer, "Always the problem is one of achieving a balance between what we want and what we get. We all want things, but the more adult among us learn to master our frustrations and to recognize that we cannot have what we want when we want it. To be truly adult and efficient persons, we have to learn to find satisfaction in daily life."[50]

The basis of behavior is attitudes learned and reinforced throughout life by experiences with other people. Attitudes may be changed by changing either feelings or thinking which are the basis of the attitudes or by resorting to some sort of discipline in an attempt to change the behavior itself. In most instances, interviewers lack time, training, or opportunity to materially change interviewee attitudes at least not in a significant or long-lasting way. Hoped-for change is temporary and disciplining interviewees is out of place (see Self-Fulfilling Prophecy and Authority).

Interviewers are behavioral scientists collecting data which can rarely, if ever, meet criterion of indisputable universality. Not usually working in the perfectly controlled environment of a laboratory, they cannot extrapolate with rigid authority; they do not deal with properties and conditions that remain constant; they cannot control the quality and quantity of variables. In short, the properties interviewers work with are the most complex of all organisms; physically, mentally, and emotionally . . . people.[22] As with behavioral science, proficient interviewers are interested in studying behavior, specifically human behavior, in response to various stimuli—internal and mental or external and physical. Behavioral science connotes all the factors that go into man's fundamental personality —needs, emotions, thinking, ability to relate thoughts and feelings. Actions are a result and a composite of all these factors. Success in influencing interviewee behavior begins by attempting to understand causes of behavior. When sensing their behavior is not looked upon as distasteful and totally unacceptable, interviewees will probably feel more like complying with requests for information.

Human Needs

Interview participant needs include: need for security, for recognition and social approval, for fair treatment and a chance for advancement, for prestige, for a sense of accomplishment. By actively listening, interviewers exhibit understanding and positive attitude related to those needs. Human behavior may, at first, appear disorganized, haphazard, chaotic because it is made up of habits, instincts, and intelligence or learning; these traits or characteristics overlap and are not clear-cut.[52 p. 35]

Human needs, largely fulfilled through conversation, are the basis of the tenet that people move in the direction expected and will lead to the personal satisfaction of needs.[52] Unless fulfilling basic needs in a reciprocal flow, interviews will be little more than a waste of time.

Individuals try to satisfy needs by maintaining physical comfort, avoiding the unsafe, attempting to gain understanding, detesting anonymity, desiring to be boredom free, fearing the unknown, and hating

disorder. Underlying every interview action and counteraction is a desire
to satisfy basic needs, a goal common to all people.[52p.22]

The anticipation and satisfaction of needs is central to effective
interviewing. Understanding human nature, preparation, strategy, all
combine to help satisfy needs.[53] Satisfying needs is based on emotion not
reason. Perceive those needs! Human beings function mostly on feelings
and not logic. French novelist, Anatole France (1844–1924), Nobel Peace
Prize winner, 1921, in literature, is quoted as saying, "It is human nature
to think wisely and act foolishly." According to the journalist, Henry
Holmes Smith: People tend to believe it is personal experience, their
own feelings, the richness of perception of the feelings, and things that
brought the feelings alive, that believing these are the most important
things in their life, all they really have in the end.

According to A. H. Maslow, "Man is a wanting animal." Because social
needs are comparatively unsatisfied, they have become a dominant force,
a primary motive for behavior. I conclude that Americans are trying to
compensate for the loss of social roots that once gave a sense of belonging.
Underneath differences of culture, people everywhere are the same.
"Human beings are all equipped with the same emotional repertoire, the
same basic needs, the same basic defenses."[6p.93] Thus, there is "a fundamental law of human behavior; emotional values and needs and intellectual knowledge are inextricably interwoven in all but the most trivial
human acts."[6p.5] Every human spirit is endowed with the same basic
qualities, but it is the quantity of each characteristic and how these
abilities develop and are employed to make us unique.

Social needs determine behavior as related to self-esteem and esteem.
Desiring personal worth, dignity, strength, competence, achievement,
mastery, independence, and freedom are included in the need for self-
esteem. Desiring attention, recognition, status, prestige, reputation,
importance, and power are included in the need for esteem from others.

Esteem consists of worth in the eyes of colleagues, peers, subordinates,
and superiors. It is tied, not to the position occupied, but to personal
qualities of contribution, expertise, and warmth. Esteem is worth to
others; self-esteem is worth to self. Esteem is gained from others by
showing you:

1. Know what you are doing.
2. Are using technical and practical applications of knowledge.
3. Care what happens to other people.[13]

Individuals have three basic interpersonal needs:

1. The need for inclusion—belongingness.
2. The need for control to maintain a satisfactory relationship with other people with respect to power and influence.
3. The need for affection-love and affection.[6p.16]

William Schultz analyzed and isolated basic interpersonal orientations, needs people have toward others: (1) inclusion, (2) affection, and (3) control.[59] David McClelland identified basic needs: (1) affiliation, (2) power, and (3) achievement.[47]

Interview participants are neither motivated in the same way nor are their needs just alike. They protect and enhance self-image as an overriding motivation to react in whatever way necessary to defend it. Maslow presents seven categories of human needs as basic to human behavior.[46] Satisfaction of essential and predictable needs motivates every type of human behavior. Interpersonal needs of interviewees are security, warmth, intimacy, and meaningfulness in relations with others.[72p.124] Interviewee needs include affection, approval, encouragement, praise, understanding, empathy, responsiveness, and acceptance of weaknesses along with respect for strengths.

When investigative matters become intense, distressful enough to cause emotional involvement, proficient interviewers try to be desensitized, detached. The potential for anger or lack of clear thinking may cause an avoidance of some distressful inquiries.[53] If participants feel threatened, inferior, or ridiculous, it is understandable they may try to increase feelings of security, acceptance, and self-regard. Like you, interviewees do not want to feel rejected and excluded.[35] Interview participants desperately seek approval and reassurance of being in control of their actions and of being worthy.

Confirming their abstracted view of life, interviewees associate with those who share and thus confirm their perceptions, attitudes, opinions, and beliefs. While conforming, they have the illusion it is done of their own free will. By not living up to, or conforming to, the norms and standards of peers, they may have feelings of guilt.

Again, cultural values are rules or accepted routes followed while fulfilling needs. Kingsley Davis distinguished six general American values he calls basic philosophical concepts of the Protestant ethic. He has considered American society dominated by general values.[51]

Individuals have a common bond worldwide. Interview participants belong to a family of mankind taught to be perceptive, to have feelings attached to self and a self expressed through face, to have pride, honor, and dignity, to have considerateness, to have tact, and a certain amount of poise.

Proficient interviewers encourage respondents to look at circumstances more optimistically.[71] The more basic the interviewee need you deal with, the more probable your success in gleaning necessary information.[52] It has been said that man's greatest fear is not of dying, but of feeling unfit to live (author unknown). Feelings of inferiority are in everyone from time to time. Thus, seek out hidden bits of fact by nourishing interviewees with feelings of security, friendship, and dignity in order to encourage them as they strive to satisfy needs.

In some situations, interviewees feel abandoned. Their vulnerability may have a disruptive effect upon cooperation. Although interviewers cannot, realistically, take the place of neighbors and close kin to reduce their sense of abandonment, interviewers can exhibit humanness and thereby psychologically comfort them enough to encourage temporary compliance.

Erving Goffman developed a concept in which he considers territoriality as particularly egocentric; wherever you go, you take them with you. Included are certain assumed rights: not to be touched, not to be dragged into a stranger's conversation, and the right to informational privacy which partly refers to the questions you don't expect to be asked. Those rights are universal and apply to human nature generally, a certain expectation of how interviewees anticipate you will treat them.[20 p. 180]

Frequently, interviewees comment, "I don't want to get involved," implying not wanting to breach moral conduct to hurt another human. There seems to be a deeply ingrained behavior disposition not to want to harm another human being or provide information that may potentially cause harm; therefore, interviewees may resist your questions.

In fact, the Bible commands people to "love thy neighbor as thyself."[41] To me, love of self is not a sin; therefore, if you love or like yourself, you may share love for your neighbor and feel uncomfortable in telling what you know of that neighbor, even in a criminal investigation. Many recall the admonition, "Judge not, lest ye be judged."

Neighbors who usually do not communicate will often inform one another of your inquiries. Spreading news of your inquiry is doing for others as you would want them to do for you. You can use neighborliness to sow positive seeds of your attitude, persistence, and general determination along the investigative path.

People are reluctant to have their inner self known; they avoid self-disclosure.[6p.542] Although you think of yourself as unique and your inner self totally different than the inner self of other human beings, realize the universality of human nature. The self has subjective characteristics, what you think, feel, believe, want, worry about; the kind of things someone else could never know unless you told them. You get to know another person's self when it's disclosed to you.[6p.541] Hence, people regard their assumptions and conclusions to be sensible and valid, tending to adhere dogmatically to their chosen ways.[7p.144] Thus, they may be defensive and make excuses for their actions.[71] Knowing the inner self of someone else, respondents hesitate to reveal it because it is a sacred trust. Revealing someone else's self is almost as difficult as revealing your own.

Predicting and controlling the interview environment is based upon precious generalizations accumulated from personal experience. Whether they work or not, they give an illusion of power and are greatly cherished. Faulty, misleading generalizations can influence accuracy. Judge each situation on its own merits using generalizations validated by either scientific authority or personal experience or both.[53] Although scientific research has high probability of being accurate, many research findings are subject to bias and open to serious question therefore, place the highest value on your experience.[19p.22]

Most people maintain the illusion of being independent, reasonable and thinking; thus, try not to make them appear foolish.[7p.247] Their temperamental disposition is subtle and imperceptible, even unconscious. There is only a thin line between what they are and what they want.[6p.12] Some interviewees have been taken advantage of, victimized; they may feel uncomfortable, embarrassed, and distressful. Not liking to think they have lost control in any way, they don't like to admit being taken advantage of; they don't like to appear foolish.[6p.195]

Chapter Four

DECEPTION

Deceit is an intentional act or practice; a perversion, concealment, or distortion of the truth for the purpose of misleading. It is a deliberate twisting of true meaning to lead an inquirer into mental error or false judgment, willfully determined to cover, hide, or keep from sight true reasons or explanations. To be truthful is to be honest without deceit, to have integrity.

> The essence of lying is in deception, not in words. A lie may be told by silence, by equivocation, by the accent on a syllable, by a glance of the eyes attaching a peculiar significance to a sentence, and all these kinds of lies are worse and baser by many degrees than a lie plainly worded. — John Ruskin.

Convincing liars are often self-assured with a cunning character. Their comments are not too strong, too defensive, or out of context. Their motivation to lie is not based upon anger or hostility, for that weakens the basis of their confidence; if they are trying to be helpful to someone by lying they will be more at ease as they construct comments to be natural in the situation. Because they are not too intense in their efforts to lie and they have reasonably justified their purposes, personally, they maintain both confidence and peace of mind. They have resolved the values of lying and suffer little or no pangs of conscience.

To bamboozle is a slang term from the 1700s having to do with tricking or swindling; to misdirect or deceive. It is to trick or deceive by elaborate misinformation; to get the better of someone by trickery, flattery, or the like; to hoodwink. Other terms regarding bamboozle:

Beat	Deceive	Hoax
Beguile	Defraud	Hoodwink
Bilk	Dupe	Hustle
Burn	Embezzle	Inveigle
Cajole	Fleece	Screw
Cheat	Flimflam	Sham
Chicane	Foist	Shaft
Chisel	Fool	Swindle

| Con | Fob | Trick |
| Cross | Gyp | Victimize |

The truthful display consistent recollection of details and attempt to dig up related specifics, often offering more than requested. They seem challenged to present needed facts without needing to protect themselves.

The truthful allow you to see their mental wheels moving in search of details. They are open and relaxed in manner of speech and thoughts even though somewhat uneasy. They clearly explain sequence of events wanting to be correct. With encouragement, they bring out things thought to be forgotten.

In contrast, deceptive-type individuals characteristically answer questions in a limited manner without volunteering additional data, taking a protected stance, knowing the less said the less likely they will be caught in a lie. Although they smile and look somewhat composed, deceptive individuals act unnatural in tone of voice and physical actions.

Truthfulness is signaled by perceptual recounting of facts, flowing narration, and acuteness of interviewee memory. Most interviewees have been taught acceptable social norms to include virtues of treating a stranger courteously, behaving hospitably toward a visitor, answering when spoken to, telling the truth and conforming to the reasonable requests of persons in authority. All things being equal, interviewees prefer to answer rather than remain silent, and to tell the truth rather than fabricate. Violating these social norms may cause interviewees distress and promotes related nonverbal signals.

The deceptive are often bound up, not free-flowing in arm, hand, and body gestures; their spontaneity and flexibility of thought and motion are not free moving, but overly controlled and stifled. Generally rigid in dealings with others, their movements tend to lack complexity and do not vary in intensity; their movements tend to be repetitive in nature.

A lack of clear thinking may be a signal of deception and related evasiveness. Thus, when interviewees express themselves in a calculated, dissociated, or awkward manner rather than in a smooth, flowing way, realize that something, somewhere, is not altogether right. Only a skilled actor can present himself in a believable way and then only with very limited expression of the facts. A mere twitch ("kine") or effort to control such a slightly perceptible movement is enough indication to warn that something is inconsistent and possibly a fabrication.[20 p. 25]

Interviewees leak the truth as they speak. Paralinguistic signals may convey internal struggles of the deceptive trying to cover outward signs of truth emerging in subtle ways. Tip-offs in facial expression and bodily movements may appear when interviewees twist true meanings. Attempts to deceive create stress. While some interviewees are capable of maintaining astonishingly good control of both verbal and nonverbal responses to questioning, others display telltale signs of deception. Some can't stand the tension of even trying to deceive, readily admitting the truth. My experience emphasizes that most "people do not readily admit to having fabricated."[10p.118]

When interviewees begin responses or statements with "To be honest," "To tell the truth," "Frankly," or "Honestly" they are most likely not frank or honest. Such beginnings are evasive and noncommittal replies. Inappropriate smiles or compliments toward you signal efforts to appease and possibly throw you off the track. Some females, acting in a precocious manner toward male interviewers, may be trying to mislead with out of place seductive action to cause loss of concentration.

Behavior that is not smooth-flowing or spontaneous stands out as contrived. Interviewees engaging in rehearsed gestures, without putting their bodies into motion in a smooth, convincing manner, signal their accompanying verbal remarks as probably contrived, false, phony, deceptive. The deceptive present a false image for you to believe. Their efforts are complex, fine shades of change, perceptible, awkward attempts signaling intent.

Interviewees expressing objections, rather than denials when suspected, are probably not completely truthful.

Because of inconvenience, loss of face, or other reasons, truthful individuals, at times, become angry. Their anger can be quelled by your controlled, smooth-talking so that clear thinking can be restored. Conversely, deceptive interviewees may feign anger to hide deception, intending to put you on the defensive; they will often not be calmed down while attempting to make it appear that your further effort is hopeless. Their anger may be a defense ploy.

While attempting to deceive, some interviewees answer questions and immediately look searchingly at your eyes and face for any signs that you don't accept the answer, trying to see if you are skeptical. That is a lingering, searching, questioning, probing, subconscious, wide-open look done in a fraction of a moment of tension to check nonverbal responses to see if the interviewer notices their deception.

Without announcing you noticed, add up verbal and nonverbal signals and merely go on seeking response patterns that may convince you that deception is being practiced. Challenging veracity, without first accumulating sufficient data upon which to make a conclusive decision, may hinder interview progress. Also, deceptive interviewees may ponder questions before responding and engage in physical actions during or immediately after pondering as a form of tension relieving, evasive in nature. They often avoid eye-to-eye contact by looking around the room or at the floor, frequently picking lint (real or imagined) from their clothes (see Terminal Phase, Polyphasic Flow Chart).

They use deliberation or contemplation to avoid timely answers. They may be uneasy, shuffling feet or crossing legs or both. Covering their eyes with their hands is also a typical means of escape from the situation. They may appear calm but in a forced way. By arm and leg movements they imply wanting to leave the interview environment, if not actually, then mentally. The deceptive may be uneasy, evasive, not balanced.

Answers by deceptive interviewees are general in nature and broad in content. Their desire, apparently, is to answer only as little as possible while hiding in their self-made emotional shelter. It is not unusual for them to enter a form of shock while answering questions, exhibiting light-headedness and numbness of extremities because of lack of blood circulation. That shock may be a form of escaping, not knowing what to do.

Use patient observation while noting indications of deception as expressed through nonverbal, physiological cues such as: burping, sweating, crying, indicating they are in a state of turmoil. Truthful individuals generally do not undergo such turmoil when questioned, particularly when interviewers try not to cause disruption. More than a gut feel is required to detect deception. You need subconscious recognition of observable signals as part of an automatic mental computer or intuition registering an imbalance warning of deception. Imbalance represented through inconsistent, evasive responses may be emphasized and punctuated by nonverbal signals.

Truthful interviewees present easy eye-to-eye contact, a freedom of eye movement, a flowing verbal exchange, not forced in any way, not rigid. Eye blink in deceptive individuals is quicker than with the truthful; also, blink frequency increases in the deceptive. The deceptive have their verbal and nonverbal communication disengaged from their intuition; they rely on instinctive responses sponsored by defensiveness.

Watching for behavioral patterns indicative of deception has long been employed. Although we all cannot claim King Solomon's special wisdom, we can at least use talents as observers of certain signals to uncover true data.

Pathological liars are persons who habitually tell lies so exaggerated or bizarre they are suggestive of mental disorder. They fabricate when it would be simpler and more convenient to tell the truth. Their stories are often complex rationalizations of self-vindication. They have histories of fabrications when wish-fulfilling fantasies developed and were appropriate in childhood. Such liars are recognized because of their continued performance throughout life.[16]

Maintaining self-esteem, saving face, is central to interview participants. Face or self-esteem is a sacred thing and sustained by engaging in various rituals based upon cultural background.[6p.182]

Not wanting to be humiliated in the eyes of those around them, people act in a defensive manner.[6p.298] Proper interview planning prevents interviewees looking foolish in front of friends or associates. Some respondents act as a stand-in for a second party not even present, trying to maintain a second party's self-image.[6p.181]

Interviewees do not want to be considered ignorant or unable to make decisions; they don't want to be considered uninformed, immature, unwise, or possessed of wrong or inadequate attitudes.[6p.491]

Feeling acceptable, interviewees comply.[72p.140] When sensing they cannot change a story to be more truthful, it is for fear of looking bad; hence, allow opportunity for them to give a fresh, more accurate story. They need a sense of comfort, a feeling of being understood, to change, alter, modify, elaborate, clear up their story of the facts. " . . . once having made a general conclusion, a witness is not likely to report individual facts inconsistent with that conclusion."[10]

Interviewees act in accordance with their own individual rational, reasoning powers; they tend to invent plausible explanations for their acts, rationalization.[52] Thus, they use rationalization to typically preserve their self-image.[7p.252]

People want to feel capable, normal, and worthwhile compared to others, disliking feeling different. Few are self-sufficient enough to be completely indifferent to insults and critical remarks; therefore, strive to help interviewees feel moderately confident and by so doing you are more likely to gain needed information. Because respondents rationalize involvement in particular situations or actions, assist in lessening their feelings of self-doubt to gain more cooperation.[53]

Respondents protect themselves with rationalizations when they have buried images of themselves which the facts of their status do not support.[52p.39] Sense if the investigation process is causing respondents to realize they have not lived up to personal expectations.[6p.274] They maintain a self-concept by conforming; they rationalize such conformity. Hence, when interviewees sense losing control, they rationalize their actions, not wanting to expose their dependency.[7p.247]

In unfavorable situations, interviewees try to rationalize involvement. Although playing down the significance of their acts, you are not overlooking the total effect of the acts on society and on their lives.[26p.34] Momentary reduction or playing down of unfavorable situations through your appropriate look or gesture helps reduce their reluctance to reveal needed data. Hence, reflect assurances that their action or lack of action is not so unique after all and that many have temporarily lost control at various times.[71]

Strive to allow respondents to relinquish blame to other people, things, or the very situation itself. Subtly assist them to blame others in their effort to save face—their overall responsibility is not changed. However, your action merely allows for a freer flow of data.[6p.312]

Interviewees try to appear reasonable to themselves and others by doing things that are proper and acceptable. Their defense mechanism projection is closely related to rationalization in its dynamics. With projection, they try to act in ways designed to make their behavior understandable and socially acceptable. Thus, in projection it is the other guy's fault; they use blaming.[82] People generally rationalize responsibilities not adequately handled.[71] "Characteristically, people look to themselves as the source of their successes and to the situation as the source for their failures."[25p.224]

At times, respondents are concerned about what is in it for me? Because of self-interest, compliance may cause them to lose face if cooperation cannot be justified. They must face themselves after cooperation. If cooperation has a high price tag of low self-esteem, it will probably not be forthcoming. They use on-going self-evaluation, through self-talk. Guilt feelings may cause them to be too off balance and less likely to truthfully comply; bias may be created.

Most interviewees desire to preserve reputation or ranking among peers. They strive continuously to preserve distinction among other human beings by engaging in whatever action is appropriate to save prestige or dignity; they try to save face. They appreciate being allowed to save face in embarrassing situations.

Chapter Five

SELECTION OF INTERVIEWERS

Ralph Waldo Emerson said: "What you are speaks so loudly I cannot hear what you say."[52]

Selection of effective interviewer is based more upon positive human equalities and deep understanding of human nature than upon academic achievement. It is essential to recruit interviewer applicants who are emotionally mature, mild-mannered, likable, impassive, soft-spoken persons whose appearance and voice are firm, but polite, possessing magnetic charisma to invoke others to feel comfortable. It is important for interviewers to possess humanness and be able to display feelings and compassion.

Those who are prejudiced breed hostility, annoyance, irritability, caustic remarks, and tactless behavior in dealing with others.

Individuals likely to succeed as interviewers have sensitivity, awareness, empathy, and the ability to relate to those in distress compassionately, meaningfully, and constructively.

Emotional maturity is an important prerequisite, without which interviewers may suffer feelings of anxiety, frustration, irritation, and rejection unacceptable to the role. The emotionally immature may attempt to rid themselves of those feelings by projecting them on others. Ultimately, this immature behavior fails, rendering them ineffective, exclusive of potential injury the victim may suffer.

Observable symptoms of the emotionally immature are stupidity, apathy, sullenness, resentment, arrogance, and so forth. They may cause dissension, friction, impairment of morale, injury to the good name of the organization, etc. Their potential damage is incalculable because they are obtuse, unaware of shortcomings, or indifferent to modifying their behavior. Emotional maturity encompasses appropriate emotions both qualitatively and quantitatively, governing emotions and impulses. The emotionally mature are at ease in a variety of situations and relate well with others.

Truth-seeking always implies responsibilities. With responsibility, maintain the highest standards of moral, ethical, and professional conduct and be governed by laws of equity and justice in the performance of all functions.

Realizing cultural backgrounds vary widely, skillful interviewers recognize variances for what they are and practice self-restraint when confronted with social behavior inconsistent with their own. Being acutely sensitive and responsive to group norms they recognize the essential arbitrariness, particularity, and limited relevance of all moral imperatives while interviewing.

Proficient interviewers cope with cultural differences because they possess:

- Confidence in face-to-face situations
- Quick thinking and perspective
- Subtlety of approach
- Keen insight into others

If interviewers can plan, organize, and evoke cooperation in social situations, they probably possess basic qualities of leadership and can inspire confidence, establish rapport, elicit information, and keep interviews under control. Adaptable interviewers cope with the unexpected instead of floundering because events do not conform to a plan.

Many things contribute to being a versatile interviewer. Following is a list of the more important items:

- Knowledge of human nature to know what people are likely to do and why they do the things they do.
- Interest in psychology in order to know why people think, feel, and act as they do.
- Knowledge of the elements constituting the situation under investigation.
- Possession of the following personal qualities:
  Average intelligence and common sense
  Keen power of observation
  Resourcefulness, persistence, and tireless capacity for work
- Suspicious nature . . . inquisitive, imaginative
- Quick mind
- Unlimited patience,
- Possession of the following arts:
  Practice of deception
  Astute questioner

Dissemble without being a liar
Inspire trust in others without trusting others
Assert and charm others without succumbing to others' charm
Dispassionate judgment of interviewee
Beguile interviewee into letting down his guard without frustration
if he fails to comply

Interview strategy comprises both the plan and the execution. However, the best plan in the world is of little value unless you have the science or art to execute it successfully. This is particularly true in interviewing because interviewees, as individuals, can frequently be unpredictable. Try to anticipate all possible conditions that could arise dealing with people, the unexpected can, and often does, occur.

Inexperienced interviewers usually maintain and develop a few obvious techniques limiting the degree of their success. To become experts and employ a wide variety of techniques they need to continually strive to broaden their scope of variations, shades of gray between right and wrong, rather than stay in the rut of stereotyping people and situations.

Good competitors, characterized as conservative, independent, and well-adjusted, have basic qualities to become skilled interviewers. On the contrary, poor competitors are characterized as liberal, self-abasing, lacking confidence, deferent, and adverse to social conflict.

Interview participants are made up of an interesting combination of characteristics: personality, habits, virtues, vices, feelings, emotions, skills, etc., that must be nurtured, merged, and channeled into a whole and healthy person. In your unique position, impose a personal discipline being competitive without threatening interviewees. Play your role with warmth and dignity, tapping all of your resources. Through trained experience, interviewers can develop the discipline and objectivity important to establishing skilled techniques.

Personal development is restricted only by self-imposed limitations such as energy, initiative, intelligence, psychological intuition, and insight. The combination of the following will encourage you to strengthen, or change, habits related to techniques used. Improvement is generally that of discovering the nature of a stranger (conceptualization) rather than recognizing an old acquaintance (apperception). Self-motivation involves:

- High energy reserve to physically and mentally handle the job.
- Initiative to be a self-starter.
- Intelligence to continually gather useful information.

- Intuition to second guess what others fail to recognize.
- Insight to understand others and situations.

Continuously strive to broaden your knowledge and awareness of people in order to improve upon your ability to imagine the unimaginable. Wisdom must first be developed, but along with it comes kindness, love, patience, understanding, and, finally, success (see Self-beliefs, SFP).

Training of interviewers: Effective training programs for forensic interviewers provide knowledge of the job, comprehension of the process, and experiences from which to develop practical interviewing skills. The most productive programs focus on the purpose of various styles of approach, dynamics of human interaction, psychological forces at work, and the process of communication in didactic instruction.

There is an old saying that two heads are better than one, and it applies to interviewing. Discussions among small groups of peers are highly effective in influencing changes of opinions and attitudes. Two or more imaginative interviewers pooling ideas (synergism) is an excellent method for developing practical interviewing skills. Once developed, role playing within the group can be used to test them. This approach also provides the less imaginative and less assertive members to benefit from those, who for one reason or another, reached a higher degree of confidence.

Proficient interviewers cultivate a quiet confidence. Ideally, a training program will assist interviewers to develop a balance of aesthetic sensibility and technical knowledge along with a sense of warmth interwoven with technically proven tactics and techniques.

The most successful investigators learn to act within the law, without allowing legal restrictions to appear obvious or stifling. Every year, citizens' rights are more clearly defined and thus challenge interviewers to conform to tighter guidelines. Civil and human rights have become permanent considerations, and of specific concern to you to keep informed and to conform. Legal restrictions tend to strengthen society and safeguard the general population.

Image and Motivation

Self-esteem, frequently referred to as self-image, is the core of personality; self-respect of and confidence in oneself.[13] Environmental factors play a large role in building and/or destroying groundroots of self-esteem. Developing and/or improving self-esteem lies almost entirely within you, demanding a strong commitment and arduous work.

Competent interviewers reflect positive concern toward interviewees, constantly striving to exhibit a serenity and warmth signaling cultural understanding and technical competence. They create a trustworthy, dependable, and consistent image.

When highly aroused internally, proficient interviewers maintain such an intelligent control over their behavior to be judged poised, a master of the situation, resourceful, well adjusted. They attempt to recover in outward poise, in control of their total behavior following removal of stress situations. Adequate control of themselves during stress and quick recovery after stress is removed are positive qualities.[77]

You can be better than you are! Your attitude regarding yourself and others influences your behavior and treatment of others and in turn influences their reaction to you and your objective. The exciting thing about interviewing is that each achievement can impel you on to seeking greater achievements, if not in deed, at least in mental awareness. Determination and steady progress are part of the secret.

Personal motivation is based upon the principle that you are the end result of what you think. Wanting to develop skills to achieve outstanding success comes from innerstrength, conscious willpower, overwhelming desire, and unwavering determination to succeed. With these you can develop courage, enthusiasm, confidence, and belief in your ability. Self-belief is explored, subsequently, when we consider the Self-Fulfilling Prophecy.

Chapter Six

ATTITUDE

An attitude is a predisposition toward behaving in certain ways. Interview participants may have attitudes of trust, skepticism or dislike, or prejudice or tolerance, toward each other.[35] Attitudes are "frozen," and it is with great effort that an "unfreezing process" takes place to change those attitudes.[6p.290] Interviewer expertise, attitudes, and personality definitely affect the outcome of interviews.[72p.160] Even if dealing with so-called rag-bottom, scrot, puke, scum-bag-type interviewees, select a positive accepting attitude.

While obtaining truthful evidence, strive for an underlying result as well; help improve the interviewee's lot in life in some way.[72p.122] Your attitude helps determine your image. By knocking or degrading interviewees, their possessions or efforts, antagonism is promoted. People are proud of their things. Shakespeare said, "A poor thing, but mine own."[52] Assume perceptive interviewees sense your attitude as expressed through your question formulation and presentation. Uncooperative interviewees are willing to terminate interviews as soon as comfortably possible, particularly if they sense you doubt your own abilities to gain data. All they need is some encouragement in the form of questions asked in a negative way such as, "You wouldn't happen to know _____ would you?" That negative approach is typically accompanied by you shaking your head from side to side as a signal of no.

Attitude is critical. Your responses to interviewees will be automatic (intuitive) and correct if your attitude, is effective. A positive attitude includes:

Congruence: Awareness of your feelings, comfortable with them and the ability to communicate with them in a constructive way to express your humanness.

Unconditional Positive Regard: Outgoing positive feeling without reservations of judgments. But never lose sight of your personal values; accept other human beings.

Empathic Understanding: Sensing the feelings and personal meanings of interviewees moment by moment as if to perceive them from within the interviewees and then convey this understanding to them.[72 p. 131]

Procedures and techniques take a lesser role to the more essential position of your attitudes and feelings.[6 p. 226] The purpose of most interviews is to help interviewees, as accomplished through your "congruent, suitable feelings displayed through words and actions" to show you are using nonjudgmental acceptance.[72 p. 231]

Your "lack of interest, remoteness or distance, and an overdegree of sympathy are perceived as unhelpful."[72 p. 226] Interviewees are keenly aware of your verbal and nonverbal signals expressing negative, unhelpful interactions. Your desire to understand is crucial.[72] Maintain a calm understanding attitude without being ruffled or shocked; be permissive to promote cooperation.[35]

The mood of interviewees should not adversely alter your neutral tone of voice.[53] Thus, your success is achieved by providing "warm regard for fellow human beings" even though you have prejudices and shortcomings.[5 p. 25] Avoid condemning behavior that conflicts with your own standards and avoid displaying prejudice.[29 p. 26]

Develop personality characteristics of "warmth, empathy, acceptance, caring, liking, interest, respect regarding others,"[16 p. 233] as well as the ability to behave in a nonjudgmental fashion.[72 p. 183] If you do not possess those characteristics, strive to attain them. Have a genuine liking for people. Be a sophisticated (worldly-wise, not naive) interviewer tolerant of man's weaknesses. Thus, "genuinely like your fellow man, be a warm, interested, caring, and involved person;" like others and yourself.[5 p. 41]

Avoid an attitude of condescension or contempt toward interviewees.[54 p. 16] Avoid an arrogant voyeuristic attitude that is counterproductive.[72 p. 211] Thus, contribute a meaningful human give and take to increase your effective productive qualities.

Genuine attitude change is based upon your predisposition, desire, to change. If your peer group is being convinced or is convinced and are working toward a positive changing of attitudes, join in.[6 p. 295] A supportive effort of your associates can materially assist in causing your attitude change.

Unspoken attitude is communicated by the ways interviewers listen and ask questions. Thus, it is flattering for you to ask for opinions. Doing so compliments interviewee's views and strengthens rapport; it also exhibits your respect.[53]p.23

Control your positive and negative feelings about those with whom you come in contact.[29]p.19 So interviewees lie to you! Don't be vindictive in your comments, for if you are, you most likely will not gain further information. If I internally forgive the interviewee and move on, I am better off and will probably accomplish the desired goal of gaining needed testimonial evidence.[71] Forgiveness requires forgetting pride and acting in an unselfish manner.[6]p.140 Forgetting self or selflessness implies considering goal accomplishment more important than building or fortifying self-esteem.

As participant observers, it is inappropriate for interviewers to register surprise or shock at any statement made by interviewees.[72]p.126 Having preexisting attitudes, interviewers may generalize too much about categories of people and situations restricting application of helpful tactics.[53] The successful are open to comments of facts, feelings, speculation, or interpretation by interviewees without becoming annoyed or irritated; again, being nonjudgmental is important.[23]p.36

If antagonism develops in interview interactions, be sure you have not given objective grounds for it to develop.[29]p.21 Merely work toward gathering truthful information for a worthy goal.[6]p.278 It is important to be a fact gatherer, not a judge.[71] Hence, learn the truth and try to help resolve the matter under investigation.[71]

When regularly placed in the middle between the organization you represent and those investigated, be emotionally and intellectually strong. Becoming resentful of the bureaucratic climate in which you work and the limitations it places upon you is self-defeating. Avoid using such a climate as an excuse for your lack of proficiency.[6]p.204

As a type of negotiator, avoid maintaining the I-must-win stance; or, at least not allow it to become too evident to cause interviewee defensiveness. Interviewing is not combat, it may be a friendly interaction. Truly, the inquiry, any investigation, is to be handled so interviewees will not lose the game.

Through subtlety and innuendo, with ulterior messages, manage to convey that it is safe to participate in your fact-gathering event. An interview is a behavioral process, not a game.[52]p.29 Avoid the chip on your shoulder and the okay, show me stance that encourages interviewees to become defensive and stressful, not cooperative.

Causing interviewees to ask themselves "what's in it for me" sparks an intuitive sensing: "not much but the pain of tension."[52] Being rigidly competitive causes a feeling that you must win totally in each interview. Even if you are without a so-called victory each time, your self-esteem should not weaken. Thus, if overly aggressive, thinking of yourself as highly skilled in dealing with people, you may learn to your dismay there are interviewees who, when compared to you, are more intelligent, more imaginative and more aware.[52] Being rigidly suspicious of all things and their aspects is not appropriate; but, maintain a questioning attitude.[53] I consider interviewees potentially deceptive where truth is being sought.

Forensic interviewers are not held in high regard by some of society because they are considered to be experiencing the joy of seeing through the story of interviewees, discovering hidden motives or influence.[29 p.47] I recommend that you enjoy your work or duty and become more enthusiastic. Each profession can contribute to society; you belong to the brotherhood of mankind!

> *The greatest revolution in our generation is the discovery that human beings, by changing the inner attitudes of their minds, can change the outer aspects of their lives.*
>
> *William James (1842–1910)*

If inconsistencies or contradictions develop in the information provided in interviews, proficient interviewers may deem it necessary to bring them to the attention of the interviewees (possibly between points *F* and *G* of the Polyphasic Flow Chart). However, to directly confront them with implications of their statements may cause a barrier to further communication. Although most inconsistencies and contradictions may be explained rationally, use care in challenging. Through inadvertence, lying, or incompetent, misleading data be provided. Being alert for inconsistencies and contradictions, interviewers may avoid tainted, misleading information.

To avoid making crude, abusive, emotional confrontations upon interviewees regarding veracity, skillful interviewers use unobtrusive means to confirm information so as not to end communication.

Interviewer bias is an obstacle projected consciously or unconsciously, verbally or nonverbally through gestures, shifts of posture, tone of voice, and intensity of expression.[80] "Biases and prejudices can distort perceptual judgments without any conscious awareness or intent to distort information."[10 p.50]

While some psychologists promote the idea that conversation is the primary vehicle to express feelings/ideas, some fail to consider nonverbal communication as a part of expression. No expression is exclusive. I believe every spoken word is dependent upon the psychological set and the environmental setting in which the spoken word, intonation, and associated nonverbal signs are communicated.

There is some thought that each participant of a conversation is pulled in opposing directions. But I have found an intermixing of logic and emotion at work in which there is a commingling of clear thinking, introspection, muddled confusion, potential embarrassment, and other related elements in each interview.

Anthropologist and professor Ray Birdwhistell says communication isn't like a sending set and a receiver: "It's a negotiation between two people, a creative art. It's not measured by the fact that you get precisely what I say, but that you contribute your part to it, that both of us exchange by the act. And then when we do communicate, we're an interacting and reacting, beautifully integrated system."[20 p.11]

Chapter Seven

AUTHORITY

People have a driving need to control and dominate their environment.[90] They have three prevailing needs: for belonging or inclusion, for affection or intimacy, and for control of circumstances. The need to control things is basic to everyone.[6 p. 16, 59, 47]

Authority is the vested, conveyed right or title of empowerment, delegated to command, enforce laws, exact obedience, determine, or judge and may be legal, traditional, or social. Having authoritative power, interviewers function on behalf of a segment of a community.[6 p. 62] In contrast, authoritarian interviewers demand absolute obedience without regard for individual rights and freedoms of those with whom they communicate.[6]

Correctly used, authority is applied in accordance with or conformable to justice, law, morality, or positive standards and based upon fact, reason, or truth without violating interviewee civil or human rights. At its worst, it causes some vested people to become "paranoid and demanding, authoritarian in pursuit of an elusive purity, and sometimes violent in the enforcement of their own sense of righteousness."[72 p. 77]

Although power is not an absolute finite, fixed commodity, people have a quest or drive to express power negatively or positively. In its simplest form, power is the ability to control, influence or cause others to do what you want done.[90] Society and status determine the impact of your control, allowing you to use power more or less in relation to others. Proficient interviewers use power in positive ways striving toward personal growth, self-affirmation, and self-assertion, rather than negatively because of insecure and inadequate feelings.

Positive style promotes confidence and accomplishment, encouraging self-esteem and interviewee cooperation. Legitimate power emanates from the role or position held, not from within. Some wrongly consider power a possession, rather than temporarily vested. Threatening punishment and promising penalties is coercive, abusive, authoritarian pressure.

When participant powers clash or conflict, develop a strategy to your advantage, applying referent power in subtle ways. To verbally fight or argue with interviewees is self-defeating, as would be running away. Giving up power is of no constructive advantage unless participants are willing to negotiate to reach a point of agreement to share or collaborate efforts. Interviewees may seek assurance in providing data in return for confidentiality, protection, or some other concession.

Aggressive interviewers, using power in negative ways, stimulate respondents to feel wrong and guilty, stripping them of self-respect. Causing defensiveness, expect a backlash of interviewee power.

Millions of people follow rules of conduct which may be founded in such books as the Holy Bible, the Koran, and other similar so-called rule books that guide human behavior. People may view interviewers and others using legitimate authority in light of Romans 13:1–10:

> Let every person be subject to the governing authorities. For there is no authority except from God, and those that exist have been instituted by God. Therefore, he who resists the authorities resists what God has appointed, and those who resist will incur judgment. For rulers are not a terror to good conduct, but to bad. Would you have no fear of him who is in authority? Then do what is good, and you will receive his approval, for he is God's servant for your good. But if you do wrong, be afraid, for he does not bear the sword in vain; he is the servant of God to execute his wrath on the wrong-doer. Therefore one must be subject, not only to avoid God's wrath but also for the sake of conscience. For the same reason you also pay taxes, for the authorities are ministers of God, attending to this very thing. Pay all of them their dues, taxes to whom taxes are due, revenue to whom revenue is due, respect to whom respect is due, honor to whom honor is due.

> Owe no one anything, except to love one another, for he who loves his neighbor has fulfilled the law. The commandments, "You shall not commit adultery, You shall not kill, You shall not steal, You shall not covet," and any other commandment, are summed up in this sentence, "You shall love your neighbor as yourself." Love does no wrong to a neighbor; therefore love is the fulfilling of the law.[41]

Interviewers are God's servants for the good of interviewees. Do you identify with that thought? Wrath, as mentioned above, does not give the right to be abusive in any way. Swift and sure legal punishment is wrath enough.

Why don't they want to give you information? Why don't they want to comply? Not wanting to testify in court because of embarrassment, fearing possible retaliation by the bad guys; these are two traditional reasons why interviewees do not comply with requests for data. But, it all really

comes down to not wanting to hurt the neighbor! In most cases. Mom
and Dad said it is not nice to speak against another person; don't bear
false witness, they instructed. Often, interviewees fear what they say may
be false. They don't want blame or guilt on their shoulders for telling
something that may help cause a problem for another human being, or
may be misleading or false in some way. They don't want to point a finger
at anyone. It is repugnant to tell something that may cause their neighbor
possible pain, injury, arrest, inconvenience, imposition, embarrassment.

First rate interviewers avoid operating on a simple punishment and
reward system; they avoid promoting McGregors Theory X only.[49] When
considered to be lazy, dumb, dishonest, passive, and simple hedonists,
interviewees will probably act that way.[6p.509] Such probabilities have
roots in the Pygmalion Effect mentioned at length elsewhere in this
presentation.

So as not to act in a stem, imperious, harsh manner, proficient interviewers speak and act out of the intuition of their soul, not from guesses;
they use intuition as a method of observing based upon experience that
is "direct and immediate."[73] Dealing in notions or speculations is not
recommended. It is beneficial to use substantial verities that strike home
to what is deepest, best in man . . . the conscience; the loftiest sentiments
. . . the heart.

"All men need authority . . . an idea long accepted by philosophers of
religion, philosophers of politics, and political scientists. Social order
needs effective authority."[7p.232] Functioning in unthreatening ways, proficient interviewers exercise authority so as not to be overly aggressive or
judgmental placing interviewees in a defensive stance.[29p.60,6p.233] Using
methods causing useless anxiety and distress encourages naive, sensitive
interviewees to be deeply hurt and anxious while encouraging sophisticated, cynical interviewees to become even more alienated and distrust-
ful in contact with adult authorities in the future.[6p.76,71] When defensive,
interviewees may feel helplessness, relative impotence, fear, and threat,
viewing interviewers as having all of the power.[6p.252]

In some investigative situations, interviewers may be treated like gods;
hence, it is easy to see how they assume a superior stance, having the
power to effect or change lives. If ever put in a godlike image, have
concern over your human responsibilities to interviewees.[29p.20-21] The
more I understand what is happening in the interview, the more likely
I will respond in a constructive manner.[54p.171] Hence, it is beneficial
not to appear too inquisitive or too authoritative; display a helping

attitude.[29p.59] An interviewer's use of power in any form may provoke interviewee defensive behavior.[72p.170] Interview success should not appear secondary to the incentive to look good.

Interviewers may be internalized as omnipotent figures who must be pleased at all costs, therefore, some interviewees may fabricate information in an effort to be cooperative.[72p.175] Some interviewees have sensitivity to my opinions at times; thus, my viewpoint could alter information obtained.[7p.147] Although it may seem impossible to eliminate assertiveness from your approach, be assertive in a pleasant kind of way and not in a threatening way.[23p.36] Try not to abuse your position of authority. Some interviewers are aggressive by nature; having been chosen because they have leadership qualities to include aggressiveness. I suggest trying to avoid entering into a power struggle with interviewees creating alienation in place of friendly rapport.[53] The "aggressive individual is expressive and self-enhancing."[25p.156]

Assertive persons having the ability to express feelings honestly probably have a healthy self-respect, confidence, and a general feeling of being okay and can usually avoid using abusive tactics that degrade others.

It seems to me that nonassertive persons tend to be anxious, inhibited, and use self-denial. Rarely achieving their own goals because they put other people's goals first, they may act like some adopted children having feelings of guilt and anger, expressing negative self-assessment.

I recommend using leadership qualities including courage, self-control, a keen sense of justice, ability to make decisions and plans, a pleasing personality, empathy and understanding, and mastery of detail. Misuse of those qualities may cause some interviewees tension and encourage their blanking of memory.[6p.565]

If, when communicating, I display a superior stance, interviewees will probably become defensive. An exhibited, superior attitude tells interviewees that I am not seeking a problem-solving relationship, that their positive feedback is not desired, that their help is not desired, and that it is likely their power, status, or worth will be reduced.[6p.492]

Although sometimes reluctant, most interviewees tend to trust and obey those in authority; most do not refuse to be interviewed. They have the right to assume that their dignity, security, and self-esteem will be protected even though unique interview features may reveal their initial anxiety. Interview tactics promoting humiliation, insecurity, alienation, or hostility are to be avoided.

Using compassion, respect, gratitude, and common sense assist to accomplish interviewing tasks. It is, unfortunately, commonplace for some interviewers to manipulate, embarrass and cause discomfort for interviewees rather than treating them with respect; resentfulness is the basic result.[6p.74] If interviewers use moralizing, judging ways, interviewees sense rejection and are unlikely to provide desired compliance; they will probably carefully limit cooperation until they can "slip" away.[35] Being rejected is a painful experience for anyone.

When interviewers test competence by throwing their weight around to dominate others, it is probably an attempt to counteract fear of not being effective.[6p.70] If they demand obedience to authority, they lose sight of how their actions are viewed by interviewees.[6] Fear may cause interviewees to mimic and imitate your behavior and attitudes.[6p.252] Some interviewers actually help create the dangerous situation they face by provoking a "showdown." It is not to my better interests to act against my own values, punishing (verbally, mentally, and physically) interviewees.[6p.70]

A forensic interview is more than a conversation with a purpose; it is characteristically a one-sided event which tends to be an evaluative process. Interviewees, however, maintain their own kind of evaluation of the interviewer (see I.E.P., Polyphasic Flow Chart), and govern their compliance accordingly.

Interviewee compliance is built on a thin, frail structure of interviewer skill, competence, and unimpeachable reputation. Your respectability helps support that structure linking you with interviewees.[6] By not disciplining or admonishing, but gently guiding interviewees through the inquiry, the interview develops into the desired direction. I remind myself: Take time! Be patient! Avoid bone-breaking, Gestapo tactics.

Interviewees who have been pushed, pressured, bribed, and at times overpowered by parents may become guarded, extremely uncomfortable, and uncooperative. And yet, their resistance to authority may be typical action in "asserting autonomy or self-determination."[72p.219] Interviewees may oppose you because of their "subconscious motivation and not a thought-out process."[15p.25] Background experience may have created a parataxic distortion of authority types and they may carry related feelings about those experiences causing them undue tension.[71] Tension, eliminates or diminishes desired rapport and the acquisition of truthful data. Anxieties, insecurity, and deprivations relating to parents and other authorities may cause interviewees to have negative feelings about interviewers. If unsophisticated, you may be alarmed by such expressions of interviewee feelings and some interviewers react defensively.[29 p. 20]

Ultimate authoritarianism is Gestapo tactics which breed interviewee resentment, retaliation, and reluctance or refusal to cooperate. Authoritarianism is based to great extent upon prejudice, and the attitude of "I'm okay, you're not okay."[8,84,1] To change authoritarian habits, interviewers need to increase capacity to see themselves more clearly. Their potential to change increases with knowledge and understanding of how such discriminatory actions affect others.[1 p. 975]

In a free society, interviewees often rebel when faced by seemingly repulsive or threatening tactics. It is repugnant to present a veiled threat of possible physical injury against interviewees. Threats produce fear, increase anxiety, and sponsor interviewee reluctance or hostility.

Gestapo tactics characterize insensitive, unskilled, crude, hollow methods which may boast self-image with meaningless attempts to feed self-centeredness and relieve inferiority feelings. Interviewees sense underhanded, terrorist or authoritarian tactics, responding only to the extent they think necessary to avoid actually being the recipient of veiled physical threat. To cross authoritarians causes them frustration because they are not tolerant. They seem all powerful having a main function of critically unveiling interviewee secrets to cause embarrassment or humiliation.[1]

Interviewees having poor self-images, feeling inadequacy and helplessness may feel duress and express annoyance, resentment, or anger; they may show attitudes of detachment, boredom, and hostility. They may engage in lengthy pauses, sudden silence, and unexplained inability to discuss pertinent detail.[72 p. 163]

Interviewers fulfilling egocentristic, personal childish needs may become frustrated, confused; they may act out personal tension by a misuse of authority.[6 p. 201] Freud stated: "Impeded aggressiveness seems to involve grave injury. It really seems as though it is necessary for us to destroy some things or person in order not to destroy ourselves, in order to guard against the impulse of self-destruction. A sad disclosure for the moralist."

Interviewers may be seen as corrupt, prejudiced, sadistic opportunists exploiting positions of power to earn the respect of peers. Exploiters show up in all organizations and it is often difficult to weed them out; they are clever enough to protect their position whenever necessary. They may demand respect based upon their "idiosyncratic egomania"[1] presenting themselves as being more than legitimate, above or better than power vested.

Power misusers lack awareness of their real self. Knowing their real self helps them understand other people more and in turn allows them to communicate on a wider adult basis with a broader range of individuals.[9] Unfortunately, authoritarian dogmatists see everything in black-white dichotomies and beware the unbeliever.[1] They operate in rigid con- trolled guidelines, adhering to proprietary symptoms which influence all judgmental situations. They don't realize tough guy tactics work only if they do not care about the answers to questions or if they already know the answers. Few people respond favorably to overly aggressive tactics.

Speaking from their critical Parent ego state authoritarians talk down to, belittle, or downgrade others; their manner becomes the basis of interviewee confusion and frustration.[72 p.156] Their behavior includes changes in speech intonation and tempo; it may be rapid or they may become silent gradually or suddenly.[72 p.171]

Sensing interviewer behavior as negative, interviewees will be on "good behavior," careful about what is said and done; they strengthen defenses.[72 p.198] If you plan to use coercing tactics, expect resistance and only limited compliance.[23 p.32] Manipulate rather than dominate; to dominate and intimidate interviewees is self-defeating.

It is self-defeating to feed off the interview situation to help support a sagging self-image. Feeling engaged in a combat of animal prowess, dominated respondents take defensive or submissive roles not conducive to fact-gathering.

Chastising respondents who lie or to become emotionally upset to feel justified in seeking revenge as misguided pleasure and is out of place. Realizing they have been treated kindly, even though they lied, inter- viewees are more willing to assist you in your efforts toward your objective. To reprimand or discipline interviewees is to invoke rebellious responses or encourage their use of a quiet protective covering.

Authoritarians may threaten, giving notification of the steps to be taken if interviewees continue in their current behavior. Threats imply mustered power against interviewees, warning of consequences if the interviewee persists. Using "verbal thrashing to react to ideas, feelings, and actions" from interviewees, they command through "unequivocal orders" using scolding. Abrupt and impatient, they may discipline or admonish rather than gently guide interviewees through areas in devel- oping needed data.[71]

Using punishment proves "skills are weak; using punishment is playing your last 'trump' on the premise that if this approach does not work nothing will" . . . poor thinking.[5 p.149] Respondents can sense if you have a "readiness to break into violence" which "does not promote cooperation."[1 p.972] Don't harm interviewees!![23 p.69]

The displacement of anger toward respondents rather than toward the real causes of distress may be brought about by pressures, real or imagined.[52 p.40] Frustrated, some interviewers unintentionally lose their temper; their utter lack of control may be expressed by hitting interviewees. Feeling foolish and miserable at times, proficient interviewers control themselves even when interviewees try to incite anger and impulsiveness. They try to keep an "unruffled exterior" faced with insult and lack of cooperation.[54 p.111] Control of oneself is the key.[83]

Research indicates: overt "prejudice is closely correlated with certain personality traits of a destructive nihilistic nature, suggested by an irrationally pessimistic ideology of the intolerant."[1]

Anger is expressed resentment directed against someone perceived to be unworthy. Ill-chosen words, tone of voice, or gestures may provoke participants placing them in a mood to retaliate. Some interviewees will not be reasoned with in any way; many will not allow truth to penetrate their shell of protective defenses. Their preconceived notions may promote irrational actions. Participant anger and compliance do not go hand-in-hand toward revealing the truth.

Successful interviewers are hardy enough emotionally not to be "destroyed" by interviewee anger.[6 p.233] They develop their self-esteem strong enough to withstand hostile antagonistic comments and hesitation of reluctant interviewees. They are not vulnerable to attacks by nasty interviewees having no intention of complying.

Having a controlled temper is important, although on rare occasions allowing it to show as a ploy or tactic is useful but then only to apologize quickly.[71] Used as a momentary emotional outburst toward the situation or facts but not directed against interviewees personally.

An angry, unplanned emotional blast, outburst, because of frustration or exasperation will in all probability place interviewees in a defensive role and could halt further cooperation. It can be an expression of planned frustration, and not to draw battle lines, it is mainly intended to show humanness, self-disclosure not an attack to reduce interviewee self-esteem the more fear, the less compliance.[53]

Using logic to dispel interviewee fear or anger is futile, hence if perceived, I recommend expressing empathic understanding rather than logical antidotes to establish a greater sense of rapport. Quelling emotion permits clear thinking.[53]

Generally, anger is a two-edged sword according to Michael E. Cavanagh, Ph.D.: "The emotion of anger is extremely important for our mental health. It occurs when one of our psychological needs becomes threatened or blocked. For example, if my sense of safety, acceptance, or effectiveness is shaken, one of my emotional responses will be anger."[17] Anger has a bad reputation, according to Cavanagh, "Many people have a real problem with anger. Some report they never feel it. Others cannot connect the word 'anger' with any feeling they experience. They use such words as 'upset,' 'frustrated,' 'disappointed,' 'confused,' 'annoyed,' and 'hurt,' but deny any of these emotions are connected with anger. Still others, while in the midst of rage, deny that they are angry."

Dr. Cavanagh continues, "Some of the more typical rationalizations used to avoid expressing anger constructively include the following:

1. It's not nice (Christian, mature) to get angry at another person.
2. If I expressed the anger I feel, it would hurt or demolish our relationship.
3. It wouldn't do any good anyhow—it won't change anything."

"We have two options. We can deny our anger or keep it to ourselves, which will cause us to violate ourselves and others in subtle and destructive ways. Or, we can express our anger directly and constructively, which will, at least, create mutual growth experience and at worst will create one-tenth of the stress caused by its denial or repression," according to Dr. Cavanagh.

Chapter Eight

INTERVIEWER ACCEPTANCE

Understanding vs. Comprehension

Proficient interviewers are probably perceived as likely to understand, accept, and not reject interviewees;[35] although unfamiliar or uncongenial circumstances might provoke some interviewers to express character defects.[54p.171] By being understanding, noncondemnatory, trustworthy, and genuinely interested, you may promote a nonretaliatory, permissive, and honest form of human interaction. An awesome feat for interviewers is to become desensitized so as to cope with interviewees who cause disgust, fear, infuriation, or distress.

The appearance or actions of some people promotes a sense of interviewer revulsion; a repugnance might develop. Successful interviewers develop capacity to treat visibly scarred interviewees with the same kindness shown internally disfigured interviewees. Dealing with interviewee internal struggles may be less difficult than dealing with exterior disfigurement and malfunctions such as speech impediments and birth defects. Warm, considerate, human conversation signals acceptance. All methods, tactics, and attitudes expressed in this presentation apply to all interviewing. After all, it is dealing with human minds whether in normal bodies or in disfigured ones.

Sensitization applies to your efforts to tune in to their attitudes and not allow different people to bother you to a point that you are overcome with distress. Being somewhat depersonalized assists the interviewer to react with calm acceptance and sense how the influence of personality affects interview outcome.[72p.136] Interviewees are not all good or all bad; therefore, profit by not easily condemning or becoming indignant.[29p.16] The less acceptance given interviewees, the more they will feel threatened.[6p.226]

When you are receptive, understanding, warm, responsive, interested and involved, interviewees will probably enter a dialogue. They are responsive in a productive, permissive counseling atmosphere. Without being moralistic or judgmental, maintain that no attitude is too aggressive, no feeling too guilty or shameful for interviewees to bring into the interviews. When interviewees feel freedom from pressure or coercion, their need for defensiveness is reduced.[35]

> The interviewer who exhibits non-judgmental understanding, a listener who provides empathic responses, will encourage people to be strongly motivated to continue to communicate. People will tend to provide an ever-increasing amount of information without realizing it. The exact reason non-judgmental understanding assists in the increased inducement to communicate is not specifically known. The fact remains that it does have a self-propelling effect.[57]

Offenders are not significantly different from the rest of the population. Because society tends to reinforce resistance to temptation by punishment and by stigmatizing a violation as odious, you may consider offenders as those who violate laws, procedures, or other restrictions. In the main, those succumbing to temptation may feel the heavy weight of disapproval when they take part in violating society's standards of cultural values. It is beneficial not to appear as a judge for society against them; restrain from speaking out or striking out against unspeakable acts of omissions or commissions.

When interviewee factual observations end and emotional interpretations begin they may distort objective reality.[53] If you notice interviewees interpreting facts rather than presenting observed details, avoid being judgmental and pouncing on them. Playing the "I gotya" game is self-defeating.

Unfortunately, some novices and some experienced interviewers think that by accepting interviewee behavior they condone or approve it in some subtle way, thus thinking it a weakness to accept some human behavior, believing it may erode their personal value system.[10 p. 34]

Implicit cultural values influence the interviewer's total inquiry.[72 p. 212] If they depend on the give-and-take of interview situations to build self-esteem, the interview objectives may be lost. I'm convinced through experience that the complex nature of interviews demands control of feelings rather than an absence of feelings.[29 p. 25] Although it is extremely unlikely to specifically predict emotions such as fear, guilt, joy, and anger, proficient interviewers can render predictions based on high probability.[53]

Inspite of its complexity, human behavior is often predictable and understandable. Without thinking, judgments are based upon life experiences. Therefore, accumulate your own research data based upon personal experiences, to develop hypotheses and decisions.[52 p. 36]

In a controlled, understanding manner, display a nonjudgmental attitude, with those exhibiting anger or anxiety. If, for example, interviewees verbally attack you, avoid retaliation. If challenged into a defensive stance, think clearly. From a semineutral role, be objective and willing to put up with certain amounts of verbal abuse from rebellious types. Nothing positive is accomplished by taking up their challenge to engage in mutual abuse. Take pride in your emotional control even when in insulting and/or threatening circumstances wherein "normal" people would probably retaliate in kind.[53]

Your morale, and personal ideological involvement in the matter under investigation are significant success factors. Interviewers are not always aware of emotionally toned judgments and reactions which have their foundation in the subconscious. Therefore, be perceptive and continually strive to understand yourself while gaining experience with other human beings.[54 p. 114] Exhibit a constancy which says "I will react to you with humanness" or "No matter what you say, I will remain the same."[72 p. 136] Hence, if a fullness of interviewee response is expected, make it clear that any point of view in any degree of enthusiasm or hostility, is equally acceptable during interviews.[35]

Clinical Humanness: Empathy, Respect, Genuineness

The degree of interviewee cooperation is directly related to the clinical approach used; analogous to the doctor's diagnosis of what happens in the human organism.[22] Its cornerstone is understanding and acceptance as reflected in respect and tolerance of human frailty. It allows interviewers to maintain an individual point of view taking for granted participant values, aims, aspirations, and reactions are in some measure unique. Clinically-oriented interviewers maintain intuitive understanding based upon assimilation of generalizations, insight collected, constructed from tested experience.

Human relations brings human dignity into the work environment, or using other synonyms, human values, human decency, and human recognition. Recognizing interviewee dignity, worth, and importance improves interview productivity when interviewees are assisted to strive for self-expression, self-realization, and self-fulfillment. Sensing the interviewer's helping, friendly attitude, they will probably comply as expected. Exhibiting an attitude of I'm okay, you're okay is effective for interviewers no matter the objective.

By effectively using active listening and exhibiting genuine interest, interviewers may avoid injecting opinions, value judgments, and criticisms. Active listening implies nonjudgmental acceptance. An effective forensic interviewer is " . . . someone who is empathic and therefore someone to be trusted with troublesome information."[10]p.57 Humanness, reflected in what you say, how you say what you say, and how you act, places ultimate value on human dignity in the here-and-now. It develops through new habits in interactions with interviewees stimulated by imagination and awareness. High levels of interviewer empathy, warmth, and genuineness express feeling and regard for interviewees as human beings. While exhibited respect opens the interviewee's thoughts, sarcastic put-downs terminate compliance.

Empathy

According to Harry A. Overstreet: "Empathy is one of our human potentials and it can go far toward saving man from psychic isolation. But the desperate plight of our world testifies that empathic potential remains chiefly a potential. Those whom it has genuinely released from immature egocentricity into mature sociocentricity are rare among us. The arrested development of the imagination is, perhaps, the most common tragedy of our human existence."

Exhibiting empathy means understanding how interviewees view their world. The first step in empathizing is to listen and attempt to grasp the meaning of what is said. By creating dialogue, interviewers can put themselves vicariously in the interviewee's "shoes" allowing for expression of feelings.[82]

Thus, interviewees feeling understood may be more compliant. Sensitive, patient, and nondefensive response to individuals in distress can stimulate dialogue in which they may vent emotions. Becoming uncontrollably angry and upset creates a barrier to a trusting relationship.

" . . . empathy, the real mortar of any relationship, requires hearing, understanding and acceptance of feelings which are part and parcel of any situation. Stated more pragmatically, we believe one cannot use the strongest of all facilitators . . . empathic understanding . . . without the ability to accept and respond to feelings."[10]p.25–26

A perceptive interviewer will be " . . . the facilitator of empathic understanding." Through " . . . the conveying of this understanding will establish the kind of rapport that will make the client feel willing to respond fully to the subsequent inquiries."[10p.61]

Asking questions is unavoidable in interviews and may interfere with warm personal contact and empathic understanding. The emotionally depressed may be able to talk about feelings even though contact is brief; empathic understanding is a powerful tool in facilitating dialogue. Respect and understanding are developed when empathy is expressed. In contrast to some notable experts, empathy, not sympathy, is needed. Feigned sympathy is useful.[34] Sensitivity to attitudes and warm interest can be expressed without emotional involvement. Empathy expressed in both word and action furthers cooperation and is heavily dependent on verbal message but not exclusive of nonverbal signals. It is mainly revealed through oral expression.

Mentally question interviewee trustworthiness; trusting completely is to be naive and inescapably fooled. However, never show suspicion to the point of causing interviewees to become offended and negatively alter compliance, at least not before reaching point *F* of the Polyphasic Flow Chart.

Avoid feeling too good to lower yourself to display acceptable forms of empathy.

"There is a belief that lawyers can adequately employ active listening techniques even though they cannot truly empathize. The belief is that, although true empathy is lacking, lawyers can proceed professionally by reflecting feelings in a way that creates the impression of non-judgmental understanding."[10p.34]

Reasons for interviewee behavior become intelligible to the extent interviewers are able to accept, see, understand, and visualize these reasons. Vicariously sensing through imagined participation allows successful interviewers to better conceive the matter under investigation. Some interviewers fear personal change brought on by understanding interviewee frailties. By attempting to enter thoroughly, completely, and emphatically into their frame of reference to comprehend their point of view helps establish a trusting relationship.

Chapter Nine

SELF-FULFILLING PROPHECY

Self-Fulfilling Prophecy (SFP) is a concept originated over a quarter century ago by Merton who based it on the notion that expectation is the cause and fulfillment of the effect; that high expectation to believe in or achieve something will cause the belief or achievement to be realized. This is commonly referred to as the Pygmalion Theory or Effect.[88]

> One of the important forces in social interaction is the tendency for one person to communicate, verbally and nonverbally, his expectations to another person. The second person then tends to respond consciously or unconsciously to those expectations. This may be viewed as one manifestation of the more general human tendency to conform to the group of peers and to the suggestion of higher status persons in society.[30 p. 84]

Your expectations and related actions can influence interviewee behavior. Applied to interviewing, high expectation of success can produce beneficial results. Your attitude toward interviewees determines how you treat them. How you treat them determines, to large extent, how they behave. The essence of the SFP is that a belief, true or false in itself, acted upon results in reality. Self-Fulfilling Prophecy can be defined as the art/gift of believing what will come as a result of your effort applied to something desired. The announcement of the "successful" venture may be a SFP if the venture is successful.[12 p. 9–12]

Believe that based upon your own efforts you will obtain truthful information. However, in order to do so, you may temporarily need to modify your methods/thinking to obtain the necessary cooperation. That is, you may have to do or say things you might normally find objectionable.

Belief and expectation are internal to the investigator before each interview interaction, regardless of the investigative circumstances. They tend to be an integral part of the proficient investigator's being, basic in his philosophical makeup. These ingredients, belief and expectation, are fundamental building blocks in the foundation of the successful, effective . . . investigator . . . interviewer . . . interrogator. Those components are practiced during the Personal Preparation Phase (see Polyphasic Flow Chart), where investigators become more and more aware of their influence in the outcome of interviews and possible subsequent interrogations.

Such practice leads the proficient to know it is vital to treat interviewees as though they are tending to be more compliant than they really are at first glance. By treating them as though they really want to and are intending to comply with requests for data, live up to your expectation. By treating interviewees as though they want to comply, interviewees do, in fact, conform to that treatment and do give greater cooperation. Present your positive expectation in a subtle manner through everything done and said by acting as though you know they truly desire to comply with requests for investigative data. By what you say and how you say what you say, how you appear and all elements about and with you, you signal your belief that they truly want to comply. Realistically imply your belief that they are ready, willing and able to comply. Treated as though they desire to comply, they will tend to live up to your expectation . . . how you treat them.

In actuality, they often do not desire to comply, at least not at first and not to the extent you expect. Thus, it is your positive expectancy and your behavior toward them that may encourage greater compliance. By acting upon an incorrect belief that is at first a false assumption, you turn the belief and expectation into reality.

Definite social and psychological processes are involved in the SFP; the power of positive thinking and magic are not, according to Dr. Merton. Positive evidence from recognized authors emphasize the benefits of applying the Self-Fulfilling Prophecy:

- Rensis Likert; Born August 5, 1903; Social Scientist, Educator; Ph.D. Columbia University, 1932.
- J. Sterling Livingston; Born June 7, 1916; Management Consultant, Educator.
- Robert K. Merton; Born July 5, 1910; Educator, Sociologist, MA. Harvard, 1932; Ph.D. 1936.
- Robert Rosenthal; Born March 2, 1933; Educator, Psychologist, AB. University of California at Los Angeles, 1953; Ph.D. 1956.
- Douglas Murray McGregor; 1906–1964, Social Scientist, President of Antioch College, Professor of Management at the School of Industrial Management, Massachusetts Institute of Technology, Developed Management Concept of Theory X and Theory Y.

In his dissertation, Rosenthal reveals that he proved, through scientific experiments, that the "power of expectation alone" significantly influences the behavior of others. Specifically, he, as a teacher, showed that:

1. He believed his students in his experiments had greater potential.
2. This belief enhanced his expectations of them.
3. As a result of transmitting his expectations to the student, they became higher achievers.

As a result of his studies and experiments, Rosenthal and Associates arrived at, following, a four-factor theory to transmit expectations through specific behavior in management situations and elsewhere: climate, feedback, input, and output.[88]

Factor 1: Climate

The climate communicates positive/negative expectations. The climate consists of all nonverbal messages, such as voice, eye contact, facial expression, and body posture.

Factor 2: Feedback

The interviewer's response to the interviewee's feedback reveals his expectations to the interviewee.

Factor 3: Input

The interviewer's contribution of information transmitted to the interviewee reveals the expectations of the interviewer.

Factor 4: Output

The interviewer's expectations of the interviewee's output is transmitted to the interviewee by encouragement of what is expected to be achieved.

McGregor reports, as a result of his finding, that underlying assumptions definitely influence managerial behavior in respect to policies, procedures, techniques, and with subtle aspects of everyday human behavior. Likert's findings in the management area reveal that to achieve a high-performance level from subordinates, the supervisor must have high-performance goals and a contagious enthusiasm to convey the importance of his regard for those goals. Livingston, indirectly, supports the SFP Theory. He states that the job of a manager is to influence his subordinates. He assumes that positive influence, in contrast to negative, is implied; however, it should be noted both are conveyed via the same method and result in corresponding positive or negative results.[88]

George Bernard Shaw, Playwright, used fine arts to portray his belief in the SFP Theory. In his play, "Pygmalion," Eliza Doolitle, the flower girl, insists she cannot become the lady Professor Higgins is training her to be until he, himself, sees her as a lady instead of a flower girl masquerading as a lady.

> " ... You see, really and truly, apart from the things anyone can pick up (the dressing and the proper way of speaking, and so on), the difference between a lady and a flower girl is not how she behaves, but how she's treated. I shall always be a flower girl to Professor Higgins, because he always treats me as a flower girl, and always will; but I know I can be a lady to you, because you always treat me as a lady, and always will."[62]

The SFP Theory has a profound effect on interpersonal communication. Industrial psychologists have long realized the necessity to create management patterns to foster motivation, improve communication, and increase productivity. In fact, millions of dollars and many manhours are currently being poured into management training courses in an effort to achieve corporate goals of improved management in order to upgrade productivity by creating better communication and improved working atmosphere.

This trend has been in vogue for a number of years and is paying off. Case studies show that high expectations lead to high performance and that low expectations result in negative or poor performance.

The general evaluation is that corporate levels of high expectations communicated through all levels of management are effective. You, like the manager in industry, fit into a chain of command within an organization resulting in your being the manager of interviews. The proven rules of management apply to your interviews because you deal with people and have specific goals to achieve. The Self-Fulfilling Prophecy (Pygmalion Effect) is a theoretical concept that can work for you. Expectations of authority figures affect the outcome of communication in management and forensic interviewing. Your expectations and encouragement of interviewees to comply are far more than verbal prodding.

They encompass your total message . . . consciously and subconsciously. Rosenthal's four-factor theory is used, following, to transmit expectations through specific behavior in interview environments. Each factor is identified and described separately for the purpose of documentation only. Each is an integral part of the others and together they represent the whole.

Factor 1: Climate

The climate communicates your expectations to interviewees through nonverbal messages; otherwise referred to as paralinguistics, body language or kinesics. Paralinguistics includes mannerisms, gestures, tone of voice, and other subtle things. Climate, as here defined, is in play from the onset to the outset of interviews. In fact, it is constantly under scrutiny and a single negative nonverbal signal has the potential of rendering interviews ineffective. Before you have a chance to verbalize, you are under scrutiny for signs of acceptance and trust. Your only hope is that you have done your homework and pass the test.

Some interviewers possess a highly accomplished use of paralinguistics; some are aware of nonverbal communication others are oblivious that such language exists. The first group is fortunate, the second has positive signs, but the third has a long row to hoe to excel. There are three basic methods of possessing a high-level body language through applied intuition, the school of hard knocks, and down-right pursuit. All require effort in varying degrees.

Intuition in and of itself is of little value; it must be applied. In the school of hard knocks, growth comes from evaluating failures/successes in an attempt to discover what caused them to occur, and to modify, or enhance behavior accordingly. Those who have the long row to hoe need to start by reading, talking to those who possess the skill, observe others, and practice with everyone with whom they come in contact. In the interview itself, deliberate communication of paralinguistics requires subtle delivery to avoid the appearance of pretense or to arouse interviewee suspicion.

Factor 2: Feedback

Responding to interviewee feedback though body language is on-going, concentrating on verbal and nonverbal communication. Feedback, according to J. Reusch, refers to "the process of correction through incorporation of information about effects received. When a person perceives the results produced by his own actions, the information so derived will influence subsequent actions. Feedback thus becomes a steering device upon which learning and the correction of errors are based."[56 p. 4]

Communication directly related to interviewee feedback responses are difficult to prepare for because of some unpredictability of interviewee. Therefore, carefully prepare yourself to meet and handle the unexpected. Again, while all preparations contribute, place emphasis on listening, hearing, flexibility, adaptability, and being in control. To a great extent, the input factor is important in channeling feedback.

Factor 3: Input (see Initial Phase)

Communicating expectations is your input and through it you can exercise control of interview situations. Prepare your verbal input such that you establish a clear picture of what you expect from interviewees.

The goal is to set the stage so that interviewee surprises and diversions are virtually impossible. Your neutral stance in explaining details and how interviewees can assist in the total effort of your inquiry is vital to your accomplishment. Interviewees continuously read verbal and non-verbal input and make interpretation relative to their own situation.

Factor 4: Output

Interviewee output is influenced by your input of expectations. The success of achieving the expected output is your reward for applying the Pygmalion Theory of positive expectation transmittal. Distinct transmittal of expectations is the key element of any interview.

The SFP draws its power from the need interview participants have to be recognized as worthwhile individuals. It is fueled by the tendency to behave in ways consistent with one's self-concept, as well as with others' expectations.

In addition to you having high expectations of success, it is mandatory Self-Fulfilling Prophecy that your supervisors have high expectations, not only for themselves, but for all of their subordinates. The inexperienced strive to live up to the expectations of those in authority. The inexperienced have few preconceptions to interfere and are easily encouraged by others who have high expectations of them.

Interpersonal Self-Fulfilling Prophecies can create greater interviewee compliance if you expect it. I try to act in a pleasant, friendly, and encouraging manner to promote clear thinking on the part of interviewees. Unintentional communication can be incredibly subtle and complex both in negative and positive ways. It seems that many interviews are equivalent to a parent talking to a child because of the emotionally tense character of some interviews. Hence, I try to recognize and comprehend emotions that could produce fears and anxieties that interrupt or restrict clear thinking.

I recommend that you develop a positive, humane, and interactional style that signals respondents to comply. Your expectation of interviewee behavior can unwittingly become an accurate prediction. Treating interviewees as though they want to provide the greatest degree of truthful compliance establishes high probability they will do so. Belief! Expectation! Action! Reaction!

Belief: Believe in yourself and your ability to verbally and nonverbally obtain truthful data. Also, believe interviewees are ready, willing, and able to share truthful data.

Expectation: Maintain a positive expectancy of success. Have faith in your abilities. By everything you do and say exhibit that you anticipate receiving cooperation. Be a positive Pygmalion!

Action: Express an I'm okay, you're okay attitude. Treat interviewees as having value as human beings, regardless of the inquiry. How you treat them greatly determines the received.

Reaction: Interviewees, respond, tend to live up to your expectation. If your tactics are positive, they will probably comply with your requests for data; if negative, they may refuse to comply. Either you are a positive Pygmalion or a negative Pygmalion, one or the other. As long as you have a choice, please select to be a positive Pygmalion to be most effective, a first class forensic interviewer.

The following comments about the Galatea effect are intended for investigators who strive to be better interviewers than they are now. I function under the persuasion that interviewers can become more confident as they attain positive experiences. Dealing with specific situations successfully tends to increase interviewer capacity generally.

Galatea Effect

Self-beliefs predict motivation and task performance in organizational settings. Self-efficacy (one's belief in one's capability to perform a task) affects a task effort, persistence, expressed interest, and the level of goal difficulty selected for performance. Self-efficacy arises from the gradual acquisition of complex cognitive, social, linguistic, and/or physical skills through experience. Mastery is facilitated when gradual accomplishments build the skills, coping abilities, and exposure needed for task performance. Groups with specific and challenging goals consistently have shown higher levels of performance than groups with no goals, easy goals, or "do your best" goals. A sense of personal efficacy in mastering challenges is apt to generate greater interest in the activity than is self-perceived inefficacy in producing competent performances.

Interest is developed via satisfaction from success, and an increase in self-efficacy is developed from a sense of personal causation. Interest may be induced externally for repetitive tasks, but is intrinsic for problem-solving tasks. It appears that high self-efficacy leads to self-administered reward and individuals who reward themselves perform better than those who do not. An efficacy expectation is a judgment, belief, of one's ability to execute a certain behavior pattern.

Self-efficacy may be involved in the Pygmalion effect (see Self-Fulfilling Prophecy) through the persuasive influence of others holding positive expectations. Persuasion is an important source of efficacy information. The following types of information affect the success of persuasion: credibility and expertness of the source, consensus among multiple sources, and familiarity of the source with task demands.

Self-efficacy is task specific, examining the individual's conviction that he or she can perform a specific task at a specific level of expertise. Behavioral changes that are brought about by reinforcement are influenced by many things, including self-monitoring, goal setting, social surveillance, and the causal influence of anticipatory thought.

There may be a significant correlation between perceived and actual competencies (performance) because perceived competency has much in common with self-efficacy. A perceived competency could be defined as generalized self-efficacy, the conviction that one can successfully carry out a range of actions. Self-efficacy is task specific, arising primarily from the influences of mastery, modeling, and persuasion. One possibility in predicting success is an individual's conviction that he or she can master new situations.[78]

The Galatea effect is a boost in performance caused by raising self-expectation. Expectations are the key to producing the Pygmalion effect, the Galatea effect is a result of the interviewer's performance expectations. Pygmalion and Galatea effects often occur together in nature and are difficult to disentangle.

A key to the willingness to commit oneself to a highly demanding undertaking is one's belief in one's capacity to mobilize the physical, intellectual, and emotional resources needed to succeed, that is, self-efficacy. Self-efficacy is emerging as an important determinant of work motivation. Expecting to do well motivates greater effort and culminates in improved performance. Self-efficacy, self-confidence, and self-assurance are nearly synonymous with each other and with self-esteem.

Expectancy is defined as a momentary belief concerning the likelihood that a particular act will be followed by a particular outcome. Self-efficacy tends to be situation specific, at first. Once established, enhanced self-efficacy tends to generalize to other situations. Self-efficacy has been defined as people's judgments of their capabilities to organize and execute courses of action required to

attain designated types of performances. It is concerned not with the skills one
has but with judgments of what one can do with whatever skills one possesses.

Self-confidence in one's skills, self-efficacy, belief you can do it, is built primarily upon successful performances; however, vicarious experience, verbal
persuasion, and physiological state also influence the establishment of self-
efficacy. Physiological state refers to the commensurate inferences about self-
efficacy that can be drawn from some of the visceral reactions that accompany
the threat of failure and the exhilaration of success."[75]

Both the Pygmalion and Galatea effects are based upon expectations.
The Pygmalion effect has to do with expectations others have of us while
the Galatea effect deals with expectations we have for ourselves. Self-
expectations are an intrinsic part of developing, making dreams reality.
We are influenced by both effects. At times the Galatea effect may be
negated by the expectations others have of us. Solid effort and commitment are needed for the Galatea effect to work through acceptance and
respect of self-expectations. It takes courage to discover what is possible
for ourselves.[91]

While applying the Pygmalion effect (SFP) during investigations, it is
vital to understand the requirements and meet the expectations of those
we investigate (see Needs). It takes extraordinary drive and determination to be successful as you commit yourself to greater proficiency.
Productivity and personal development are the goals.[91]

The Polyphasic Flow Chart, following, is offered as a type of guide or
road map. Don't let it throw you. Yes, it's a challenge to ponder the many
pieces of this presentation; but, having done so, you will probably find
you have more confidence in conducting interviews and you may even,
partly because of it, become a more first rate interrogator. The intent is to
consider essential pieces of the interviewing process so as to give you a
strong grasp of some workable tactics. All of what you gather from this
writing bears upon and is interrelated with the process suggested by the
Polyphasic Flow Chart. Any and all tactics offered are intended to
encourage you to think about interviewing in ways you may not have
considered before. We can all be better than we are!

Chapter Ten

POLYPHASIC FLOW CHART

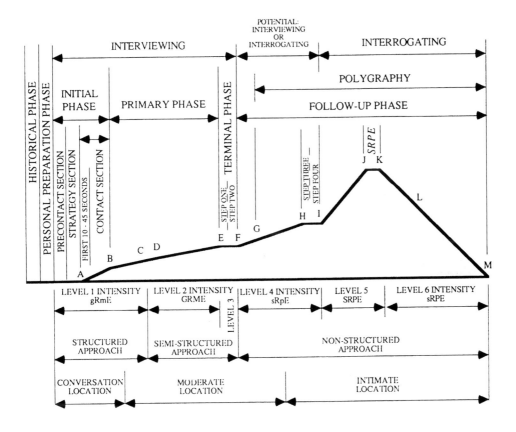

A broad overview of interviewing consists of six phases of a Polyphasic Flow Chart: Historical, Personal Preparation, Initial, Primary, Terminal, and Follow-up.

Before reviewing each phase of the Polyphasic, Flow Chart, please visualize their relationships. The Historical and Personal Preparation Phases and two sections, Precontact and Strategy, of the Initial Phase are to be considered before entering into problem-solving interviews with witnesses, suspects, or even victims, for that matter.

Historical and Personal Preparation Phases

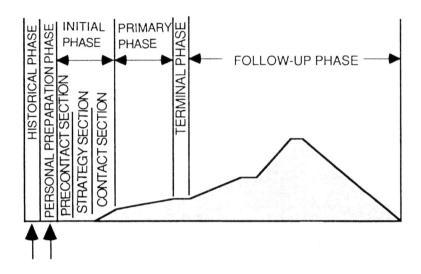

Historical Phase

The Historical Phase and its effect is influenced by participant culture, education, and experience. Investigative problems bring together a mix of participant characteristics. With few exceptions, people advance taught cultural progress based upon life's *tried and true* methods of human interaction.

The Historical Phase involves all of the influences that impact investigators and the interviewees. Someone has packed our emotional luggage for life, so to speak. As we are growing up, our parents or whoever raised us has directly or indirectly taught us certain things. Some of us carry a great deal of garbage in the emotional compartment of our luggage. That garbage, consisting of biases, prejudices, and so forth, can hamper our productivity and effectiveness in life, if, in our Personal Preparation Phase, we don't take a look in our luggage to modify its contents. We may, however, take opportunity to discard much of that garbage to lead to a healthier life. Through education, training and experience we can decide to modify our contents and thereby probably become more proficient as investigators, or whatever else we choose.

Self-beliefs (see Self-Fulfilling Prophecy) are developed or destroyed, to large extent by those who raise us. Our self-esteem is built or bludgeoned when we are young. Those of us with gumption make it inspite of those around us bent upon keeping us down by butchering our self-image. Likewise, our esteem for others can be damaged in these formative years and forever alter our perspectives in communication. This possible damage to self-esteem and esteem for others can be corrected during our Personal Preparation Phase where we can make a decided effort to modify our attitudes and related behavior.

Effective investigators come to terms with all of this sorting through of luggage before handling any investigations. The successful ones don't knowingly bring biases and prejudice into inquiries that might lead to misguided observations, evaluation, and assessments. They become aware that how they treat people is greatly influenced by what happened to them in their Historical and Personal Preparation Phases. Ultimately, we are completely in control of our behavior!

Personal Preparation Phase

Interviewers can be applied scientists, emotionally mature individuals using practical qualities to develop skill and proficiency. Their ethical behavior becomes evident as their leadership qualities develop. Professional adaptability is expressed in willingness to modify behavior in a never-ending learning process.

While sorting through any garbage in our luggage of life, we may have opportunity to learn how to use certain tactics to assist us in gathering vital information. I call the listed tactics, following, Filter Factors. By using them, investigators will probably enhance the effectiveness of their communication during interviews.

If the factors, following, are applied in sensitive, delicately skillful ways they will have significant and positive affects on the outcome of the interview process. They are listed as vital tools, tactics, for any interview interaction. I call them filter factors because they assist the interviewer to show, display favorable characteristics and to screen out or mute less favorable ones. They are factors, elements of a facade, presented to interviewees to help the interviewer look okay. Without doubt, most interviews contain at least one hidden agenda. Certainly, the interviewer, depending on the organization represented, has unpublished, unannounced reasons for conducting the interview. The idea is that use of such filter factors may cloud or fog over the interviewee's clear view of the interviewer's hidden agenda and what is happening during the interview.

In the real world, individuals have opportunity to modify what they learned while growing up. As investigators, or before, we can take a close look at ourselves and change those things about us we and others consider destructive to the process of communication. In our personal rebuilding, we can pilot our abilities using tactics suggested in this and other writings. It's up to us!

To be competent, resourceful, in the use of the filter factors, following, first rate interviewers practice long and hard in using them in preparation for each next time they are called on to conduct an interview.

Filter Factors for interviewers:

1. Consider the human needs of interview participants!
2. Use nonjudgmental acceptance!
3. Continue to build and maintain rapport!
4. Avoid antagonizing or harassing interviewees!
5. Avoid using coercive behavior!
6. Use empathy!
7. Use respect!
8. Use genuineness!
9. Use active, attentive listening!
10. Use patience!
11. Use positive silence!
12. Use positive eye contact!
13. Maintain a positive, neutral stance!
14. Use positive proximics!
15. Use positive kinesics!
16. Use positive haptics where appropriate!
17. Use positive power!
18. Use positive control!
19. Use a positive attitude!
20. Apply flexible methods!
21. Control personal anger!
22. Cover personal values!
23. Cover suspiciousness!
24. Use creative imagination!
25. Apply the Self-Fulfilling Prophecy!
26. Exhibit human warmth—sensitivity!
27. Use observation!
28. Use evaluation!
29. Use assessment!

30. Avoid third-degree questioning!
31. Use closed questions when appropriate!
32. Use open questions when appropriate!
33. Use simple questions!
34. Avoid using double meaning questions!
35. Dare to ask tough questions!
36. Use unasked questions (assume answered yes)!
37. Properly use leading questions!
38. Use self-appraisal questions!
39. Handle trial-balloon questions!
40. Assume more data is available!

Initial Phase

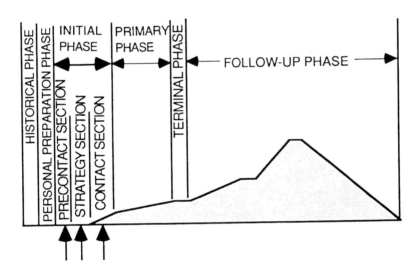

The Initial Phase consists of Precontact Strategy and Contact Sections. Although the Historical and Personal Preparation Phases, without question, subtly influence our behavior during the Initial and subsequent phases, they do not deal directly with the investigative problem.

Of the three sections of the Initial Phase, two deal with details of information regarding the matter under investigation . . . the people possibly involved in the matter . . . conditions under which interviews take place. The third, the Contact Section, has to do with the first few critical minutes of contact with the interviewee.

Initial Phase—Precontact Section

The Precontact Section of the Initial Phase generally involves the interviewer becoming familiar with available information as the beginning of a flexible interview plan. A plan includes a Floating Point Strategy (F.P.S.) and a *clear* picture of interview objectives. Determination of the interviewee's personality regarding habits and hobbies based upon available data is vital to effective, flexible planning. Seasoned interviewers know luck is merely what is left over after careful planning and proper preparation.

During a Preliminary Inquiry, Precontact Section—Initial Phase details of an investigative problem are obtained. That inquiry might reveal which of the interviewees had significant knowledge, access, opportunity, or motivation to cause the problem. Evidence is collected and, or, reviewed as gathered from the complainant . . . victim, witness. Success of the investigation is often based upon how thoroughly investigators gather such foundation data. Learning the details of the predication of the inquiry will fortify the investigator throughout the investigation. Through this important inquiry, investigators gather information to establish details as to time, date, and other information specific to the investigative problem. In light of all available information, the investigator formulates why someone would do those things causing the investigation. Possible motivation is reflected in interviewee life style; habits, hobbies, stressors.

Initial Phase—Strategic Planning Section

In most instances, interviewers have little or no specific knowledge of potential interviewees before reviewing the investigative problem. Planning interviews includes conducting a sufficient background check of potential interviewees, when possible, to determine strategic information about interviewees and the problem under investigation. Having such information allows the interviewer to anticipate why interviewees may or may not comply with requests for truthful information. Knowing their cultural attitudes and feelings can help mold yourself more adequately to meet their personalities and potential reluctance. Preparing for reluctance is vital while expecting compliance.

Prevailing participant personality characteristics include the mixture of the Parent, Adult and Child Ego States predominate in each.[39] I consider personality: behavior patterns deeply ingrained, including

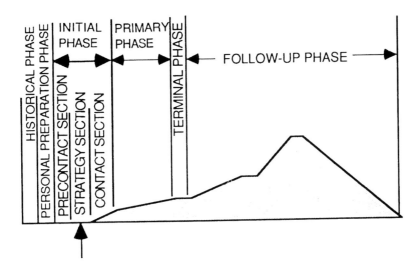

ways one thinks about, perceives, and relates to the environment and oneself.[9]

It is better to be over prepared than under prepared, especially when dealing with people who may try to deceive you.[56] "The novice interviewer watches the casual performance of the experienced interviewer and wrongly assumes that the relaxed atmosphere indicates no appreciable planning or research."[24]

Environmental Setting: In the Strategic Planning Section of the Initial Phase determine where best to interview people to gain their greatest compliance. Ideally, interviewing away from the hustle and noise of some environments is best. Often, however, transporting employees any distance to some ideal site might disrupt the work flow of a business setting with minimal gain. The key factor in any interview is privacy and most sites allowing that are probably suitable.

Proximics: Sometimes space limitations prevent moving closer to the interviewee than the Moderate Location and, often, beginning an interview in the Conversation Location is not critical. I always try to begin interviews in the Conversational Location and then gradually move into the Moderate Location where most of my interviews are conducted. The Intimate Location is usually not used in interviewing unless dealing with an interviewee who needs consoling, comforting, or when using Level 4 Intensity of review and encouragement or other portions of the Follow-up Phase.

In my view, moving closer to interviewees is intended to assist participates to focus more fully on the topics of discussion. The advantage of such closeness is in the human warmth conveyed. Positive motives displayed generally spark productive results.

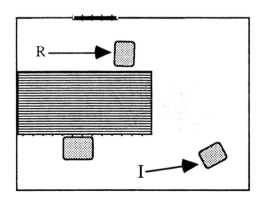

Plan view, typical interview room, 10'X12'

Illustrating participants in Conversation Location
I=Interviewer situated about six feet from R (Respondent).

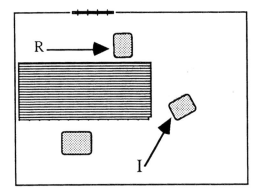

Plan view, typical interview room, 10'X12'

Illustrating participants in Moderate Location
I=Interviewer situated about four feet from R (Respondent).

The above illustrations represent typical participant locations.

How likely is it that the interviewee will comply with my request for information? Well, who knows for sure. I make an educated guess based upon certain indicators, premises. That's where the Forensic Formula, mentally, comes in handy:

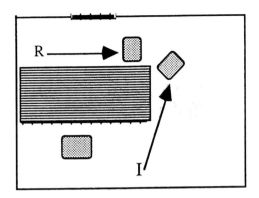

Plan view, typical interview room, 10'X12'

Illustrating participants in Intimate Location
I=Interviewer situated about two feet from R (Respondent).

Forensic Formula

$$R = 2(T + A + N + P + \frac{V + B}{2}) = W.N.$$

$$I = H + T + A + N + P + 2(E + U) + \frac{V + B}{2} = W.N.$$

$$\frac{R + 2I}{3} = \% T.I.C.$$

Details of the Forensic Formula will be explored subsequently.

The following list of some behavior characteristics may be indicators of potential interviewee cooperation. Such characteristics are part of the basis of Forensic Formula Calculations. Thus, the degree of possible interviewee cooperation, is relative to and based upon behavior as reflected in known habits of interviewee character, loyalty, and reputation.

Behavior Consideration in Establishing Interviewee Type

Abrupt	Doubting	Masterful	Restless
Adventurous	Dramatic	Mellow	Reverent
Affluent	Dynamic	Methodical	Righteous
Aggressive	Egotistical	Meticulous	Scholarly
Altruistic	Emotional	Mild	Scrappy
Anxious	Exceptional	Modest	Secretive

Apprehensive	Extravagant	Nonconforming	Self-educated
Argumentative	Extroverted	Opinionated	Self-sacrificing
Blunt	Fearless	Opportunistic	Self-sufficient
Boisterous	Fluent	Ordinary	Sensitive
Bold	Forceful	Orthodox	Shrewd
Calm	Forward	Outspoken	Shy
Carefree	Funny	Outstanding	Skeptical
Cautious	Fussy	Over critical	Sophisticated
Changeable	Gifted	Overeager	Stalwart
Clear-thinking	Guarded	Painstaking	Stern
Clever	Happy-go-lucky	Perfectionist	Stimulating
Complacent	Hardheaded	Permissive	Strict
Compromising	Harmless	Pessimistic	Stubborn
Conforming	Headstrong	Philosophical	Studious
Constrained	Humble	Polished	Subordinate
Contemplative	Humorous	Possessive	Subtle
Conventional	Hurried	Preoccupied	Suggestible
Critical	Idealistic	Presumptuous	Suspicious
Cultured	Impatient	Profound	Talkative
Cynical	Impersonal	Prominent	Temperamental
Defensive	Impulsive	Prosperous	Tenderhearted
Defiant	Influential	Provocative	Thrifty
Deliberate	Inoffensive	Prudent	Tough
Demanding	Intellectual	Rational	Unassuming
Dependent	Inventive	Reactionary	Unbiased
Discerning	Judicious	Religious	Uncomplaining
Distinguished	Lighthearted	Remarkable	Unprejudiced
Domineering	Limited	Reserved	Unpretentious

Forensic Formula Factors

When evaluating interviewees (usually sight unseen) based upon the potential of available information, I'm guided in assigning numerical values to the Factors of the Forensic Formula. Insight gained from available data assists me to calculate mentally, *probably not actually,* the weighted number for me and for each interviewee to determine the chances of gaining truthful testimonial evidence.

Formula Factors Regarding Interview Participants

I = Interviewer; person in an authority role seeking truthful data (testimonial evidence) to use in decision making and action taking.

R = Interviewee (Respondent); victim, witness, or suspect; someone possibly possessing investigative information. An interviewee can become an interrogatee as the information gathering process unfolds. Hence, a suspect can become a subject.

H = Applies to the interviewer. Clinical Humanness; recognition of interviewee uniqueness through applied empathy, respect, and genuineness.

T = Trust; combined: self-image, self-esteem, self-control, self-confidence degree of self-worth, positive self-regard.

A = Attitude; predisposed basis of self-esteem and dispensed esteem. Degree of I'm okay — You're okay.

N = Predominant social human needs, foremost of which are inclusion, control, and intimacy.

P = Personality; ego states mixture (via Transactional Analysis Theory).

E = Applies to the interviewer. Degree of positive expectancy as expressed in Belief, Expectation, Action, and Response (B.E.A.R.); (see the Self-Fulfilling Prophecy).

U = Applies to the interviewer. Understanding; degree of Nonjudgmental acceptance used.

V = Degree to which cultural values are maintained based upon customs and mores.

B = Balance (emotional equilibrium); individual psychological uniqueness. The degree of development within the range from impulsive, ego-centered childishness with low tolerance for frustration to patient, collaborative altruism, with control of impulses.

Formula Factors Regarding Interviewees: Factor values in the following examples are arbitrary, subjective at best. I view most interviewees as average in all factor categories and assign values accordingly. Values are based on gut feel or intuition influenced by available information. Now, if you think such value assignments are not relevant or valid, ponder that I have had relatively high success in solving complicated investigations using this subjective methodology.

Calculation of %T.I.C.: As I've said, the calculation is a subjective foreground estimate of my chances (%T.I.C.) of gaining truthful data from the interviewee. The idea is to think about my chances or how likely it is that I will gain a high degree of truthful interviewee compliance.

All of this formula consideration is nothing more than some deep thought as to the amount of possible interviewee compliance and which interviewee might have the necessary knowledge, access, opportunity, and motivation to be involved in the matter under investigation. The goal is to gain truthful compliance.

Formula Factors are measured (evaluated) between 1 & 10, with 5 as the median (as many below 5 as above 5). The evaluation of 10 (perfect) is not used because interview participants are thought not to have reached that state of accomplishment. The "2" in the weighted number portion of the Forensic Formula is used to make results come out in percentages for easier evaluation and application.

In other words, I assign numbers, values, to each factor related to the potential interviewee. For example, if I sense low interviewee self-esteem, I might assign a number value of 3 or 4 when considering the "T" factor in the interviewee's formula. Again, all of this calculation is purely mental on my part . . . gauging the probability of interviewee cooperation . . . attempting to anticipate the Percentage of *T*ruthful *I*nterviewee *C*ompliance.

Forensic Formula

$$R = 2(T + A + N + P + \frac{V + B}{2}) = W.N. \text{ (This represents the interviewee)}$$

$$I = H + T + A + N + P + 2(E + U) + \frac{V + B}{2} = W.N. \text{ (This represents the interviewer)}$$

$$\%T.I.C. = \frac{R + 2I}{3} = \text{(This represents the combined influence of both participants)}$$

Calculation regarding interviewees: In calculating the interviewee (*R*espondent) portion of the Forensic Formula please consider the following evaluations. I'm only using 6s in the following to illustrate how this thing is intended to work:

These values have to do with the previously listed factors for the Forensic Formula related to interviewees. The 6s represent values I might give to the interviewee. The 6s could be 2s or 9s or any other number ranging from one to ten all based upon what I *sense* about the interviewee. If I feel the interviewee has a bad attitude, for example, I might assign a value of 2 or 3 in the interviewee's formula regarding

Interviewee (R) portion of the Forensic Formula

TRUST ATTITUDE NEEDS PERSONALITY VALUES BALANCE

6   6   6   6   6   6

$$R = 2(T + A + N + P + \frac{V + B}{2}) = W.N.$$

$$R = 2(6 + 6 + 6 + 6 + \frac{6 + 6}{2}) = 60$$

$R = 60$ (This is the weighted number for the interviewee in this example).

attitude; (A). However, if I sense the interviewee has a positive attitude, I might assign a value of 8 or 9 in the formula for the interviewee regarding attitude. This value assigning takes place based upon what I learn during the preliminary inquiry (Initial Phase—Precontact Section). I consider which values to use as I review case data and speak with people who claim to know the individuals I will probably interview during the course of the investigation. Through the eyes, ears, and sensing of those who provide information, I gain a feeling of who will be the most cooperative interviewees.

Calculation regarding the interviewer . . . me, in this example: Now, as you might guess, I consider myself pretty good as an interviewer, so, I put high numbers into the formula for myself. At least I believe I'm usually treating interviewees, interacting with people, in a consistently positive fashion. I try to personally maintain about the same values in each interview.

When I evaluate myself before conducting interviews, I envision certain values for me as factors in the Forensic Formula. Using these values reminds and encourages me to display the most professional demeanor I can.

Also, these values have to do with the previously listed factors for the Forensic Formula related to interviewers. Please notice that I too show T.A.N.P.V.B. values; but, in addition, H.U.E. are evaluated. Even the least educated, least sophisticated interviewees notice how I'm coming across to them as a person. If I don't score well in their eyes, I don't get the information. If I'm not okay in their evaluation, then they withhold data, probably. I can do all the scoring of myself I want; but, I realize the

Interviewer (I) portion of the Forensic Formula

HUMANNESS TRUST ATTITUDE NEEDS PERSONALITY EXPECTATION UNDERSTANDING VALUES BALANCE

8   8   8   8   8   9   9   8   8

$$I = H + T + A + N + P + 2(E + U) + \frac{V + B}{2} = W.N.$$

$$I = 8 + 8 + 8 + 8 + 8 + 2(9 + 9) + \frac{8 + 8}{2} = W.N.$$

$I = 84$ (This is the weighted number for the interviewer in this example).

most important scoring is done by the interviewee, of me. The interviewee doesn't need a formula to rate me, just a gut feeling of if I'm okay or not okay to talk to. Let's not overlook the power of intuition.

The 84 represents a weighed number (W.N.) for me. Meaning that when I consider all of the factors for me, I come up with a number (W.N.) representing my part in the total interaction with the interviewee. My weighed number represents my relative influence on the success of the interview. The key issue is how I influence the outcome of the interview. After all, the only one I can, or try to, control in the interview is me.

In the following, the R stands for the weighted number for the respondent and the I stands for the weighted number for the interviewer. As part of the formula, I = 84 and R = 60, with R + 2I indicating the weighted number for the respondent (R) be added to two times the weighted number for the interviewer (I), or 60 + two times 84. In other words, 60 plus 168 which equals 228. Then, 228 divided by three. With all of that, I'm trying to show the influence of the interviewer in the interview. By suggesting the use of two times the weighted number of the interviewer in the formula, I'm trying to announce how what the interviewer says and does has a great impact on the success of the interview than what the interviewee says and/or does.

$$\%T.I.C. = \frac{R + 2I}{3} = \frac{60 + 168}{3} = \frac{228}{3} = 68.4$$

$$\%T.I.C. = 68.4$$

As an example, the 68.4 represents the probability of me gaining this interviewee's truthful cooperation or the percent of possibility that the interviewee will comply with my request for information.

By placing higher values in the formula for interviewee factors, I would be indicating I felt a greater possibility existed that the interviewee was going to comply more truthfully in answering my questions. In contrast, the more I sense, feel, interviewees are less likely to cooperate, the lower the values I place in the formula for them.

Again, the goal of an interview is to gain the highest percentage of truthful interviewee compliance (%T.I.C.). I want interviewees to tell me all they know about the circumstances of the matter under investigation. Therefore, I calculate how the interviewee and I will probably blend in the interview, how we will get along. My hope is to encourage interviewees to reveal everything. So, all factors are considered together, with awareness of the interviewer's major role in the process.

In all inquiries, interviewees were considered separately, in advance of their interviews. The foreground is that time when I have yet to communicate with the interviewee, it's the sideline action before going onto the playing field to try fancy plays. The foreground is the time to determine and study strategy. No contact yet. That's what I mean by the foreground estimate . . . my chances of gaining truthful data from interviewees . . . not completely based on chance. Such estimating applies to each interviewee.

Fundamental considerations before contact with interviewees: The collection, evaluation, and preservation of information is vital to any investigation. Without pressure or suggestion, effective interviewers encourage interviewees to provide a narrative account of their observations regarding the investigative problem. Once the interviewee narrative account has been presented, it's vital to review and summarize details to ensure the report is complete. Allow unrestricted recall then ask more specific questions to gain details while taking notes. Doing so shows the interviewer has been attentive. The quality of information gained depends upon the interviewer's interpersonal skills.

Showing concern and developing rapport helps in gathering data. Directing full attention to the interviewee and avoiding an indifferent attitude is vitally important. By speaking softly, slowly, and firmly, effective interviewers communicate that they are capable of both understanding and solving the investigative problem. Rather than use rapid-fire questions, proficient interviewers allow interviewees time to answer fully without interruption, thereby showing interest and attentiveness.

Used properly, eye contact is an effective factor in establishing and maintaining communication; however, if the interviewer stares at the interviewee, there may be undue strain placed upon the interviewee which may interfere with communication.

Many interviewees are completely impartial and relate what they know, while others are influenced by physical and emotional factors distorting their perception and affecting the reliability of their information.

At a crime scene, locate witnesses and record their identity and their observations. When contacting witnesses, effective interviewers identify themselves, explain the reason for the contact, relate the time of the crime, and ask the witness to recall everything observed during that period without contaminating information provided. At times, interviewers lack extensive preparation because of the urgency of the situation. In adverse conditions of distraction and confusion, gather basic, pertinent information immediately and, later, in a recontact interview, gain specific facts under more favorable conditions. Often, even without clear preparation, it is necessary to forge ahead and interview.

People tend to seek group consensus and often will conclude the group as right and they are wrong. If not separated quickly and interviewed, witnesses may compare stories and may adopt parts of the accounts of others at the crime scene. Interviewing alibi witnesses promptly helps reduce opportunity for anyone to corroborate stories and prevents a suspect from covering up participation in the crime.

Fear of reprisal and intimidation may prevent interviewees from cooperating; therefore, gain identification and interview witnesses away from suspects to prevent unnecessary witness apprehension. Proper regard for the feelings of victims, emotionally upset even if uninjured, facilitates questioning and fosters their cooperation. Fear is perhaps the most common and strongest emotional reaction of victims. Above all else, reducing victim fear requires patience. Fear is an indication of physical and emotional imbalance that cannot be dissipated by the exercise of self-control alone. A hurried approach will only confuse and apply more distress, increasing rather than reducing emotional reaction. Calm the victim by saying things such as: "You're safe now."

Interviewee credibility is based upon truthfulness, believability, as related to observation and accuracy in reporting. Four possible tests regarding such credibility are:

1. Was the interviewee present and aware of circumstances?
2. Was the interviewee attentive during what happened? Distinguish actual interviewee experience from feelings related to what was observed.
3. Determine interviewee powers of observation and ability to relate facts briefly, correctly, and clearly without emotional disturbance.
4. Do nonverbal signs indicate interviewee deception?

Plausibility of witness observation is critical to the overall investigation. What are the specific interviewee abilities, physical functioning, to see and hear what was reportedly observed?

Gaining interviewee cooperation may be a frustrating effort for some investigators. Interviewees may not want to become involved in the investigate efforts. Some dissatisfactions regarding the system held by some interviewees are:

1. Callous or indifferent treatment.
2. Fear of reprisals.
3. Inconvenient criminal or civil court continuances.
4. Confusion and fear owing to not being properly prepared to provide depositions or court testimony.

To some interviewees, an unnecessary burden on time and energy seems endless with numerous appearances and related fear of authorities and others connected to the process; not to mention possible related fatigue and potential financial loss.

The greater the time lapse between the incident and the location of witnesses, the less chance they will be able to accurately report what they observed. In addition, they may be reluctant to cooperate fully once the excitement of the situation has subsided.

Initial Phase—Contact Section

The First Four Minutes: A time frame of interview interaction as depicted between points *A* and *B* of the Flow Chart. Within this time frame, I begin using the Filter Factors such as active listening and so forth, and continue using them into the Primary Phase and throughout the inquiry, even into the Follow-up Phase where confrontation may take place, where inconsistencies are resolved, and during which admissions and confessions may be sought.

On occasion, an interviewee will confess or make some significant admission within the first four minutes of interview beginning with-

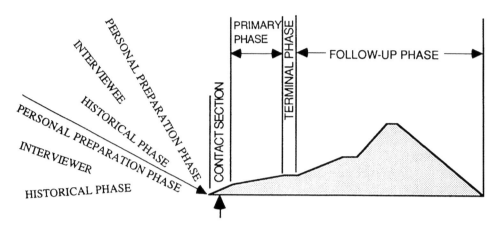

Both partipants converge on point A with whatever they have learned, practiced, and adapted in life to that point. We have hopes the interviewer has honorable intentions to provide professional service, and that the interviewee is ready, willing, able to provide truthful information. We know, however, these hopes may not be realistic in some situations.

out being specifically encouraged to do so. Be ready for such an event.

Introduction: The first 10 to 45 seconds of interview interaction between points *A* and *B* of the Flow Chart is mainly the time frame in which to begin exhibiting that you are calm, cool, collected, friendly, firm, fair, human, compassionate, okay, and subtle. In telephone interviews, your unseen qualities are expressed through tone of voice, timing, silences and other paralinguistics. Face-to-face interviews are preferred.

Greeting: Intentions are conveyed through nonverbal messages in those first few seconds of human interaction. Human warmth is expressed in tone of voice, gestures, and mannerisms paralinguistics significantly affect the interview outcome. Important rituals help interviewers warmly display a polite beginning of fact-finding interviews. During the first few minutes, an interview tone is determined, which may last for minutes or even hours.

Seating: Predetermine the seating arrangements in a location allowing privacy and comfort. Learning how and when to use the Conversation, Moderate, and Intimate locations is vital to your success. How and when to use those locations are subsequently explored, as is the concept of space between people during communication (see previous illustrations).

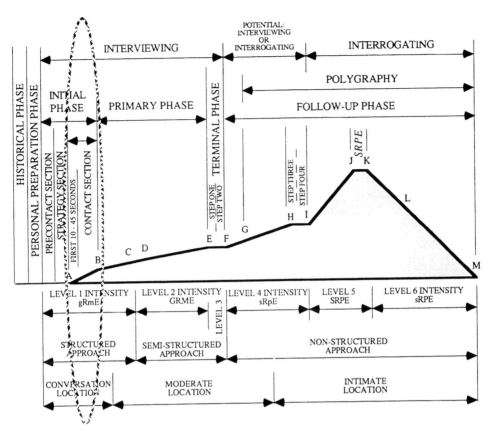

Observation, Evaluation, Assessment, and Intuition: These are vital and often subconscious elements in all phases of investigative problem solving. They usually begin between participants with the first verbal and, or, nonverbal communication . . . not ending until their last communication.

Tone Setting: Your intonation of voice and exhibited behavior (non verbal signals) can express a particular meaning or feeling showing attitude through use of words or phrases. This is the time to exhibit prevailing or predominant style, the hue of your *true colors,* your intended friendly interaction. This is when the interviewee Interaction Evaluation Process (I.E.P.) begins and consciously or subconsciously continues throughout the interaction; interview and, or, interrogation. The I.E.P. is a way in which the interviewee looks over the total circumstances of the interview, including the interviewer, to determine if the conditions are correct to reveal information. Whether you like it or not, I.E.P. happens. Even the dumbest, least educated interviewees sense if you are okay.

Again, I.E.P. is not limited to the interview; it applies in all aspects of the Follow-up Phase as well.

Announcement of Objective: When beginning any interview, it is important to state an interview objective while providing an invitation for interviewees to present statements, observations, opinions, or facts.

Determining how the reported event happened and how it can be prevented in the future may be your expressed intention, part of your announced objective accomplishment of the goal of the interaction begins with your first communication with the interviewee. While seeking interviewees' opinions, insights, antidotes, to assist in finding pieces to the investigative puzzle, show appreciation of their agreement to be interviewed regarding the problem. There is some strategic advantage when interviewees are not under arrest when interviewed . . . cooperation seems more likely . . . certainly there is less distress.

Although the interviewee may be uncomfortable to speak with some interviewers, your professional demeanor and friendly ways soon estab-lish your suitability as a recipient of important information unavailable elsewhere. It seems only polite to announce the purpose of an interview to the interviewee. Hence, you might say something such as:

> The purpose of our talk today is to discuss the report about _____ happening. I'm looking for information that will assist me in making clear recommendations. I'm involved in interviewing several people; therefore, I need your assistance to get a better view of the circumstances. First, let me get a little background data about you to get to know you a little better (moving into the Structured Approach).

Whenever stating the objective of your interview and discussing the circumstances of the reported event, I recommend you use the word *if* to soften any questioning method. Using *if* tends to prevent accusations that might seem implied or sensed in your voice. Please notice the use of *if* as related to the Semi-Structured Approach, following.

A Floating Point Strategy (F.P.S.): Applied as soon as you compre-hend most of the basis of the investigative problem, as learned in the Precontact Section—Preliminary Inquiry of the Initial Phase. F.P.S. is any point in time during the problem solution process when strategy, hypothesis, may need reevaluation and possible modification in light of developing evidence. Probability estimating is the essence of F.P.S. Pic-ture your problem-solving process with numerous points at which you can take a renewed view of your progress, evaluating to determine if you are on the right track toward the objective. Your strategy floats from point to point without setting anchor or certain course without first being reasonably sure of most conditions affecting your assessment of the evidence. Through it all, it is important to assist the interviewee to rationalize and save face as the foundation for cooperation.

Intensity Levels

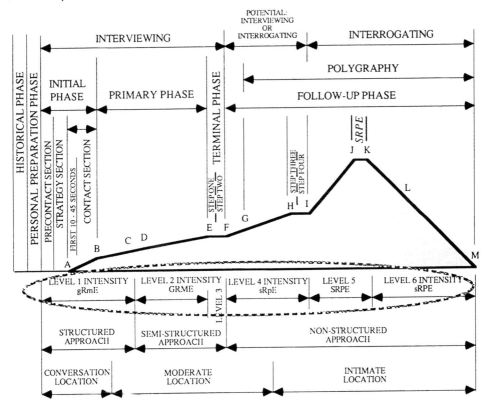

Dictionary definitions of certain words, following, may help explain certain parts of the Polyphasic Flow Chart as they apply to this way of looking at the topic of interviewing (also see Self-beliefs, SFP):

Intensity: The degree or extent to which something is intense . . . The quality or condition of being intense . . . Energy, strength, concentration of activity, thought or feeling.

Intense: Acute or strong, as in sensations, feelings, or emotions . . . Having characteristic quality in high degree . . . Strenuous or earnest, as activity, exertion, diligence, thought . . . Having or showing great strength, strong feeling, or tension, as a person, the face, language.

Review: The process of going over a subject again in study or recitation in order to fix it in the memory or summarize the facts . . . An inspiration or examination by viewing . . . A viewing of the past; contemplation or consideration of past events, circumstances, or facts . . . A general survey of something . . . To look upon.

Encouragement: To inspire with courage, spirit, or confidence . . . To stimulate by assistance, approval.[45]

Those definitions, above, shed some light on the suggested positive behavior necessary if interviewers are to reach sufficient proficiency in gathering truthful information. Excellent interviewers modify their behavior to inspire and convince interviewees to provide information, hopefully the truth. With sufficient practice and dedication, many interviewers develop into capable interrogators. By applying honed interviewing skills and focusing their energies upon improvement, interviewers can become more and more competent in solving complicated investigative problems. It's not force, but finesse that counts in human interaction.

When we consider intensity of review and encouragement, talismanic incantation comes to mind in that intensity, really, is the verbal and nonverbal communication used to influence the interviewee to reveal information, or influence the interrogatee to own up to an admission or confession. Intensity is the remarkable or powerful presentation which influences the actions of the interviewee or the interrogatee. Degrees of intensity imply amount of effort put into how remarkable or powerful the presentation will be. It's all in how we treat them. Never coerce anyone during an inquiry.

Levels of Intensity

Level 1 Intensity: gRmE (basically used from point A to between points C and D in all interviews, but also in preliminary inquiries); *g*eneral *R*eview and *m*inimal *E*ncouragement; representing the least amount of review and encouragement.

Level 2 Intensity: GRME (used starting between points C and D to point E); representing the most amount of *G*eneral *R*eview and *M*inimal *E*ncouragement.

Level 3 Intensity: GRME (continued use between point E and point F).

Level 4 Intensity: sRpE (used between points F and I representing the least amount of *s*pecific *R*eview and *p*ersistent *E*ncouragement.

I try to avoid immediately using sRpE (Level 4 Intensity) with interviewees to resolve inconsistencies. I make it a general rule to notice inconsistencies and *tune in* to them without *pouncing* on interviewees because of them. It is self-defeating to play the *I got ya game!*

Level 5 Intensity: SRPE (used between points I and K representing more than sRpE in the amount of *S*pecific *R*eview and *P*ersistent *E*ncouragement but less than *SRPE*.

SRPE (used between points J and K of Level 5 Intensity); representing the most amount of *S*pecific *R*eview and *P*ersistent *E*ncouragement used by the interrogator whose objective is to gain a confession or admission. A confession deals with several significant inculpatory statements or all such statements while an admission deals with one or more inculpatory statement. This level, mainly, includes efforts to assist interrogatees to rationalize and save face while they confess total or partial responsibility for the problem under investigation.

Level 6 Intensity: sRPE (used between points K and M); representing the least amount of *s*pecific *R*eview, but the same intensity of *P*ersistent *E*ncouragement ... as in Level 4.

Approaches

Initial Phase — Structured Approach

The Structured Approach essentially begins at point A and continues to a time between C and D. In addition, that mode is used during the Preliminary Inquiry of the Precontact Section of the Initial Phase. Used at the beginning of the interview interaction as the basis of your direct observation, evaluation, and assessment of the interviewee. The Structured Mode (Approach) permits use of closed questions involving: What, Where, When, How, and Who without accusation or intimidation. With this approach, I encourage interviewees to provide answers to questions designed for easy answer; I use routine questions the answers to which are without doubt available to interviewees, such as spelling of the family name, how many years of schooling they have completed, what type of work they have done in the past, and so forth. These are topics to which interviewees may easily respond while sensing their interactional

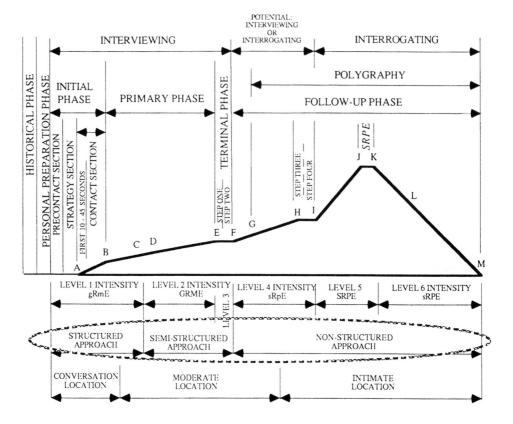

status. This is when they can sense how I'm treating them, if I'm ruthless or not, okay or not.

However, the mere fact interviewees respond to any question begins an encouragement to continue to do so when you seek more flexibility in answers to your subsequently asked problem-solving, fact-finding questions of the Semistructured Mode. Less deep thought is sought from interviewees during the Structured Mode than in the Semistructured or Nonstructured Modes.

I try immediately to blend rapport into the Initial Phase—Contact Section while using the Structured Approach. The Structured Mode, Approach, is similar to the approach used in many employment application procedures where in the interviewee is asked to provide information by completing a written application in which yes and no or multiple-choice questions are asked. Limited flexible fact-finding interaction is sought from interviewees using the Structured Mode between points *A* and *C.* Factual information regarding the matter under investigation is not requested in the first four minutes, or so, of the interview.

Interviewee delay in responding, at first, is expected and not necessarily considered a significant part of a pattern of potential deception. The degree of interviewee clear thinking, however, can be noted to assist in determining the pattern of the interviewee's ability to handle structured questions. In this approach, questions are not related to solving the investigative problem directly. The Structured Mode can help establish the relative status of the interview participants and assists in creating a type of secure feeling for both. It allows interviewees to sense an awareness of you, if you are okay to receive information.

Between points *B* and *C* of the interview process, I review certain of the case information with the interviewee as a prelude to actually asking fact-finding questions, all the while reinforcing the positive tone or mood of the interaction, building rapport.

Primary Phase—Structured Approach

After the first four minutes, at point *B*, I try to develop a fluid hypothesis, Floating Point Strategy. I become more focused on the issues of the case between *C* and *D* and, by then, most of the time, I have moved my chair closer to the interviewee as in the Moderate Location.

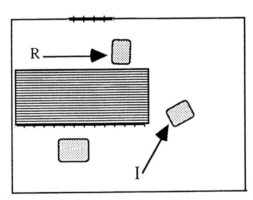

Plan view, typical interview room, 10'X12'
Illustrating participants in Moderate Location
I=Interviewer situated about four feet from R (Respondent).

Skeletal Constructs: A construct is used to form build, frame, devise a complex image or idea from a number of simpler images or ideas. Constructs are simple ideas from which more complex images or ideas are built.

This approach, Semistructured Approach, contains the skeletal questions (bones, constructs, simple ideas) basic to all interviews of a fact-finding nature in which spontaneous response is sought but *not* insisted upon. Formulation of questions depends upon the interaction as much as upon the factual content of the investigative problem. The problem prescribes basic foundation questions, while the skeletal *bones* of the Semistructured Approach guide efforts toward reaching the interview objective and eventual problem solution.

Primary Phase—Semistructured Approach

Level 2 Intensity begins between C and D to point F. As a lead into the Semi-structured Approach, between points C and D, you might consider saying to the interviewee: As I've mentioned, my main objective is to get a clear idea of the reasons for the reported _____.

Seek deep thought from interviewees in this mode regarding details; allow time for thought without insisting on any certain amount of response. The Semistructured Approach implies your desire to receive information from interviewees in an immediate way; however, it does not imply use of coercion, abuse, or intimidation. As a matter of fact, this mode mainly refers to how you sense the interaction and are tuned-in perceptively to what is happening moment by moment; the pressure is on you to be aware and alert for signals of truth showing itself, assisting you to determine the interviewee's veracity. Accusation toward interviewees is not appropriate in this mode.

Formulation of questions in this mode is not materially altered by the interviewee's responses. Their formulation is partly intended to encourage the presentation of responses which might reveal the interviewee's verbal and, or, nonverbal behavior that may be indicative of deception. The skeletal constructs of *bones* remains the guide posts to follow. Therefore, maintaining the use of those bones is helpful, unless and until you are confident the patterns (subsequently considered) of interviewee response, verbally and, or, nonverbally, signal deception.

Waiting until the Terminal Phase (between points E and F of the Polyphasic Flow Chart) to draw your conclusion regarding interviewee veracity is most productive, allowing you more time to establish your confidence. It follows that, by then, you will have had a more complete look at patterns provided and probably gained solid observation, evaluation and assessment of the interviewee.

Skeletal elements . . . constructs, bones . . . presented to interviewees, Semistructured Approach questions, might be used as follows (please keep in mind the value of the Floating Point Strategy and interviewer flexibility in all interview interactions):

Bones: While applying the following constructs it is important to imply to interviewees that you are seeking permission to ask the questions as you proceed. To be useful, such seeking should neither be overdone nor too obvious. Between the *You* construct and the *Borrow* construct, it is suggested that question formulation contain some indication that you are not barging into the mental ground of the interviewee to snatch information, but rather, you are calling to the truth to show or reveal itself.

Between those Bones, move with compassion as you continue to use positive Filter Factors in your transition from the Structured Approach into and through the Semi-structured Approach, beginning between points *C* and *D* of the Flow Chart. At no time in using the Bones is it suggested you make any accusation against the interviewee avoid expressing you have decided or have drawn a conclusion regarding the interviewee's veracity pertaining the issue under investigation.

You: You might say: "It's important to get this matter cleared up (name interviewee)." After a basic review of the reported abuse, comment that you are asking these questions in an effort to determine what, if anything, happened. All of this done as a lead into the You question: "I'd like you to work with me on this to resolve this report. *If,* you had any _____ contact with _____, it's important to get it straightened out and clear things up. (name if interviewee) let me ask—How do you stand on this matter, did you have any _____ _____ with _____ as the report claims?"

On some occasions interviewees provide full confessions. Usually, however, such is not the case.

The interaction is not conducted in an accusatory way but in an open, positive, neutral way with no assumption displayed that the interviewee committed the delinquent action or is deceptive. If the interviewee is deceptive, however, your delivery of the questions is intended to reveal interviewee uneasiness prompting him/her to reveal evasiveness though verbal and, or, nonverbal response; outward signs such as squirming, preening and other releases of internal distress not appropriate to the interaction if truthful. Such evasive signals, possible signs of deception, take place in about one one-hundredth of a second or less. Your attentiveness is required to sense such signals without making it obvious. Don't stare. When using the Semistructured Approach, seek pieces to the pattern of interviewee responses upon which you can eventually draw your assessment regarding interviewee veracity.

Who: Then you might say: (Preamble—"Knowing for sure who did have _____ contact with _____ is one thing, but having suspicions is something else"). With no challenge to the interviewee's probable answer of "no" to the You question, then: "Well, let me ask you: Do you know for sure who did _____?"

Suspect: Then you might say: "Okay then, even though you don't know for sure who did _____, let me ask—Do you have any suspicions of who may have _____ even though you don't know for sure who did it?" With quickly added: "Keep in mind that I'm not asking you to point a finger at anyone or anything like that because that wouldn't be fair; I'm wondering if anyone has done anything or said anything to cause you to think they may have (name action under investigation). Can you think of anyone who could have been involved in that _____?" Typical of the truthful: "I can't imagine who it is or that it even happened here." If someone among fellow employees did (named action), "That person would have to be a Jekyll and Hyde personality."

Trust: Then you might say: "Okay then, who comes to mind that you trust; that you think would not have done the _____ with _____?" Or: "Of all the people that did have opportunity, who do you think would *not* have caused the _____, if they did?"

Event happening: Then you might say: "After considering the situation, do you really think the _____ actually did _____ with anyone or do you think there is some other reason for that report to take place?"

Approach: Then you might say: "Life presents many temptation for all of us. Let me ask you this: Has _____ ever asked you to _____?"

Think: Then you might say: "People have thoughts of doing many things in their life. There are many demands and pressures on everyone day to day. Now, as far as your concerned: Do you recall ever thinking of having _____ with _____ even though you never actually did?"

Instruction: Then you might say: "Many people teach their kids things about _____ as a part of them growing up. After all, it is the responsibility of a parent (as appropriate) to teach certain things!

What comes to mind about telling or showing _____ things about
_____."

Clear up matter: Then you might say: "If the investigation shows that
you actually did have some _____ with _____, would you
be willing to explain things about that and get this thing straightened
out?"

Happen to false accuser: Then you might say: "Let's assume that we
find out the report was not true, what should happen to _____?"

Happen to doer: Then you might say: "If it is learned who did have
_____ with _____, what should happen to that person?"

Jail for doer: Then you might say: (Depending on the to the Happen
to the Doer question; if jail or prosecution not mentioned by the
interviewee) "How about jail for that person?" The response of the
truthful type interviewee has been: "I should think so! That pervert!"
Or: "Yes, whatever the law says" or something to that effect (provided
smoothly without hesitation; in a matter-of-fact way; as though to imply
a judgment). The deceptive tend to be lenient toward the molester or
wrong doer as expressed in answering: "Well, jail seems to be a little
harsh; it really depends on the reason it happened." Or: "I'm not one to
know, it really depends on the circumstances, I can't say, maybe the
person is under a lot of personal strain (and other such ramblings)."

Kind to do it: Then you might say: "What kind of person do you think
did this thing?" (You may expect the deceptive to respond: Personal
problems! or: Under pressure! or: Having tough times! or: I'm not that
kind of person; I'm not a pervert! While the truthful tend to respond:
Sick person! or: Perverted, I'd say! or: Not caring about us going through
this.)

Why happened: Then you might say: "Why do you think that report
was made?" (You might expect the deceptive to respond: I have no idea.
or: I'm not the kind to do that!" While the truthful might respond: No
reason! or: There's a divorce case!).

Say you did it: Then you might say: "Is there any reason for anyone to
say they think you did (as reported)?" The truthful type might respond:
"No, I don't think so, I didn't do it." (Nonverbally indicating a mental
search under way regarding how he could have given any type reason to
anyone for such confusion.) The mental search is not accompanied by
worming and squirming as though being poked from the inside by the
truth trying to get out to be seen and heard. Rather, there is seen a
furrowed brow, squinted eyes, a contemplated silence of thought, all

signaling a mental search for a basis of such a confusion. All so quick, all so fleeting.

Witness view you: Then you might say: "Is there any reason that anyone might say they saw you (as reported)?"

Say to doer now: Then you might say as a prelude: "Let's assume _____ with _____ actually did happen. If that person was here standing before you, what would you say to that person?" Truthful often respond: "It's not right!" Or: "That was a stupid thing to do!" "You sicko/pervert!" (Provided quickly and smoothly, often as an angry blast of indignation. A type of judgment conveyed.)

Outside inquiry: Then you might say: "Do you mind having the investigation extend beyond the family into your (job, social friends or what ever)?"

Polygraphy available: Once interviewees finally provide data claimed to be truthful, detection of deception examinations might be made available.

Investigators face some problems when intending to use polygraphy. Some individuals will not agree to undergo a polygraph examination no matter how helpful it is reported to be. Some are reluctant, but eventually submit to such testing.

Before using polygraphy as an investigative aid, there are two important things to consider. First, be convinced the use of polygraphy is a practical, functional, and trustworthy investigative tool. Second, be convinced the polygraph examiner (polygraphist) chosen to administer polygraph examinations will provide the highest available professional service.

Useful Methods in Asking Someone to Undergo a Polygraph Examination

1. *Where should the request be made?*

Privacy is an important element to consider when asking someone to participate in a polygraph examination. If potential examinees are among peers they may find it necessary to refuse to undergo the examination for fear of losing face or group approval. They may be truthful in their statements but "look bad" if cooperating too much. Approaching a group of individuals to ask them to undergo such an examination may meet with rejection and probably universal refusal. Requesting someone to take a polygraph examination must be on an individual basis during which time adequate explanation may be rendered by the interviewer to allow for skillfully handling of reluctance. Only on an individual basis can the true responses, both verbal and nonverbal, be noted and evaluated.

2. *How should the request be made?*

Requesting someone undergo a polygraph examination can take place when logical avenues of investigative effort narrow inquiry focus to a logical specific "hub" of responsibility. When specific suspects are developed and interviewed, the use of polygraphy may be an appropriate step in strategy. Flexible use of polygraphy depends on the circumstances. Discretion is the key. Personally prepare to ask for cooperation of interviewees to undergo the examination and be able to supply the polygraphist with personality data regarding each potential examinee. Based on findings regarding the potential examinee's personality, habits, hobbies, and so forth, an approach is made, requesting the interviewee to undergo the polygraph examination.

Effective investigators appeal to potential examinees in such a manner that they will realize the importance of their cooperation. They're told polygraph examinations can logically clear them of further consideration in the investigation as potential suspects or responsible participants in the case matter under investigation. Naturally, each potential examinee will have been interviewed to establish his or her individual statements pertaining to knowledge and/or participation in the case. Those interview results are provided to the polygraph examiner for review well in advance of any scheduled examination.

3. *What are typical interviewee replies to being requested to undergo a polygraph examination?*

It can be assumed that there are as many replies, positive and negative, as there are individuals who are asked to undergo a polygraph examination. There are, however, some typical replies expressed by potential examinees. Let's consider the cooperative, seemingly truthful individuals who have not given reason to doubt their veracity. Possibly the relative position of some cooperative interviewees cannot be verified through logical means of investigation. Those individuals usually continue to cooperate by agreeing to "stand on their heads" if necessary to prove truthfulness. That type interviewee is in the majority and is generally a pleasure to deal with. The exception is truthful individuals caused to become upset because they have become a part of the investigation, any investigation. They may be indignant that they are questioned in any way; they probably will cooperate by submitting to a polygraph examination if treated kindly, with appreciation.

Next, response or reply of deceptive . . . culpable . . . potential examinees (untruthful types) when requested to undergo a polygraph examination can take many forms. Deceptive (untruthful in statements to investigator) are generally lacking in cooperation. They may "play games" to avoid undergoing the examination. Initially, they may agree as requested; but, later refuse for some contrived reasons. They may even attempt to change the minds of their peers (fellow employees, possible suspects) who have agreed to undergo the examination. They are often evasive.

4. *How should investigators evaluate interviewee replies?*

Skilled investigators view each reply to requests to undergo polygraph examinations as additional bits of investigative data fitting the big puzzle of the investigation. They are to be met with appropriate reassurances or related comments. Interviewee reluctance is the basis of thorough explain of procedures and questions to be used in the polygraph examination. Some people have fear they will be asked questions unrelated to the investigation. To those who fear their general nervous condition will unfavorably affect the results of the testing, proficient interviewers point out that it is typical for everyone to be somewhat nervous during such an examination and that general nervousness will not cause unfavorable results. Again, truly cooperative potential examinees will see the logic and necessity of polygraph examinations.

Evasive, deceptive interviewees will not be convinced of the usefulness of the polygraph as an investigative tool. Maintain reasonable boundaries in responding to potential examinees' objections. It's not appropriate to "oversell" the reliability of polygraphy. To do so might actually convince untruthful interviewees not to undergo the examination. Making a second attempt to request interviewees to undertake the examination seems appropriate. Some reluctant examinees might want to speak with anyone else to assist in deciding. It seems that many reluctant potential examinees, if given time to think about it, will become more cooperative and eventually submit to the examination.

It is important to take a neutral stance when first asking someone to undergo such an examination because, merely being asked may cause them tension. Such tension may be enough to interfere with clear thinking to cause refusal.

Up to the point of the challenge or confrontation, the investigator played the part of the understanding, empathic interviewer, but now there is a changed role. The interviewee may be a little confused with the request to undergo the polygraph examination. The emotional shift of investigator intensity in making the request may "throw" some inter-viewees. Even some interviewers become shaken when changing the intensity of their efforts to confront interviewees to undergo polygraph examinations. People are complicated!

Do whatever has to be done so as not to damage rapport. Most interviewees accept the offer of the examination to avoid looking bad and to prove their truthfulness.

Nervous or Apprehensive Type

There is a tendency for some to fear what is not understood. A group of our society continually fear life in general and many things connected with it. Their's is a painful existence. Some individuals become anxious (tense and nervous) to even make the most uncomplicated decisions. Approaching this type individual to ask him to undergo a polygraph examination should be thought out thoroughly. The cooperation of tense insecure interviewees may not be gained if not handled in a smooth way. It is within this group of insecure individuals we find the potential examinee, even though truthful, who may refuse to undergo the exami-nation and become incensed by being considered a suspect.

Nervous Types May Fear False Results

Some will not be convinced polygraph examinations are reliable. They may think the polygraph may render a false result. It will require considerable skill and patience in a calm, confident manner to gently guide such interviewees toward accepting the use of the polygraph. They may need to discuss the proposed examination with a relative or friend to gain confidence or to at least gain an awareness of the usefulness of the polygraph.

Alleviating the Fear of the Nervous Type

Effective investigators anticipate causes of interviewee nervousness and attempt to answer their many questions even though not verbalized. This type of individual characteristically *needs* to know the basic proce-dure of the total polygraph examination including the fact that:

1. The examinee can answer whatever questions he chooses.
2. Examinee is free to leave the examination room at any time.
3. All questions will be reviewed and discussed with the polygraphist in advance of their actual use so as to prevent misunderstandings.

4. The polygraphist will only ask questions necessary to the proper application of the examination.
5. There will be no surprise or shocking questions utilized during the examination.
6. There will be no electrical shocks applied to the examinee at any time.
7. The attachments used in the examination will be thoroughly explained and they cause little or no discomfort.
8. The investigator should express through spoken and unspoken means confidence in the usefulness of the polygraph examination generally and in the ability of the polygraphist specifically.
9. The polygraph procedure is similar for each examinee and will not be unusual for this one.

Usually, truly nervous types will be convinced of the usefulness of complying with the investigator's request to undergo the polygraph examination. The potential examinee who persists in refusal based upon nervousness claims may be using that claim to avoid the examination. This is particularly evident if the claim cannot be substantiated by other interviewee personality traits. Deceptive individuals may fake nervousness.

Investigator Response to or Evaluation of Nervous Type

When indications exist that the nervous type is not truly nervous but merely dodging, the investigator might concentrate more of his investigative abilities upon that person. This is especially appropriate when most or all other suspects or potentially responsible individuals have been cleared of suspicion through investigative means, including the use of polygraphy. Such evasive tactics are generally considered typical of deceptive individuals.

The Protesting Type

Indignation is not an uncommon position to see the interviewee take when involved in the middle of an investigation. Such a stance is not uncommon, specifically when veracity is challenged by being asked to undergo a polygraph examination. Some protest to the point of being angry with the investigator/interviewer, but such indignation is usually not long-lived. If of reasonable intelligence, the interviewee will see that particular "tools" must be employed to make advancement in the total investigation. Feelings may be hurt, but they too will see how the polygraph examination serves a useful function and how cooperation is needed. They may not like the idea of it, but will usually submit to save time and facilitate exoneration.

The continual protester type who can in no way be brought to the awareness of the utility of the polygraph is in most instances again "dodging." They do not want the discovery of their involvement. Unreasonable protests (trained indignation) by some interviewees is a signal to the skilled investigator that there is more to the protests than is evident on the surface.

Cooperative Type

Many law-abiding citizens find themselves to be a part of some type of investigation in their lives. It is not unusual to consider that a great many people, at one time or another in their lives, have been an interviewee regarding some matter, possibly minor, but possibly tragic in nature. Generally, most people are cooperative. The cooperative ones will take part in the routine investigation process, if not with enthusiasm then with curiosity. They may feel a little put out about the whole thing. Although somewhat impatient because their daily routine is disrupted, they generally comply with requests for reasonable cooperation.

Typical Bluffs of Deceptive Potential Examinees

Yes! They may say. I'll take a polygraph examination to assist in the investigation to verify my veracity. That may simply be a bluff, agreeing to undergo the examination. So-called street-sharp interviewees live a life of bluff and the confidence game. Street-sharp individuals know how and when to agree as investigators tread their way over the rocky road of investigation.

If the offer of the polygraph examination was merely a bait question asked of each interviewee without ever intending to use it, then bluffing might work for the deceptive. If agreement to undergo the examination misleads the investigator, then the bluff worked. But, if the investigator is prepared to provide and actually does provide such an examination then the bluff is called.

Understandably, there are times when street-sharp deceptive interviewees agree to take polygraph examinations or even suggest that it be provided but they may never appear for the scheduled appointment. They may, in fact, continue agreement up until the last moments when they will demand payment for their time. If monetary payment is not immediately provided, they may decline the examination claiming they fulfilled their part of the agreement and if not immediately paid for their time and inconvenience, they will not undergo the examination.

A characteristic "dodge" or "bluff" of some deceptive interviewees is to agree to undergo the examination, but they must first consult a spouse or attorney before the actual scheduling of the examination. This is a diversion to allow time in which to think of a way out of such an examination.

Health problems are also the basis for refusal of the polygraph examination. Deceptive interviewees will often claim to have a bad heart and must consult a doctor before giving agreement to undergo such a stressful examination. Truthful interviewees do not generally use health problems to dodge or bluff their way out of cooperating. Deceptive individuals are often quick to find a way to refuse or delay taking a polygraph examination while the truthful interviewee is generally most cooperative.

Some individuals think their veracity should not be questioned by anyone in any way for any reason. They are offended by the mere fact that they, in any way, are a part of an investigation. Somehow they think investigators should know them as truthful by merely looking at them, considering them honest in every way. They think of themselves as above reproach and think everyone should also consider them so. They think that their honesty is somehow written on their foreheads. Possibly this is a naive position to hold but, nonetheless, one held by some.

Naturally, effective investigators use a most tactful personality in dealing with individuals refusing a polygraph examination on moral grounds. Usually such an interviewee will eventually comply with the request, seeing the necessity for participation in such a meaningful investigative endeavor. The deceptive individuals, however, who has used the moral issue as a bluff will stand fast and not see how such an examination is necessary and certainly not in his or her case. Experience teaches investigators how various methods are used by interviewees in an attempt to bluff their way.

The bluffers play for time, knowing, hoping they can avoid being found out for an extended period . . . possibly even escape the eventual day of discovery. They know investigators usually have limited time available to expend on any investigation and if the investigation is prolonged, the likelihood of its solution is diminished.

There are no easy answers for investigators; there are only complicated questions which might frustrate and discourage. The more investigators understand about polygraphy, the more likely they can apply its functional values.

Terminal Phase

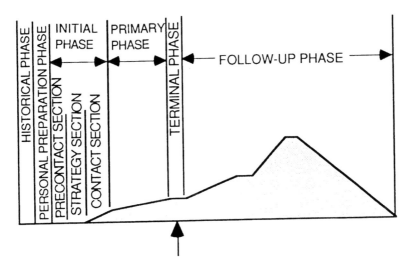

Between points *E* and *F* of the Polyphasic Flow Chart is a juncture called the Terminal Phase, a turning point, at which the interviewer will probably draw a conclusion that the interviewee's verbal and, or, nonverbal patterns of response indicate one of: truthfulness, deception, possible deception or probable deception. The Terminal Phase, as I consider it, has two steps.

Step One—Terminal Phase: A time and place to realize a conclusion reached as to whether the interviewee is providing the highest percentage of truthful information possible ... a place and time for deduction.

Successful interviewers realize ... a conclusion is a deduction ... a decision ... an idea based upon constructs ... a judgment based on something that goes beyond what you actually know. A conclusion is a conjecture, a presumption, an inference ... it is making a statement about something you do not know for sure. Investigators deal with probabilities, they make inferences. They reach conclusions, make decisions ... they use deductions.

A dictionary defines deduction: assumption, conjecture, opinion, supposition, surmise; reasoning, conclusion, guess, inference, summation;

theory, explanation, guess, hypothesis, postulate, presumption, proposition, speculation.

In logic, deduction is a process of reasoning in which a conclusion follows necessarily from the premises presented so that the conclusions cannot be false if the premises are true. A conclusion is reached by this process.

To deduce is to derive a conclusion from something known or assumed; to infer, derive by reasoning, conclude or judge from premises or evidence; to hint, imply, suggest; to guess, speculate, surmise. To draw a conclusion as by reasoning.

An inference is the act or process of inferring. In logic it is the process of deriving the strict logical consequences of assumed premises. The process of arriving at some conclusion which, though it is not logically derivable from the assumed premises, possesses some degree of probability relative to the premises.

Premise is to assume, either explicitly or implicitly (a proposition), as a premise for a conclusion. A proposition is supporting or helping to support a conclusion.

Between points E and F, a conclusion can be reached based upon behavioral indicators provided by the interviewee. Interviewees provide those indicators, behavior signals, depending on circumstances created in the interview leading up to point E. To report that interviewees never or always produce certain behavior would be misleading. I think it is fair to say, based upon my experience, that certain behavior signals are characteristic of deceptive individuals while other such signals characterize truthful interviewees.

In a limited way, the following scale and chart indicate some typical behavioral signals and their frequency of appearance during interviews regarding interviewee veracity based upon interviewer observation, evaluation, and assessment. It is by using those signals in conjunction with other essential constructs that the investigator draws a conclusion as to interviewee veracity and determines subsequent action to take.

The chart, following, represents only a portion of the many behavioral signals possible and in no way represents the majority of such signals. A twitch, blink, or change of skin coloration at the right moment may assist the investigator to reach a conclusion. It is the totality of interviewee behavior which takes on meaning, not merely a single action. All of what an interviewee says and does assists the investigator to reach a conclusion. The interviewer's challenge is to notice without being noticed noticing.

Questions asked are constructs. Responses are constructs. I present my constructs and watch for constructs presented by the interviewee. I want to display positive constructs so as to stimulate interviewees to reveal constructs which reflect upon their veracity. When interviewees are inconsistent or deceptive, it is as though they are trying to force a blue puzzle piece into a space intended for a brown piece, all the while hoping I will not notice. Or, it seems they are trying, when really obvious, to offer a puzzle piece of the correct size and shape for a space but it is eye-catchingly blue rather than brown. In some situations, the piece offered is the correct size and shape and brown in tone but enough off in shading to be noticed by the trained eye of the investigator. The subtle color difference of the piece becomes evident when placed in the total puzzle, in contrast with other pieces . . . circumstances of the investigation.

The total of everything I present to the interviewee signals if I'm okay to confide in. Each and every part of my presentation encourages or discourages the interviewee to comply. Certainly, if the interviewee is hostile by nature to all in authority or is deceptive, much of what I do and say during the interview may make little difference. So often, however, my effort will nudge reluctant ones into a more compliant stance and even nurture deceptive ones into a position to admit or confess.

The chart and scale, following, are not directly connected to the Forensic Formula. They are intended to reflect some behavior observed in actions of some interviewees relative to veracity. The real question is: Can we have confidence in behavior signals provided by interviewees as indicators of veracity? My experience tends to indicate Yes! Certainly there are no absolutes in such assessments, but I'm convinced nonverbal signals are meaningful in the detection of deception. When thinking about such signals, consider the scale and the chart.

Step Two—Terminal Phase: A time and place to decide what to do next in the process.

By point *F* in the Terminal Phase, after using both Structured and Semistructured Approaches, evaluate if there is need for further Interviewing using a Nonstructured Approach (Level 4 Intensity) for the purpose of drawing out indepth, concealed information or, when appropriate, to seek an admission or confession by interrogation using the Intensity Levels 4 through 6.

The interviewer assesses interviewee candor up to and including point *F*, essentially, the last moment of nonaccusatory interview interaction. At times you may decide to continue the inquiry from point *F* to clear up

Interviewee Behavior	Truthful	Probably Truthful	Probably Deceptive	Deceptive	Informant
Embarrassed					
Afraid					
Clammy Hands					
Ashen/Pale Appearance					
Belchs					
Nervous Giggle					
Compliments					
Covers Mouth					
Covers Face					
Covers Eyes					
Shifty eyes					
Limited Eye Contact					
Schoid Stare					
Clear Thinking					
Complete Thoughts					
Incomplete Thoughts					
Evasive - Ducks/Dodges					
Hesitant Speech					
Argumentative					
Rebellious					
Choppy Sentences					
Measured Responses					
Clear Denial					
No Denial					
Compliant					
Reluctant					
Hostile					
Preens					
Squirms/Ants in Pants					
Brushes/Picks Lint					
Controled Positions					
Smooth Movements					
Shifts in Chair					
Declines Polygraphy					

```
10 - ALWAYS
9
8 - FREQUENTLY
7
6
5 - SOMETIMES
4
3
2 - SELDOM
1
0 - NEVER
```

The scale, above, refers to how often certain behavorial signals appear, see chart at right, as related to interviewees who are subsequently concluded, deduced, to be - Truthful, Probably Truthful, Probably Deceptive, or Deceptive.

Also, Informants are included in the chart to show that they too provide behavioral signals which may be significant.

The chart, right, of interviewee behavior characteristics represents some of those signals which may help the investigator calculate if the interviewee is telling the truth or not. To be useful, such indicators are not taken as significant individually. It is the pattern they make that signals their significance during the course of the interview process between points A and E of the Flow Chart.

inconsistencies, but then you might arrange a reinterview for some; therefore, a complete interview termination is usually not appropriate. If further review and encouragement are not employed, interviewees should be left thinking that they may be contacted again with participants leaving on good terms. If this is to be the end of the interview, leave a business card and request to be contacted when anything further is recalled. Maintain rapport!

Immediate interviewee response or reaction to stimuli during the interview interaction may reveal enough to permit you to sense brief verbal and, or, nonverbal interviewee signals upon which to act. On-the-go interview interaction, moment by moment action/reaction is almost automatic.

Arranging for a second interview might be appropriate for some future time. To verify interviewee information, scheduling a polygraph examination might be in the next step; use of *s*pecific *R*eview and *p*ersistent *E*ncouragement (sRpE) might also seem a next best action to fit your Floating Point Strategy (F.P.S.). If you decide to review inconsistencies while applying Level 4 Intensity, continue to apply the Filter Factors . . . active listening, and so forth.

Inability, lack of confidence, being timid, or being too cautious might hold some investigators from reaching a conclusion as to the interviewee's veracity. In such situations, interviewees might best be told on leaving the interview that it looks like they have more on their mind. They might be told that a second interview will be set up in the near future to review a few things; giving the impression suspicion exists that weighty information is being hidden, suppressed.

Inconsistencies: Any interviewee, however cooperative, might show some indications of holding back information. Victims may not reveal all details of the situation because they are embarrassed over the fact that they allowed the bad guy to take advantage of them. They might just feel dumb for being out of control in a stressful moment. The inconsistencies they present could also indicate that they fabricated the crime and actually stole the money themselves or arranged for a buddy to steal it in a mock holdup.

A witness might actually be a coconspirator in the theft and has good reason to feel uneasy over being interviewed for details. Knowing more could have been done to caught the robber or at least pay more attention to a license number, may cause the witness to be self-conscious and appear to be holding back information.

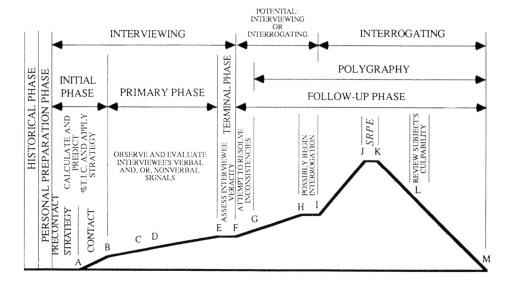

Obviously, the thief might feel it necessary to hold back information and thereby signal deception through inconsistencies or through behavior indicative of deception through verbal and, or, nonverbal communication.

Thieves with little practice, tend to stumble over routine investigative questions giving telltale signs of involvement. It is highly possible to pick out the bad guy from dozens of interviewees, suspects, using the process outlined in this writing. This process has been proven in real-world cases.

Although elements of a Floating Point Strategy are vitally important, it is not the purpose of this text to venture too far into the various possibilities of choice. Between points *F* and *M* of the Polyphasic Flow Chart there is considerable flexibility in using a Floating Point Strategy. The basic idea . . . interviews take place before, and are foundation to interrogation.

Follow-up Phase

Nonstructured Approach: The use of the Follow-up Phase, Levels 4, 5 & 6 Intensity, begins at point *F.* From that point in the interview interaction you may decide to strategically venture into specific review using persistent encouragement to resolve inconsistencies. Your action taken between *F* and *G* of the Flow Chart, to be productive, needs to be based upon sensitive awareness, not abusiveness. Level 4 Intensity is useful

SOME POSSIBLE OPTIONS		

TERMINAL PHASE	STEP 2	1. THANK THE INTERVIEWEE, END INTERVIEW
		  A. SAY NO NEED FOR MORE CONTACT
		  B. SAY NEED FOR RE-INTEVIEW
		    1. POSSIBLY INCONSISTENCIES SHOWING
		    2. MAYBE NEED FOR POLYGRAPHY
		    3. HAVE INTERVIEWEE RETHINK DATA
		2. MOVE INTO NEXT STAGE OF FLOW CHART, F-G

FOLLOW-UP PHASE	BETWEEN POINTS F AND G	ANNOUNCE INCONSISTENCIES ARE EVIDENT.
	BETWEEN POINTS G AND H	1. ASSIST INTERVIEWEE TO RATIONALIZE AND SAVE FACE. 2. AFTER INTERVIEWEE EXPLAINS AWAY BASIS OF INCONSISTENCIES, ARRANGE DETECTION OF DECEPTION EXAMINATION TO CONFIRM WHAT INTERVIEWEE CLAIMS AS TRUE. 3. CONSIDER SUSPECT NOW A SUBJECT AND VENTURE INTO INTERROGATION. SEEK AN ADMISSION OR CONFESSION. 4. MOVE INTO STEP THREE - BETWEEN POINTS H AND I.
	BETWEEN POINTS H AND I	STEP THREE: 1. TERMINATE INTERVIEW LEAVING OPPORTUNITY TO CONTINUE CONTACT IN FUTURE. 2. DECIDE TO VENTURE INTO STEP FOUR WITH FULL EFFORTS TO GAIN AN ADMISSION OR CONFESSION. STEP FOUR: CLEARLY ANNOUNCE SUBJECT BELIEVED TO BE THE ONE RESPONSIBLE, AND SO FORTH.
	BETWEEN POINTS I AND M	1. ASSIST INTERROGATEE TO RATIONALIZE AND SAVE FACE. 2. SEEK ADMISSION OR CONFESSION.

when dealing with victims and witnesses, as well as suspects, who may now, more and more, be considered subjects.

To be a valid, contributing part of the interaction, your behavior is connected to and flowing with those of the interviewee, interflowing as produced, immediate and connected. Your interviewing behavior and related interviewee behavior are inextricably interconnected with verbal and nonverbal signals. This is true in each of the three approaches, but most certainly in the Nonstructured Approach.

The Nonstructured Approach, a real time mode, signifies the *now* interaction between interview participants in which both affect the other while progressing toward the problem solution. Trajectory of a guided missile in flight can be viewed as an example of such interaction as it streaks toward its target miles away. In its flight, the missile sends back data to the sending station indicating its location in flight and if it senses obstacles in its path; in turn, the sender of the missile tells the missile to avoid the mountain it reports in its path. The sending and receiving of signals are immediate, ongoing, and now in nature, all the while the missile is in flight toward the objective.

A similar situation exists in the interview interaction when participant signals are exchanged during the striving for the truthful solution of the problem. The more compliant the interviewees, the more likely they are headed toward the objective, with you *guiding* the way. Radical direction or use of abuse, harassment, or intimidation can and often does cause interview participants to miss the mark, miss the objective, miss the truth. Observed interviewee reluctance or hostility indicates avoidance to be guided toward a collaborative objective. The deceptive ones send signals intended to mislead as you direct the inquiry; their signals are devised to send you along your way alone. While traveling toward the objective, some do not want to arrive with you at the final solution point, the truth.

Between *F* and *G*, you might decide to review, to some degree, such pattern signals of deception with the interviewee to encourage truthfulness. With caution, you might then seek the truth using Level 4 Intensity of review and encouragement at this *turning point.* Handle this matter delicately. A premature decision of interviewee deception, with related action, may only fortify and promote the interviewee into greater reluctance to reveal the truth with effort to cover it better.

A premature conclusion drawn, sensed by interviewees, may cause them to think that *the pressure is off* and there is little need to struggle to cover up the truth anymore. The interviewee's battle then will be with you alone and not with the truth and you combined; interviewee effort could become one of self-defense if it is sensed that you have prematurely concluded that deception is indicated. If you are not fortified and ready to engage in specific review and persistent encouragement of the interviewee as in Level 4 Intensity, become so before advancing.

Between points *F* and *G* of the Flow Chart, among many options available, the next thing to do might be to announce to the interviewee:

"It looks like you haven't told me the whole truth!" or "It seems to me that you are holding back something!" or "I'm uneasy about what you've told me here today. I believe you've got more to tell me!" or "I think you're the one that did this thing and it's important for us to talk about this to get it cleared up!"

Expressing a conclusion between points F and G takes some daring and skill. Although there is no need to harshly accuse or intimidate any interviewee, there is, however, a time for specific review and persistent encouragement to clear up inconsistencies or gain an admission or confession when an interview gradually flows into an interrogation. This is not the time to say anything like: "You lying son of a b_____!"

Although comments to the interviewee, between points F and G, might have been general in nature indicating that not all of the truth has been revealed, between points H and I, the interviewer, now interrogator, comments clearly and specifically to announce the interrogatee seems to be intentionally holding back information and is probably a key player in the matter under investigation . . . molester, robber, and so forth.

So then, between points F and G, the interviewer may use a more concentrated efforts of review and encouragement. How it is done, exactly, is determined by the situation, the individual, and so forth. To suggest every eventuality is not possible. Suffice it to say that it is through intuitive skill that the interviewer sorts through the complexities to solve the case.

Between points G and H effort is undertaken to convince the victim, witness, or suspect to cooperate more fully. Inconsistencies may be explored, specifically identified, and dealt with when appropriate.

Steps 3 and 4—between points H and I

Step Three: In this step, the interviewer makes a strategic conclusion. This is the time when the interviewer may realize the victim turned in a false robbery report and is really the thief. Possibly a witness is determined to be a partner in the theft, or probably gave a false story of what happened. Step 3 is a time in the process when the investigator decides to enter into an interrogation. Up to this time, efforts have been modified so as to deal with embarrassed victims and reluctant witnesses, but now may be the time to forge ahead into the interrogation to seek an admission or confession.

Step Four: During Step 4, between points H and I, a clear proclamation is made to reveal the investigator's deduction of the interrogatee's culpability in the matter under investigation. Yes, I know, interrogation might start earlier, between *F* and *G* of the process, but the most intense interrogative effort takes place beginning in Step 4 between points *H* and *I* of the Flow Chart.

Between points *I* and *J*, proficient interrogators move with polished strategy to convince the interrogatee to reveal something which could be used against his or someone else's best interest. This is no longer the time for the use of the word . . . if, for now the investigator displays confidence in the subject's involvement in the matter under investigation. The one time suspect is now a subject. The victim or witness may have gradually become a suspect in the mind of the investigator and then develops as a subject, deserving interrogation.

Between points *J* and *K* is the most intense use of review and encouragement. Efforts to assist the subject, interrogatee, to rationalize and save face are used. But, this is no time to degrade or humiliate the subject. Coercion has no place here, or anywhere in this science.

Use of *SRPE*, between points *J* and *K*, interrogation, is not for all investigators. As a matter of temperament, confidence, skill, and other elements, some are more capable than others of dealing with this concentrated search.

Between points *K* and *L* is the time when the admission or confession are put into a verbal (tacit) and, or, signed statement. Even though there may be some doubt in the investigator's mind as to if the subject told the complete story of what happened, any legal admission or partial confession is, at times, helpful to resolving the matter under investigation. So, wrapping up part of the matter is better than not having anything. That is not to say the investigator should be satisfied with a partial job done. Certainly, clear up all you can, while realizing the necessity to continue or start over in renewed effort. In a child sexual abuse case, for example, the molester may admit touching a child but deny finger penetration of her vagina or other sexual contact. Between points *J* and *L* accept whatever is offered in a confession and have it witnessed and put into written form, then, when possible, gain more details of the subject's culpability.

At about point *L* in the process, determine extent of the subject's onus by considering whether details of the full extent of the subject's involvement have been withheld? Is it time to use a detection of deception examination? These and other alternatives can be considered to suit the circumstances.

Between points *F* and *M,* depending on the circumstances, a multitude of options are available. At about point *M* of the Flow Chart, arrest followed by prosecution often takes place (see Erickson appeals).

Chapter Eleven

COMMUNICATION

Set and Setting

Careful arrangements are needed for the psychological set and environmental setting of each interview. A desirable interviewee psychological set is characterized by at least a temporary readiness to respond truthfully. Willingness to comply is dependent upon attitude, generally, influenced by interviewer expectations. Being ready, willing, and able to truthfully comply is a most desirable interviewee psychological set. Interviewer expectation impacts interviewee self-belief to encourage interviewee confidence in answering questions, even if the answers are against interviewee better interest.

Interviewee psychological set is often affected by pressure of responsibility. If they cannot easily take off their loyalty or distractive protective cloak of role playing, they may not be comfortable or secure in your interviews. If their psychological set causes a lack of cooperativeness, then find a better time or circumstances where their concentration is conducive. Pressures, loyalties, obligations, needs, and restrictions of life frequently cause interviewees to be uncomfortable and not relaxed mentally.

Some investigations provide conditions best suited for unscheduled, surprise interviews. First blush, truly surprise, unannounced interviews can reveal some distress or interviewee imbalance which may stimulate compliance. Understandably, scheduled or prearranged interviews allow interviewees to be emotionally prepared, diminishing the significance of the interviewer's authority role. Interviewees are not usually caught off balance by announced or scheduled interviews; hence, to schedule or not depends on the circumstances (see Strategy Section, Initial Phase).

Interviewing in the home ground of interviewees provides emotional strength which may hinder your efforts, but not as long as you are alert to potential handicaps. Researchers consider the impact on human communication of physical appearance, dress, arrangement of furniture, vocal cues, physical environment, and personal space: "Overwhelming evidence supports the conclusion that the environment in which an interview is held contributes to the overall outcome of the interview."[38]

Interviewees behave in accord with their perception or definition of the situation. Circumstances help determine the mood and partly indicate your expectation. Even if interviews are conducted in a crowded retail store with people walking all about, there can still be an indication of your attempt to speak privately and intimately.

Your discreet manner, the interview objectives, and the care taken not to embarrass interviewees will be clearly sensed. They assess if you understand their need to maintain self-esteem. Although interviewing in the presence of others may be productive, privacy is best. Even when three people are involved in an interview, the third person, second interviewer, or observer usually hinders progress of gathering intimate, hidden data. Three is a crowd.

Most interviews require some degree of confidentiality and intimacy. An unspoken protective barrier develops separating interview participants if privacy is not extended.

Advantages of one-on-one interviews include: persuasion tailored to one person, feedback is immediate, adaptation is easier and obstructions or counteractions to persuasive effort is not limited by another participant.[66] There is an "advantage of getting interviewees out of their own immediate work environments to a place where it is easier to relax and talk and where privacy, both physical and psychological, is ensured."[25] Interviewees in familiar surroundings may have emotional strength, comfort, and confidence. Those familiar conditions may allow or fortify them to rebel and refuse to provide needed information. However, overall comfort and privacy are better than interviewee discomfort and public embarrassment.

When interviewing in surroundings familiar to interviewees, give an honest, natural appreciation of such things as the appearance of their home or possessions. Your comments of positive recognition can help build and maintain rapport and show your humanness.

Being seen talking with an interviewer can be an interviewee violation of accepted custom in many areas and cultures, and peers may become extremely upset to learn that cooperation was given to any form of society's authority. Their need to be approved, to be included, of within their community may be strong; to violate the code of conduct established is asking not to be liked and not accepted. Disapproval is terrible to many.

Proficient interviewers try to make it easy for interviewees to respond comfortably without fear of ridicule by friends, neighbors, or significant others. Thus, through an inconspicuous approach, enhance confidentiality and earn their trust. Deciding to comply is based to large extent upon their evaluation of your style as expressed through your enthusiasm, attitude, and expectations.

With friends, interviewees often act differently, taking on an added dimension to their identity. They prehend, absorb part of their peer group rather than maintain personal identity. That action, positive or negative, depends on the circumstances and the leadership of the group.

Interviewees, cooperative if approached alone, may rebel and be uncooperative when approached while in the company of, and subtly controlled by peers. In most instances, interviewees try to live up to demands of their group which provides emotional security, acceptance, and love. Not complying with the wishes of peers produces group rejection; so, rather than lose a place in the group, and all that goes with group belonging, they usually respond as they sense the group directing.

Using Nonverbal Behavior

People learn roles which are often out of touch with what is really going on within themselves. Inconsistencies between what interviewees say they feel and what their body movements suggest they are feeling "belie" feelings of anxiety. Though the idea that interviewers deal in facts and not feelings may be appealing to some, experience reveals the concept is untenable. "How people feel strongly influences the nature and amount of information they provide and the decisions they make."[10]p. 29–32

Sensing the unique capacity of words in their world, people imitate and emulate others. Experience makes it increasingly clear to me that true messages are conveyed nonverbally and language is often a ritual obscuring communication.

By using language, people pursue truth, love, self-realization, power, and success. However, mature individuals learn that language conceals as much as it reveals of true feelings, motives, and attitudes. With awareness that actions convey true messages, interviewers can tune into the feelings of others while overlooking words. "We must never forget that the most powerful communication isn't what you say, it's what you do."[76]p.495, 34

Although verbal communication is the most distinctive of human achievements, feelings and intentions are conveyed through facial expressions, gestures, and intonations. Observed unintentional nonverbal cues can assist you to make decisions about other people. The human face may directly mirror anxiety or exhilaration without any deliberate decision. Expectations are conveyed mostly through nonverbal communication.

Relevant findings of social scientists indicate vocal intonations, timing, silences, facial expressions, eye movements, and body positioning may confirm, or obscure, or contradict spoken words. While words deliver explicit, objective information, nonverbal messages convey how you really feel. As you evaluate clues, cues, and messages from interviewees, avoid being preoccupied with the actual words spoken, but with all aspects of communication, including intonation.[72]p.125

Attune yourself to meanings. Words may elude you, but beneath words are intonations which carry much of the emotional sense of their message. Again, intonation and gestures are called paralinguistics. Psychologists Leuses and Gerald Davitz asked different actors to express various emotions while simply reciting the alphabet. They asked individuals to guess which emotions were being expressed. Pride was identified correctly 20 percent of the time while 60 percent of the individuals identified anger.[20]

Robert Rosenthal of Harvard University has devised a multichanneled test of nonverbal perception. Eleven channels of different nonverbal communication were administered to two hundred groups in different parts of the world. One of the most outstanding, most reliable results found by Rosenthal is that women always seem to do better than men. That seems to be true no matter where the women are tested. Women are more sensitive to nonverbal cues than men, not only in Rosenthal's testing, but also on other tests as well.[88]

People use nonverbal behavior to express three basic emotional sets and attitudes: (1) the degree of liking and disliking felt toward others; (2) the degree of dominance or submissiveness felt in a relationship; and (3), the degree of responsiveness, the sheer amount of reaction, positive or negative, or mixed, that other people arouse in you.[81]

Avoid conveying nonverbal messages that interviewees are ignorant or stupid. Such unfortunate messages are displayed implicitly through gestures or intonations; (paralinguistics). Although explicit questioning may be direct enough and seemingly specific, you may be displaying a judgmental message that is intuitively read.[53]

What you do and how you do it signals a great deal to interviewees. Tension and relaxation, strength and lightness, suddenness, directness, and so on, all signal something to interview participants.[20] The way I stand and move provides clues to my character, emotions, and reactions to interviewees. Interviewers are rewarded with truthful information in direct proportion to the impression made upon interviewees.[20] The language of emotion is subtle but powerful; it doesn't need words. Looks, tone, and deeds transmit feelings and attitude. Participants have a built-in receiver especially tuned to the wavelengths of their needs.

The prime object of dread in childhood is not angry words or an angry-sounding voice, but an angry disapproving face. Tomkins explains: "Children seem to dread the angry, unloving, shaming face of the parent much more greatly than a spanking."[20] If you present an habitual authoritarian expression of anger or discontent, you send out unfavorable signals which may cause the child in the interviewee to respond in an emotional way.

Freud wrote: "He that has eyes to see and ears to hear may convince himself that no mortal can keep a secret. If his lips are silent, he chatters with his fingertips; betrayal oozes out of him at every pore."[20p.54]

When interview participants enter into efforts to display forced actions and expressions trying to be convincing, clumsiness is revealed.[20p.79] Clumsiness is based upon stress of the moment. If you put on a "good act," you may fool some people into believing you, but your body odor may subconsciously signal your insecurity and lack of self-confidence.[20p.131]

Haptics

In some cultures even visual intrusion of personal space is felt by interviewees.[6p.78] Many interviewees sense space as an extension of their ego and may go to almost any length to preserve a private sphere of space. Some do not want anyone close to them and certainly they do not want to be touched by anyone. Their restraint has nothing to do with you personally, usually.

Touching another human being in a gentle reassuring way tends to indicate concern, warmth, and closeness not conveyed in any other way. When it seems to fit, your touch can be a flowing part of an interview, signaling a special caring unavailable in words. A complicated combination of things happen when two human beings touch; hence, sense when it is appropriate to touch interviewees, be able to strengthen interpersonal communication. Proficient interviewers learn to use reassuring touch (haptics) during interviews to exhibit humanness and strengthen interpersonal communication.[68]

At times it is helpful if you merely place your hand upon the interviewee's hand, arm, or shoulder in a reassuring way. Reassurance by touch may strengthen bonds of rapport. A mere touch can signal acceptance. However, realize that not every interviewee or every interview situation will allow or permit touching to take place.

Hostile or extremely reluctant interviewees will usually not allow themselves to be touched other than possibly to allow a handshake. Even a handshake may send signals regarding personal confidence and/or apprehensiveness.

Locations

Anthropologist Edward Hall reports definite distances are maintained between people for different purposes differing from culture to culture.[32] Proximics is the study of interpersonal distances between human beings. According to Mehrabian, people of high status assume and are granted more free space around them than those of lower status. Whatever your status, you carry a kind of bubble of personal space from one encounter to another. Anthropologist Edward Hall is credited with the concept of the personal space bubble.[86, 20] Mehrabian reports: Out to about a foot-and-a-half most Americans reserve the space for intimate conversation, whispers, and secrets. From about a foot-and-a-half to about four feet, nominal, casual interactions. Beyond about four feet out to the limit of hearing, impersonal transactions. Extreme dislike, high assertion of dominance and responsiveness are all expressed through tone of voice, deliberate silences, variations in eye contact, facial expressions, distancing and posture.[81]

My experience suggests three distances between interview participants. In the Intimate Location, the sound, smell, and feel of interview participants signal involvement with another body. This distance is reserved for in-depth type interviews requiring intense interpersonal communication and also for interrogation situations in which confessions and admissions are sought. The Moderate Location brings participants close enough to allow a gentle touch of an arm or shoulder if appropriate. Most interviews take place within the Moderate or Conversation distances.

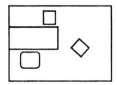

In the Conversation Location participants are situated in a safe location just outside easy physical reach. In it there is preferably no obstruction between participants other than possibly a corner of a desk. In the Conversation Location, you may lean back or forward in your chair depending upon the context of the interview. The general location of your chair in relationship to the interviewee's chair is to the left front or right front at an angle of about forty-five degrees. Avoid leaning or propping the back of your chair against a nearby wall in a casual manner or placing your feet conveniently upon a desk. Keep your body position alert in appearance and attentive, projecting a professional appearance at all times.

The Conversation Location allows participants opportunity to lean forward and enough room to move their legs comfortably. It permits viewing interviewees for nonverbal communication at critical moments for floating point strategy. In that location, you could lean forward moderately and not be able to touch their shoulder unless they also leaned forward. Avoid squarely facing interviewees in this location presenting yourself symbolically as a threat.

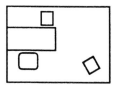

In the Moderate Location participants sit with chairs situated at a forty-five degree angle, as in the conversation position. The Moderate Location allows the interviewee's upper body to be reached by leaning forward slightly; crossing of legs by participants can be accomplished carefully. Most interviews and many interrogations can be conducted from the Moderate Location.

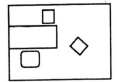

The Intimate Location may be the most stress-producing or most reassuring, depending upon how interviews are conducted. In that location, interviewees can be touched easily because your chair is situated squarely in front of interviewees or slightly to either side so that your knees can be next to their knees. In it, crossing of legs is next to impossible and you can easily touch their upper body. Use of that location creates the greatest of interpersonal dynamics and is reserved for interviews of the most concentrated human interaction requiring expression of deepest human empathy and encouragement.

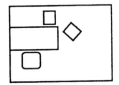

Whether standing or seated during interview situations, you can sense a critical distance and a flight distance with each interviewee. Interviewees have private space around them, enter it with particular care so as not to put them into a stance for danger.

The Conversation Location is four to six feet between participants. At first, position yourself about six feet away from interviewees, don't offend or violate their critical distance. If you go past that invisible line of the critical distance and step into their flight area they will generally back off to create room between themselves and you. The flight area is somewhere in that Moderate Location. First secure a foothold in the Conversation Location. Avoid rushing into the use of the Moderate Location. Your quick action to move toward them may cause undue stress. Recognize that there is a commonly accepted, invisible boundary around interviewees—a protective wall of privacy.[6 p. 78] Although stress is built into every interview, creating undue stress may block the flow of communication; it is unnecessary and self-defeating.[20 p. 180] Do not work over interviewees in a type of stress interview.[77] Try to feel safe in having positive regard for others.[13]

When people talk, they rarely overlap each other in conversation. Psychologist Adam Canden says that gestures play a part in regulating turn-taking in conversation. Anthropologist Birdwhistell has made similar observations. Canden found that when you relax a gesture while talking it is a signal to others that you are finished. Even if you have stopped talking, but hold your gesture, it is a signal not to interrupt you. Canden also found that your eye contact, like gestures, works to control the flow of conversation. You often look away for a few seconds before you finish speaking and look back just as you finish, signaling that it is the next person's turn to speak.[20]

Nonverbal behavior may nullify what your words say. Mehrabian points out that sometimes a pleasant set of words is delivered in an unpleasant tone.[81] The tone can undercut the verbal message, explicit messages versus implicit meanings. You can use a polite term of sir (explicit message) when addressing someone when you are really calling him a son-of-a-bitch. At times you could refer to someone and call him a son-of-a-bitch, but really mean it as a friendly greeting. Words depend on your tone of voice and gesture to take on their meaning. Meaning is in people not words.

There is increasing evidence that gestures and facial expressions are not simply learned. Eibl-Eibesfeldt has collected extraordinary evidence of inborn, natural facial expression by studying children who are born blind and deaf. Many facial expressions are inborn, such as smiling, laughing, and crying. Also, stamping feet in anger in the blind child is viewed as inborn. The blind child would have had no opportunity to learn those things as a sighted child would through visual imitation. Many facial expressions are inborn . . . a product of evolution, reports Eibl-Elbesfeldt.[86]

Interviewers gain self-control and proficiency while slowly attaining professional security, acceptance, and confidence by taking full responsibility for their actions.[72 p. 352] Always try to know what you are doing.[72 p. 126] It is vital to ensure interview communication takes place frankly and freely, but, in addition, to realize forensic interviews are special communication so focused and controlled that the initial problem-solving purpose is achieved.[35]

Control

Command or control of an interview requires you to concentrate or you will lose, so-to-speak.[71] Making all effort to maintain a chain of thought is vital when interviewees try to create diversions to completely sidetrack you from your goal.[71]

It is solid evidence of aggressiveness when a person interrupts someone else; it is an attempt to dominate. Used appropriately, interrupting interviewees can help direct interviews toward a desired end and keep some level of tension alive without trying to create new tension.

It is important that interviewers trust themselves while guiding interviewees along the path of truthful compliance.[6p.272] Interviewees think of themselves as rational beings making their own decisions. Hence, I attempt to create the illusion that they are in reasonable command of interview situations, at least as to the direction of the flow of information. Use persuasion for "communication designed to influence others by modifying their beliefs, values, or attitudes."[64]

Environmental diversions often cause a loss in concentration: phones ringing or neighbors stopping in for a chat are not under your control on interviewee turf. Sense the beginning of diversion or the break in thought pattern, make all effort to maintain your chain of thought. Interviewees may play old "mental tapes" and fantasize about events causing concentration problems.[45] To regain the discussion, review several comments or points mentioned just prior to the time of an interruption.

Signs of losing control of the interview appear when the interviewee begins to ask questions. When that happens, attempt to return to the position of control by first realizing what has happened and then not answer those questions.

An interviewer can use silence in positive ways to indicate or signal having control. It's important to avoid a personal silence as a cry for help signaling a loss of composure or train of thought. It is not positive to be harsh or abrupt; simply stop answering questions. After looking at my notes for a few moments to regain my thought patterns, I go on without trying to hurt feelings, or without becoming frustrated.

I regain *command* without an abrupt turning off of their side tracking. Regardless of the importance of the issue, I try to be tolerant enough to be sidetracked a little, if only to be polite, but not to be lead completely away from the real investigative issues.

Counseling

Information-gathering interviews are at times counseling in nature. There are two basic schools of thought about counseling: the directive and the nondirective. They exist on a continuum with degrees of being directive and nondirective.

Directive interviews involve the interviewer in counseling, collecting information, defining and analyzing problems, giving opinions and information, suggesting solutions, and giving some specific recommendations.

In nondirective interviews there is more of a facilitator than advisor using questions but not involved in making recommendations. The degree of direction-giving in interviews depends in large part upon your objectives.

If you are a dominant, assertive-type individual, be careful how you use eye-to-eye contact so as not to frighten interviewees with patterns of looking. I recommend allowing time for interviewee clear thinking. Do not stare down or out stare them.[26p.86]

Interview participant status is reflected in freedom of using their eyes; therefore, avoid being considered too assertive by your aggressive use of eyes in a dominant manner causing interviewees to become uncomfortable. My experience indicates that easy eye contact is needed to promote rapport with interviewees. "Eye contact is also very important in communication."[25p.309]

Silence

The "silent treatment" is the ultimate form of rejection and a sure sign of displeasure.[6p.78] Improperly used, interviewer silence is a form of authoritarian punishment and is a self-defeating move; it often offends, causing defensiveness. Hence, by the use of abusive silence, more tension is usually encouraged in interviewees and thereby possibly less compliance. Because interviews are a form of evidence collection, added tension and speed are not needed unless they help in making observations and assessments.[26p.85]

At times, however, silence or pause indicates to interviewees that more is expected in response to a question. With silence, there is a built-in sense of threat or implied disapproval.[26p.85] Silence, however, can be helpful if used productively. Creating silence in the proper interview framework without an intentional threat to interviewees can strengthen rapport and encourage compliance.

They can sense the mood of the moment, the implicit meaning of silence. Thus, I try to promote silence as a warm waiting period allowing for clear thinking. Because embarrassing silence is bothersome, I keep questions simple and direct, allowing time for their thoughtful reply.[23]p. 112 When I pause between questions I permit a slight silence. Interviewees often provide further information to fill the gap of silence.[26]p. 86 That silence often produces meaningful and relevant information not available from a fast moving interview.[26]p. 85

Amateur or novice interviewers may have low personal tolerance for silence; some become distressed because of it. Research "indicates that there is positive correlation between the amount of silence used by the interviewer and the respondent's general level of spontaneity."[30]p. 188

Silence can be personally oppressive for anxious interviewers who lack self-confidence, a brief period of silence may seem almost endless. However, interviewee silence is not necessarily a hindrance.[72]p. 166 Silence can be useful to both participants at times. It should not cause a disruptive effect to strategy, but it can cause you feelings of insecurity at times. Through training and practice, interviewers can withstand varying duration of quiet in order to use it to maximum advantage.

Interviewees, at times, resent being interrupted when speaking. They can be so touchy that they may become petulant, impatient, or irritable, in that they may be unwilling to talk at all. They can hold a grudge and be resentful of your dominance and engage in long intervals of silence before answering your questions.[20]

Your silence may be equated with withdrawal and rejection and shakes up interviewees when it happens repeatedly. When there is silence, participants may clutch up and become defensive.[20] Although interviewee silence may cause you to feel uneasy, it is important not to suggest to them responses to your questions. In some instances, interviewees realize silence makes the interviewer uncomfortable and will intentionally create silent spots in the interview to trap the interviewer into proceeding without receiving answers to the proposed questions.[5]p. 25 Even though silence can cause some interviewers to feel rejected, opposed, and thwarted, it is vital to not respond in an authoritarian manner. Resist responding as if interviewee silence is a personal attack.[5]p. 25

Thus, it is sometimes helpful to introduce silence at times when interviewees least expect it, realizing, however, that practiced, self-confident interviewees can withstand it and even at times intentionally present some of their own silence in hopes of bringing out any interviewer lack of confidence and tension. Experienced, composed interviewees can handle silence by sitting patiently and expectantly or by asking questions which will detract from the interviewer's effort. Some interviewees handle silence by returning the interviewer's stare with a calm, anticipatory look. The skill of interviewees in handling silence is a signal of their ability to control distress. Hence, I try to sense their developed talent to handle such silence.

When I sense interviewees are purposefully using silence, I assume that they are using other ploys to their advantage in manipulating me. Those using such ploys are formidable competitors and need special attention; therefore, I use closer observation and assessment. Truthful, straightforward, compliant-type interviewees need not employ tactics of strategic silence.

When I select to use silence as a tactic, I glance at interviewees rather than stare. To stare is not recommended; to glance and listen is essential. Staring can be oppressive; silence without a stare is enough to bring out meaningful existing interviewee tensions.

I support using silence to keep the pot bubbling, not to antagonize or alienate interviewees. It can be a constructive part of the interviewer's tactics and need not be a harsh method. I am neither in a hurry for the answer, nor anxious to put words in their mouths when they take too long to respond.

The subtle use of silence can be a weapon for battle or a marvelous instrument of the most delicate construction. Positive use of silence permits further blending of verbal and nonverbal communication. It can be a flavorful part of an interview permitting expression of acceptance.

Being Neutral

Subtle signals may show when you decide for or against interviewees. It is nearly impossible for interviewers to eliminate prejudice, hate, envy, vanity, etc., from behavior. And yet, they can control expression of personal views and values so as not to destroy chances of gaining the desired goal, be it complex or simple.[71]

I try to encourage compliance by deliberately seeking to establish neutrality.[23 p. 25] Neutral, in not taking sides; but yet giving the impression of taking the side of interviewees, ever so slightly. The bending of my attitude from a midpoint can be sensed. It is important to demonstrate respect for interviewees and an awareness of their feelings of need for security.[35p.126] Between Flow Chart points *A-F*, I make remarks in a neutral way avoiding a critical or judgmental stand.[35]

Hence, be neutral and objective in your methods, not giving interviewees a way of relieving tensions easily, except through verbal expression of data. Encourage them to evaluate their situations on real merits and not be guided by anxiety, irritation, or other emotion in decision making.[53] Criminal victims and witnesses may cloud facts with feelings and emotions, distorting needed data. Therefore, bring interviewees from emotional responses (T.A.-Child) to factual responses (T.A.-Adult) based upon clear thinking and not clouded with a playing of old emotional "tapes."[45]

Interviewees can generally tell your "party line" by your opening words.[6p.490] It takes but a few moments, a few words, a few nonverbal signals for you to show your relative position, the categorization you hold of interviewees. By taking the position—My mind is made up! Don't confuse me with facts!—you limit your investigative progress. Your bias (attitude) and stereotyping may adversely affect interviews.[23p.150] Perceptions of you (Parataxic Distortion) are determined to large extent by images left by other interviewers. Hence, your jaundiced view or emotional involvement and bias is not neutral and will carry over to any future inquiry experienced by interviewees.[23p.120]

Elements of neutrality include nonverbal signals in the interviewer's demeanor. Tone of voice, facial expressions, language, and timing in switching from one set of consequences to another must all be congruent with the verbal assertion of neutrality. If by force or tone of voice the interviewer emphasizes certain consequences, the interviewee will quickly sense, whether it is true or not, that the interviewer does have a preference. If the interviewer repeatedly calls attention to a particular set of consequences, the same result will often occur. If the interviewer reacts to an interviewee's focus on positive consequences by quickly switching to a discussion of the negative consequences, the interviewer again may be perceived as being less than neutral.[10p.172]

Being Patient

Patience is part of an accepting attitude. When interviewees provide emotional responses, be ready to withstand the heat and not react in a defensive, defiant manner. I see your point of view, I understand what you mean may be your possible comments. Reacting to their emotional tirades with threats and insults, or by "pushing" your position of authority and demanding a "civil tongue" only alienates them.[52] Your patience is essential.[71] Benjamin Disraeli, 1804–1881, said: "Next to knowing when to seize an advantage, the most important thing in life is to know when to forego an advantage."

Being tolerant or indulgent signals acceptance, patience and understanding. Thus, being patient has built within it a form of forgiveness and respect felt by interviewees. "A mark of one's own enthusiasm and dedication is impatience with people who do not do a good job. Few interviewers would consider this a fault."[25 p. 155] Impatience toward interviewees, however, is self-defeating and can only be characterized as abusive, judgmental and does not strengthen rapport. It is often thought to be a negative sign of sarcasm, ridicule, cynicism, and intimidation.

Chapter Twelve

INTERVIEWEE TYPES

In the process of defining investigative problems based upon available information and reviewing potential interviewee types, proficient investigators determine the probable degree of interviewee cooperation. Knowing various types and their methods as to how they talk, dress, move, do business is vital. It is useful to adapt to their traits and needs by developing the ability to size up people, read their basic personality types.

The Complainer

With them, listen attentively and avoid becoming defensive, try not to argue back. Repeat what they say as a way of showing that you comprehend complaint details and exhibit understanding. If they become sarcastic and hostile, try to draw out more detail to find out the exact issue. These urgent individuals may fly off the handle and become angry. They want action and results.

The Know-It-All

They think they have all the answers, wanting to take control of everything. Thinking they know my job better than I do, I allow them to parade knowledge. By finding an area of common interest with them, I may strengthen rapport. Because this type is basically thoughtful, logical, and business-like, they respond to words such as detail, tested, orderly, and so forth. To gain their trust and respect, have facts and figures at your finger tips and use systematic, thorough methods.

The Indecisive

Most of them want to cooperate, but are restrained by anxiety over making decisions. Using some nurturing helps them gain trust in you and narrows down their anxiety to some specific problems that can be considered realistically and resolved. Being dependent, concerned how others think of them, they often want others to make their decisions. Rapport with them is strengthened gradually as you wait patiently. Interviewers exhibiting a calm, confident, professional demeanor assist them to gain strength to comply.

The Unresponsive

Not wanting to become involved, they are detached, requiring a light touch, resisting any pressure to cooperate. Standing aloof, above it all, they want to control things themselves, resisting the hard sell, and not wanting anyone to influence them. With them, try to deal in concepts rather than detailed specifics. These are tough to deal with unless they are thoughtfully approached in a respectful way. Some elite, high-status people in this group are self-motivated individualists wanting to "pull their own strings and push their own buttons."[89]

The Scatterbrain Type

These may seem incapable of serious, connected thought; although pleasant, they truly challenge any interviewer's ability. With them, painstakingly and patiently advance point by point and item by item toward your goal. Because of mental and emotional makeup, they have a serious loss in capacity to concentrate; their minds jump from one segmented thought to another to possibly frustrate you. They may act as a child with fickle and impulsive thoughts, lacking maturity and jerking in an erratic stop-and-start fashion. Their problem may be lack of confidence. By skillful techniques you can gradually sift through unnecessary chatter, feelings, and "what ifs," "isn't it too bads," and "if onlys" to find needed data. They are not complicated; therefore, they generally provide more truthful answers because of their relative inability to think in complicated terms to conger up deception.

Criminal Types

Those brutal or repetitive, true criminals have a personality problem in development. Their character defect is in development and not a sickness. They are called sociopaths. They are Narcissistic types that are self-centered, confused about reality, impulsive in their actions and have no feeling of guilt. Their actions are appropriate for most five-year-olds who want what they want when they want it, often full of aggressive hatred and have no sense of right or wrong. Hervey M. Cleckley characterizes sixteen features of the sociopath:

1. Superficial charm and good intelligence.
2. Signs of irrational thinking but no mental illness.
3. Absence of nervousness, no signs of anxiety.
4. Generally unreliable much as a child is unreliable.
5. Tends to be untruthful.
6. Lacks shame, considers actions okay.
7. Lacks control of social behavior.
8. Lives for the now, doesn't learn from experience.
9. Incapacity of love for others, only for self.
10. Shows lack of understanding, has no guilt, lacks insight.
11. Tends to be unresponsive much like a child.
12. Exhibits fantastic behavior generally, and obnoxious behavior when drinking.
13. Threatens suicide but seldom carries it out.
14. No interest in sex life because it's not developed.
15. No life plan, no future plan.
16. Full of aggressive hatred.[18]

According to Thomas Harris, psychopaths are always able to differentiate between right and wrong and usually are well acquainted with requirements of society and religion, but are absolutely unwilling to be governed by these laws. They say laws do not concern them. They have a diminished sense of guilt; absence of sense of gratitude; justification of means by the end to be attained; complete disregard for consequences of action; lack of discretion, judgment and wisdom; impulsiveness; a peculiar ability to ingratiate themselves; and inability to profit by experience.

Their only interest with laws is to see that they are not caught in their violation, and if caught, to try to secure, by some trick, minimum punishment. Thus, one symptom is complete selfishness which manifests itself in every act. The only one they think of, in fact, the only individual they completely love is themselves, and they are surprisingly hardened to the rest of the world, including members of their own family.[83]

Psychopaths relate untruths with glibness. Their total disregard for the truth causes them to fabricate; they feel no compunction about lying.[37]

From a personality standpoint, it seems to me that the kind of individual least able to resist conformity pressures, and probably investigation pressures as well, is submissive, lacking in self-confidence, less intelligent, lacking in originality, authoritarian-minded, lacking in achievement and motivation, and searching for social approval, typically maintaining the attitude of I'm not OK, you're OK. To be most effective, evaluate subjective interviewee information in light of their current emotional state, opinion, attitudes, values, hypothetical reactions (projections of what they would do, think or feel if), and their actual tendencies to behave or feel.

The Compliant

Whether interviewees have a duty to speak the truth depends upon the situation. If they are predisposed to be cooperative and truthful, you may not need most of the methods and techniques suggested in this presentation.

Interviewees, inclined to judge the desirability of cooperation on a win-or-lose concept, cooperate or not depending on how they sense the ultimate outcome of the transactions. Deciding not to cooperate, they may use tactics to confuse and/or frustrate you.[52] Degrees of interviewee cooperation range from informants who rush forward to give information to the hostile, uncooperative type not even agreeing to meet with you, let alone provide information.

The most willing, least resistant interviewees decide to become compliant. The seemingly mystical field of confidential sources, snitches, sources of information, knowledgeable sources, stool pigeons, and informants has been, throughout history, the central repository of information for interviewers. Informants may give or sell information. Their motivation may be complicated or simple, ranging from seeking a new country for their family to the most basic one of feeding a family or getting revenge against an enemy.

Part of gaining cooperation is in being kind to fellow human beings to include being polite and considerate of their position in life, their needs, and their privacy.[13] Expecting interviewee calmness and clear thinking, you will probably receive it.[52] Your professional, calm, nonjudgmental, methods signal to victims, witnesses, and suspects that it is safe to trust you and that the danger is now over or reduced. Having an it-is-time-to-talk-now tactic can assist your effort.[23]p. 11

Prominent, compliant interviewees often want to be your teacher in interview situations and that can benefit the inquiry if you are not technically prepared. In preparation to deal with intellectual, prominent, or elite interviewees, seek out and learn some jargon of their profession or trade.[23]p. 36

Overlook interviewee social status; don't be timid even though the social tendency is to seek approval or appreciation, esteem, from those you look up to who are in authoritative positions. Obviously, high status interviewees may frighten inexperienced interviewers into becoming tongue-tied. Some people intentionally promote status differences to make interviewers uncomfortable, some claiming special privileges.

Be bold enough, have enough gall, and confident to face any interviewees with questions pertinent to the inquiry without embarrassment or diminished self-image. Be ready to receive verbal and nonverbal interviewee signals of disapproval commonly displayed toward someone of lesser rank (see Self-beliefs, SFP).

Rushed and busy prominent interviewees generally find time to be interviewed. Thus, most people, including the elite, will not refuse to be interviewed.[23]p. 29 Based upon proper preparation, ask the prominent to interpret, evaluate, and render opinions where possible, for they will often help guide your investigation.[23]p. 11 They can be stimulated with encouraging comments, not necessarily questions.[23]p. 56

In most instances, the main interview purpose is not to trick but to encourage or stimulate interviewee aid in exploring and revealing truthful facts.[23]p. 82

Gaining access to business information is possible by understanding and respecting the concession provided. Legal restrictions and policies at each company vary regarding availability of information to investigators. Some employees are instructed not to provide company information under any circumstances and, if they do, their employment will be terminated. Because of such restrictions I am certain to approach high-ranking officials of the business firm to be assured my requests for information are likely to be honored.

Dying Declarations

While reviewing degrees of cooperation, I suggest a closer look at the subject of death and dying. Considering some limited points may assist in conducting inquiries with people facing that final stage of life, death.

Since the early seventeen hundreds, deathbed statements have taken on a special likelihood of truthfulness. Some have considered that impending death would make most men strongly disposed to tell the truth. Interviewees must be conscious and have an attitude, that death is near and certain; that it is certain, not merely likely. That attitude, is proven by evidence of the declarant's own statements of such belief at the time, expression of "settled hopeless expectation." The circumstances, however, can prove the hopeless situation, need not actually make such a statement. Dying declarations can be dangerous testimony, which a jury is likely to handle too emotionally.[48]p.555

The weight of particular dying declarations depends upon so many factors varying from case to case that no standardized instruction will fit all situations.[48]p.560 Uniform Rules of Evidence, R. 63, Sub 5 ... "A statement by a person unavailable as a witness because of his death ... if the judge finds that it was voluntary and in good faith and while the declarant was conscious of his impending death and believed that there was no hope of his recovery."

Many of us never consider death possible. "Death is attributed to a malicious intervention from outside yourself, it is associated with a bad act."[39] Because dealing with death causes people to realize they are not omnipotent, they consider death as a fearful, frightening happening. Fear of death is a universal fear even if you think you have mastered it on many levels. Hence, I think it is vital to develop ways of coping and dealing with death.

Although in a rush to uncover facts, try to slow your pace when dealing with the dying. At times, hold the hand of the dying person, smile, or listen to a question. Your humanness helps. Dying people may "cry out for rest, peace, and dignity."[39, 96] Sense where and when to ask questions, without a mechanical, depersonalized technique. Terminally or critically ill interviewees may cause some interviewers anxieties and confused thinking because, in some strange way, they may feel ashamed in causing additional pain through asking of even a few simple questions.

Some dying people at first are not receptive to inquiries. They may start complaining about pain and discomfort; they are often angry in the midst of sharing agony. Thus, if not steeled to this eventuality, some interviewers may "crumble with sympathy, compassion, and warm feelings."[39]

Through a personal "desensitization process,"[39] proficient interviewers try to learn how to slowly and painfully replace anger and rage with calmness and equanimity in all interview situations, most especially in dealing with death. They build and vary experiences to become psychologically toughened to emotional pain involved in many investigations.

At times dying persons are nasty and uncooperative, even abusive, but this response should not trigger frustration or related defensiveness. Remain calm, cool, and collected. If ever you seek ways to avoid interview contacts with dying persons, realize that even "highly trained hospital nurses rationalize their avoidance of dying persons."[39]

It seems to me, the thought of "no hope" or "settled hopeless expectation" appears in the fourth or depression stage when legal elements take form, in that stage dying individuals may realize they have no hope to live. According to Kubler-Ross, one thing persisting through all stages is hope. If patients stop expressing hope, it is usually a sign of imminent death. When not expressing hope, they give up; death usually comes within twenty-four hours of when patients stop expressing hope. First stage: Denial and isolation; Second stage: Anger; Third Stage: Bargaining; Fourth stage: Depression; Fifth stage: Acceptance.[39]

For deathbed statements to probably have legal significance, they must be obtained at the fourth or fifth stage of the dying process in my view. Be attentive and alert to the dying person's condition and the interview circumstances. Complete notes are necessary for later legal review to help in the evaluation of admissibility of the deathbed statements and their weight as evidence.

The Reluctant

Reluctant interviewees may have information but not want to get involved in someone else's hassle. The possible red tape of court appearances may be too much trouble or they don't want to be worked over by some attorney in a deposition situation.

Interviewee reluctance to comply may be based upon an adherence to a need to know policy, compartmented, to protect information from escaping the grasp or control of an organization. Secrecy is not restricted to government use; various organizations use it. Some interviewees use such a policy at times, not knowing how to deal with an inquiry, maintaining a veil of secrecy because they can't stand to make a decision to comply. Fearing the outcome of their potential choice to cooperate, they avoid being helpful. Secretaries and other loyal, dedicated employees may act as barriers between you and prospective interviewees. Those agents are bound to live up to instructions and are restrained as far as discretion to permit access to information or people.[52]

When interviewees give lip service, agreeing to provide needed information at some time in the near future, it may be a form of reluctance to cooperate; it is an indication that you may be wasting your time. Sensing a run-around, try to be more alert and prove to yourself if their reluctance is a defensive move to protect self-esteem or really an effort to sidetrack or mislead.[53]

Assuming reluctant interviewees have some attitude of resentment, ask questions to help melt that frozen stance. Use questions and statements bearing upon assumed hidden resentment rather than the target issue of your inquiry. I try to use questions and statements containing assumptive views based upon why interviewees don't comply. Through expressions of empathic understanding, I display that I'm aware of why some people do not respond. An interviewer's concerned attempts to skillfully convey compassion will probably thaw frozen attitudes of noncompliance, at least for a short time.

I attempt to resolve the basis of interviewee reluctance before attempting to obtain information. Interviewees not responding to questions can cause some interviewers greater frustration than facing hostile, antagonistic vocal interviewees. At least with hostile types there is often some response, even if it is negative. That quiet, unresponsive, stoic type presents the greatest challenge. Any response, any dialogue is of value, a breakthrough. Merely to have that stoic type respond in any form is stimulation enough to carry on the effort.

When interviewees argue against your advancing inquiry, your magnet may find its way through their armor. With additional effort, energy, enthusiasm, self-motivation, those holes can be enlarged for clear viewing of the contents. Intuitively sense whether or not you can expect information to develop when interviewing highly reluctant types. By using well-prepared questions and statements I try to establish interactional synchrony and gain some degree of truthful compliance. When interviewees try to argue why they should not comply they are indicating that at least some part of their attitude is favorably considering doing so, or they wouldn't argue the point. Even interviewees who show up for scheduled interviews and sit quietly without response to investigative questions signal that part of their attitude is favorably considering compliance. Each situation creates need for evaluation.[53]

Investigations are not always "neat and nice."[52p.10] The ultimate interview goal might be to legally find the basis to prosecute someone and an interviewee, a witness for example, may feel the goal unacceptable; therefore, you may select to use a cover story to avoid the interviewee's reluctance. Lessen the potential of interviewee guilt feelings regarding compliance; tell them that prosecution may not take place, while in fact, prosecution is specifically planned.[23p.32]

Allow them time to change gradually; if they hesitate to comply, consider it natural. With "irrational opposition, the real reason for noncompliance is hidden and there is an imperviousness to logical argument."[53]

Reluctance is no reason to cause humiliation. Allowed opportunity to rationalize, interviewees may render data at some future time. Hence, I avoid pushing interviewees "into a corner" to extract data. Such treatment encourages rebellion and stops any form of compliance.[52p.28]

Avoid acting as some inexperienced interviewers may who catch interviewees in small lies, berating them for lack of cooperation. That action often stimulates interviewee revenge and retaliation, showing up in distortion of any data provided.

Pretend to overlook and forgive small lies. I remind myself to be perceptive, keep an eye on the goal of developing particular information, and not be sidetracked by possible feelings of anger because interviewees may be evasive or lying. Deception is a defensive effort. Try again and again to focus your approach on the goal with several methods of questioning. In most situations, interviewee lying is not a personal attack upon you; it is merely a way to maintain balance.

I try to control my reaction to interviewee rejection so as to be "tactful and diplomatic."[54p.171] Proficient interviewers develop a keen sense of what to say and do so as not to be offended or offensive. Some interviewees feel any questions asked of them are accusations. Therefore, I always assume some resentment exists even though they may not have taken part in the matter under investigation. Such feelings can create reluctance or hostility. Those sensitive types are often reluctant as a matter of pride, responding emotionally rather than with clear reasoning.[6p.490]

Disapproval by peers sparks habits corresponding to peer goals, not individual goals.[6p.318] When facing outer-directed (having low self-esteem, low self-efficacy) interviewees, overly influenced by friends, associates, and significant others, you may find them reluctant or at least indecisive. Inner-directed (having high self-esteem) interviewees think for themselves and are not overly influenced by others. People like to be approved of, generally, and they try to please others and maintain a feeling of being appreciated.

The Hostile

Extremes on the continuum of interviewee cooperation include completely truthful open compliance on one extreme and hostile rebelliousness on the other. Hostility may be hidden or clouded over. Although interviewees may not outwardly express antagonistic comments and actions, hostility may be brewing within but under enough control so as not to burst out as a form of angry words or actions.

Having a weak sense of self-worth and a feeling of loneliness, some interviewees claim to be "fighting against the power of politics and economics that have forced them into typical roles in society."[6p.167] Thus, interviewees in similar situational roles claim they fight similar battles with society and its authorities.

Interviewers will not always face antagonistic, sullen interviewees who will not comply, but still be prepared. My challenge is to become aware of preparation and self-control faults based upon limitations in methods, techniques, tactics and canny maneuvers. With proper preparation and self-control, most interviewers can conduct productive forensic interviews.[54p.201]

Some interviewees intentionally rebel to assert independence and express resentment of all discipline and authority. With such resentment, "be patient and persistent to overcome hidden, irrational interviewee opposition."[53] With insight, quickly recognize suddenly invented, unnatural patterns of interviewee behavior. Amid the turmoil of emotions, interviewees diverge from their "original script" and may become immobilized with momentary speechlessness while engaged in mental gymnastics in an effort to avoid answering your questions. Finding they cannot successfully manipulate your interviews, they may become hostile to the point of refusing to continue their interviews.[54p.175]

Being angry, unwilling interviewees may be more aggressive and hostile than expected and may verbally attack you without provocation.

Hence, anxiety and fear caused because of their unwilling participation in the interview will not aid your effort.[72 p. 150]

Indignant interviewees may think that because they had no involvement in the investigative problem it is somehow written on their forehead or on their sleeve announcing not to be considered in any way. Facing hostile indignation, I try to use patient methods, appealing for cooperation. Through dialogue, interviewee anger and fear may be vented and reduced. However, there are no quick, easy guidelines dealing with uncooperative, argumentative, over-cautious interviewees.

Many times you are not the cause of hostility. Possibly the image of your organization stimulated their reluctant stance. Or, in some instances, associate interviewers have previously laid unfavorable ground work upon which you must function. Hence, if interviewees are committed to certain perceptions or beliefs, they go to extensive means to support those beliefs.[6 p. 216] They may even try to provoke the interviewer into becoming a heavy-handed, overly aggressive individual.

Fearing conspiracy, some interviewees consider the whole world a threat to safety and welfare, they perceive those in authority in an enemy category. Some overly sensitive individuals are enraged by relatively routine questions. If requested to undergo a polygraph examination they may be argumentative and generally uncooperative with the polygraphist. They may even try to instruct the polygraphist in how to conduct the examination; their general overall psychophysiological responses tend to lack the stable quality necessary for diagnostic evaluation. Their unfounded fear of a conspiracy may indicate possible mental disability.

With changes in current laws, interviewees seem justified in being fearful about "anonymity and confidentiality."[35] It follows that tensions and anxieties may be the basis of lack of compliance to the point of rebellious hostility.[53]

If there is any skill to be learned in the science of forensic interviewing it is in coping with terrors attending self-disclosure and the art of decoding the language, verbal and nonverbal, in which interviewees speak about inner experiences and accumulated knowledge. Their souls, their real selves, their subjective side is what they think, feel, believe, want, worry about; those things determine their behavior. It is the rare interviewer who understands those things. It is not easy to enter thoroughly, completely and empathically into their frame of reference, into their abstracted perception of life.

Chapter Thirteen

QUESTION FORMULATION

Questions, keys to knowledge and feelings, encourage compliance when their design is simple. Make them more specific and complex after evaluating the degree of interviewee compliance. Aristotle said, "Think as wise men do, but speak as the common people do." Ask questions spontaneously to express ideas in a natural and subconscious manner. Trust yourself to ask properly worded questions while exhibiting encouragement. With adaptability, make your questions specific, definite, and concrete. I believe vague, general type questions permit interviewees to wiggle and squirm away from your desired goal.

Interviewees provide opinions wherever and whenever they can; therefore, continually try to distinguish true factual data from opinionated, emotional comments. Separate their observations from interpretations, fact from fiction or opinion, facts from feelings.

Interviewees enjoy and welcome opportunity to give answers to questions for which they know the answers; they feel more free to talk when speaking about familiar topics. They do not like to appear dumb, foolish, or uninformed; they, therefore, tend to avoid answering questions making them appear so. Those embarrassed or upset over some questions avoid eye-to-eye contact and may display signs of imbalance or distress. Some interviewees turn quite shifty-eyed when they are lying, planning to lie, or asked to reveal hidden data about their self.

Questions sell, guide interviewees on the idea to decide to tell the truth. It is not a matter of telling, but a matter of selling . . . manipulate, not dominate. Thus, be a persuader of sorts, use properly phrased questions in a setting and under circumstances convincing interviewees to decide to provide truthful data.

Be a successful persuader, convincing interviewees to comply.[6 p. 247] Have a commitment to gain information through the strengthening of their obligation or sense of duty.[6 p. 70] Through a variety of canny maneuvers seek to create a new identity or altered behavior for interviewees.[6 p. 269] Maneuvers are not negative if related intentions are basically helpful and honorable. Create a temporary new identity for respondents, so to speak, persuading them to move from a relative position of limited compliance to one of more complete compliance.

A question is, in effect, your request for the interviewee to think about a particular subject matter. Even your subtle statements or comments based upon your assumptions can be types of questions presented in a manner allowing interviewees opportunity to answer or comment. Allow free association to occur rather than rely on many questions. Some interviewees elaborate more freely when fewer questions are asked, permitted a chance to ramble a bit. Once interviewees decide to provide data, you often need merely guide that flow with timely encouragement. Interviewee narrative can be the basis of determining veracity.

Your assumptions, concepts, and phrases used will cause some degree of interviewee cooperation, apathy, suspicion, and hostility. Even your vocabulary could cause embarrassment or fright. At times, interviewees lose face if not comprehending your words; they may become disturbed or insulted; their child may feel naked and vulnerable, their parent judgmental and skeptical. Their resentment may cause them to refuse to cooperate or possibly falsify answers or refuse to invest energy to think. And yet, some interviewees will be extremely cooperative in trying to answer all inquiries even though the interviewer uses crude, biased assumptions, concepts, and phrases.

By initiating the question-answer pattern, you tell interviewees as plainly as if put into words that you are the authority, the expert, and that only you know what is important and relevant. That may humiliate some interviewees and they may think it is a third degree tactic. Therefore, be sensitive or intuitive enough to realize when and when not to ask questions.

Question objectively; avoid giving impressions you have taken sides in the investigation; this, however, may be difficult for interviewers representing certain organizations, law enforcement investigators, for example. Presenting a neutral role is a difficult task. Regardless of the hat you wear, interviewees may suspect some hidden objective or ulterior motive.

Do not grill the interviewee as a prosecuting attorney might do. Ask questions in a conversational manner, because your purpose is to hold a conversation with someone who has knowledge or has experienced something that you want to know about. Holding a conversation implies a certain amount of give-and-take during the interview. Make sure that you are asking questions and not making statements that do not call for answers.[25 p. 286]

Two main types of questions generally found in interviews consist of:

1. Closed questions (typically referred to as close-ended questions) usually receive a simple yes or no answer. Their unrestricted use tends to terminate or hamper your efforts. Use this type at the beginning of interviews (see Structured Approach) to encourage affirmative responses and to put interviewees more at ease. These are narrow in the responses permitted.

2. Open questions (typically referred to as open-ended questions) start with who, where, what, when, how, and why and cannot be answered yes or no. They require clear interviewee thinking, draw out the most distress and assist in revealing the greatest amount of data. Some modifications of open type questions are as follows:

   a. Reflective questions are used to handle objections and take the form: "You feel it would be too difficult to change?" like a mirror of the interviewee's objections. There is a challenge in this type of question bouncing back to interviewees comments expressing reluctance to comply. "You feel too uncomfortable to discuss this matter now?"

   b. Directive questions are used to direct interviewees to areas of agreement. Interviewees want to know "what's in it for me?" Self-interest. "You do want to get to the bottom of this, don't you?"

   c. Pointed questions and direct questions stir interviewees into action, out of a state of inertia. They are specific in nature and design, pointing most accurately at the goal. Complex, detailed and persuasive.

   d. Indirect questions. Assumptions are voiced implying your goal, less stress revealing. Used at the beginning of interviews and as a change of pace during the course of interviews. These have diversion application.

   e. Self-appraisal questions. Used to encourage interviewees to change and to stimulate their adult ego state responses.

   f. Diversion questions. Used to reduce tension and restore rapport.

Open questions help interviews flow. Most open questions begin with the words what, why, and how. Questions beginning with why may provoke undue stress because they generate too much challenge. Under most circumstances, interviewees cannot answer the question "why?" regarding subconscious thinking or behavior to answer reveals too much of one's self. Self-disclosure may be uncomfortable.

Hold some assumptions during interviews to enable yourself to ask appropriate open, low-structured questions. First, assume interviewees have information needed and that with proper question formulation you will persuade them to reply truthfully.

To learn the cause, reason, or purpose, ask the question why to search out facts of a situation. And, through that question, probe areas not commonly touched by more complicated questions. There are times, however, when asking the question why creates a threatening situation in which interviewees may become defensive because of distress. Presented that question, they may feel rejected, misunderstood, and imposed upon. They may withdraw, prevaricate, or hit back with silence which may confuse or frustrate you.

Indirect questions draw out less fear and less defensiveness while direct questions stimulate physical expression of interviewee inner tension. Direct questions are the majority asked in forensic interviews. By asking exactly what is desired, expect that they are ready, willing, and able to respond. That method works most of the time and it is based upon the Self-Fulfilling Prophecy.

> Insofar as gaining information is concerned, narrow questions have the advantage of eliciting details. In contrast, Open-ended questions rely almost exclusively on the client's unaided ability to recall . . . narrow questions can inhibit the development of rapport . . . far too many . . . interviews consist almost exclusively of narrow questions.[10p.44]
> . . . misuse of narrow questions involves detailed probing before the client is ready. People will be willing to provide details, particularly about sensitive subjects, only if they feel comfortable in doing so. Therefore, probing too soon, without first having developed a maximum of rapport, may cause the client to feel improperly invaded.[10p.45]

Gently stimulate the interviewee's thinking and memory with pointed, creative questions (see Semi-Structured Approach). If those pointed, direct questions do not encourage cooperation, they will probably reveal a certain amount of existing stress reflected or displayed through nonverbal signals that may be indicative of truth emerging.

Pointed questions need not be offensive or accusatory in nature and design. They, on the contrary, must be thoughtfully developed and subtly applied to avoid invoking stress and related defensiveness. They take the form: On the day of the fire, how often did you smoke in the storeroom?

Use indirect questions when attempting to assist interviewees save face, allowing them to rationalize. These questions promote an expression of their hidden self, their opinions and suggestions, views, feelings, and other confidential matters while you give them a universal blessing such as . . . we all think that . . . everyone in the bank has the opinion that . . . I've talked to many of the employees and they consider that. . . . Indirect questions open avenues revealing interviewee-projected thoughts, needs, and values.

Again, people generally do not like being embarrassed because they are unable to answer questions; that uneasiness may be the foundation of some tension. Asking questions accusingly or suspiciously may arouse fear and defensiveness and not cooperation. Abruptly asked or tricky questions are not appropriate; they are mostly self-defeating.

I'm now going to ask you a few questions about such and so. That sort of lead-in will often cause potentially deceptive interviewees to show nonverbal signs of distress signaling intent to deceive. Their exhibited uneasiness is cause for you to question, mentally, the truthfulness of provided answers.

It is self-defeating to immediately confront or challenge interviewees displaying signs of uneasiness just prior to or during answers to announced questions. When a clear pattern of evasiveness becomes evident, make a gradual challenge designed to allow even more opportunity for evasiveness. Look for a pattern of evasive responses that may be indicative of deception. Isolated evasiveness, although important, must not be the basis of your challenge regarding deceptiveness (see Level 4 Intensity).

Again, some degree of unprovoked anxiety in each interviewee may be useful. Enhance tension by the use of questions or comments about the interviewee's defense mechanisms, sensitive areas of feeling, or provocative events. Insensitive confrontation, however, because of conflicting details in their stories, could more than keep the pot simmering. Aggravated levels of tension may provoke nonconstructive interviewee behavior to cause undue tension, evasiveness, and defensiveness. Avoid using overly complex or confusing questions.

At times, calm interviewees by indirect means using diversion questions. That calming process is based upon the main ingredient of diversion questions involving something or someone near and dear to the interviewee.

Diversion questions have two purposes; first, to take the 's thoughts away from the tension-producing issue, and, secondly, to cement a closer bond, restore rapport by indicating a direct or indirect compliment. Diversion questions are useful when dealing with highly emotional interviewees. Their use lessens the specific nature of the inquiry and broadens thinking toward less emotional (not anger-producing) things, to spread emotions. Diversion questions usually help relax conditions and turns off the critical part of the interviewee's Parent Ego State.

Information-gathering interviews are to be based upon factual matter rather than opinions or feelings. Novice or inexperienced interviewers collect more feelings and opinions rather than facts.[4]p.100 " . . . skillful probing differentiates effective interviewers from ineffective ones."[25]p.243 Your inquiry objective determines application of open or closed questions. Fewer tactical restrictions apply to using open questions. Their use is dependent upon the circumstances of your inquiry. Open questions can help you to:

1. Discover interviewee priorities, attitudes, needs, values, aims, and aspirations.
2. Determine interviewee frame of reference and viewpoints and assist in establishing empathic understanding.
3. Engage in active listening, stroking, positive regard, recognition, and enhance rapport.
4. Allow and encourage interviewee expression of feelings and facts without participants feeling threatened.
5. Promote catharsis or expression of interviewee emotions.
6. " . . . bring into play the rapport-building advantages . . . "[10]p.58

Closed questions are specific, restricting options in answering. Multiple-choice questions are a form of closed questions in which all alternatives are listed and their answers are accomplished by merely checking one listed such as in a school test or political survey.

The yes-no or either-or option of some closed questions limits the scope of responses and options. However, if you want to maintain maximum control over interview situations and thereby save man hours, use closed questions limiting interviewee choices. When reluctant interviewees are not expected to give detailed explanation about an event, closed questions are useful.

Words tend to communicate aspects while some may think they represent total images; words represent partial images not the total picture.

Thus, try to avoid using legal sounding words such as kill, rape, assault, and so forth, in questioning, because, misused, they tend to cause excessive tension and related defensiveness.

My experience reflects that investigators "... usually have problems asking tough or embarrassing questions and they may even avoid asking these questions to save themselves from embarrassment. There is no doubt that it takes a certain amount of gall to ask someone if he or she stole the money, killed the husband, or got drunk and ran over a neighbor's child."[25 p.288]

Although most interviewees tend to feel a personal obligation to answer appropriately formulated questions, that obligation is lessened when you are not skilled in your efforts and they realize that lack. If interviewee expectations conflict with the interviewer's questioning pattern, the interviewee may feel frustrated or annoyed. As a consequence, rapport may suffer.[10 p.65]

The more often you can induce yes answers to simple, preliminary, closed questions, the better the chances of gaining further cooperation when asking more complex specific, open questions. By conveying the impression that more information is sought, needed, and expected, you subtly promote the revealing of more data. Imply that you have considerable information accumulated against which you will check provided information; such implication is best presented without creating tension unnecessarily.

To avoid receiving answers of no to questions, such as, "Have you seen or talked with Sam Smith recently?", mentally assume that you have actually asked that question and imagine the answer to be yes. That is, you will not actually verbally ask that question, but merely assume it to have been asked and answered yes in your imagination. Then, proceed to actually ask the second question, "When was the last time you talked with or saw, communicated with, Sam Smith?"

That second question, an open type, cannot be answered yes or no; interviewees must respond with a sentence if they answer at all. That will help determine the direction of successive questions. You might then ask how many times they spoke with Sam Smith in the past two days if they did speak with Sam in the past couple of days. If they spoke to Sam two times in the past couple of days, then, what was Sam wearing when last seen? They may be helpful by providing a current description of Sam. Also, what of Sam's means of transportation and associates?

If interviewees have been permitted to answer your first question "no" because the word "recently" is considered a certain period of time, such as several hours, they could play mental games, dissemble, without revealing any needed data. Assume interviewees have desired information.

When problem-solving topics are touchy, sensitive, or threatening, restate questions to find their most suitable and acceptable form. Acknowledge to yourself that some questions contain words that trigger mental images that may be emotionally painful and may promote related thought blocking. Whether your questions are restated in their original form or reconstructed using other words and then asked, all depends on the circumstances and how you sense your progress and function in the situation.

There are times when a mild or modified version of an emotional question can first be asked before the main question is presented. Such action will intentionally forewarn interviewees of the upcoming loaded emotional question so that they can be somewhat prepared for it. And yet, on some occasions, it may be necessary to spring emotion-revealing questions unannounced to create opportunity for interviewee tension to show.

However, the main purpose of restating questions is to reduce the tension. Hence, restate or reword questions when it is not certain if interviewees comprehend their meaning. All the while, look for, listen for, and sense possible signals of deception. Be aware of patterns indicating truth emerging.

Your questions may not be answered at all or only partly. Repeat questions by varying wording or their pace to avoid being boring as well as to allow time for answers. Allow time for respondents to think without unduly challenging them. It is always a good idea to repeat questions rather than go on to another topic; to go on and leave unanswered questions can only cause you eventual frustration. Wait a reasonable time for a response and if none is forthcoming, then reword the question and ask it again. Be patient! Was the question asked in a clearly expressed manner? Preoccupations distract interviewees so they may not have heard the question as it was first expressed. The first asking of questions may trigger old emotional tapes to play, causing distraction and interference with clear thinking.[45] Or, was not answering the deceptive individual's tactic of avoiding the topic? Always maintain a certain amount of unexpressed skepticism to protect yourself from acting as a novice.

Challenging interviewees to answer questions may cause them to become defensive. Appear to overlook the lack of answer and merely reword, restate, and try again. Some perceptive interviewees are tuned in enough to provoke you to challenge them so that they then may feel justified to storm out of the interview situation, claiming your impatient challenge as an excuse to terminate the interaction. Even a victim or witness of a criminal investigation may feel insulted if challenged by a demand for an answer to a question. Thus, by patiently rewording or reasking questions, you signal persistence, patience, and humanness which strengthens the bond of interpersonal communication.

To emphasize genuine interest in details, provided and strengthen the interviewee's positive view of your thoroughness, review details during questioning to thereby allow coverage of more specific areas of interest as the need may arise. As long as reviewing does not break the train of thought, make it appear that some details provided are not as clear as they could be, claim to have missed some meaningful segments.

Pushing interviewees into a corner where they will have to stand and fight is self-defeating. Noticing the sincerity of your tone of questioning, and how you avoid asking abrasive, leading questions, they will feel less need to be defensive. Asking "Isn't it true that you were . . . " tends to be abrasive and may promote defensiveness.

Unobtrusively direct interviews, deciding when to listen, when to talk, what to observe, and so on. With over-talkative interviewees who ramble, or those who tend to wander, gently and empathically lead them back, redirecting them through leading questions to a discussion of immediate issues.

Leading questions need not be abrasive in design if thoughtfully constructed. Your assumptions apply in leading questions: "From what I hear you say, you must have had a rough time in that job last summer?" That question has assumptions, a statement and an open question built into it. Naturally, the interview objective and its participants determine the wide variety of questions and their direction. Again, intentionally maintain moderate interviewee emotional imbalance by deliberately using leading questions containing implicit messages, conveying expectation that they will answer with truthful information.

Traditionally, leading questions have been characterized in a negative fashion; they have been thought to produce invalid unreliable answers. That negative characterization applies only when you do not realize that you have used them and you receive false or misleading answers. Ulterior transactions, as mentioned elsewhere in this presentation, are typically built into your use of leading questions. Thus, formulate some questions in a leading way with the ulterior motive of encouraging the revelation of truthful data through stimulated dialogue.

Leading questions often guide interviewees toward greater compliance. They exhibit your assumption that interviewees can provide desired data. An advantage of leading questions is that they can convey interviewer acceptance and thereby enhance rapport. Novice investigators may have a problem in using leading questions because their tone of voice and related nonverbal signals may not be well-controlled. Interviewees may feel condemned in some way if you are not careful in using leading questions.

Self-appraisal questions assist in developing a hypothesis. Gaining deeper understanding of interviewee needs and opening avenues of their opinion reveal possible evasiveness and distress. Self-appraisal questions make it difficult for interviewees to snow you. In order to do so, they have to first think of an answer, decide that the answer would not be appropriate or not sound good, make up a new story, and tell it—doing all these things simultaneously. It is almost impossible for deceptive or evasive interviewees to be consistent in answering self-appraisal questions.

It can be difficult handling interviewee trial-balloon questions such as "Just say I did steal the money, what would happen to me?" or "What usually happens to a person who steals merchandise?" These may be considered game questions or what if questions reflecting an interviewee is on the brink of telling some significant fact or truth is emerging.

When trial-balloon questions develop, avoid pouncing to play the I gotya game. Instead, calmly and subtly present questions that will lead, encourage, the interviewee to a point of deciding to tell the truth. What if questions are used to test the water, so to speak, to see if the coast is clear to land. Those questions signal the need for continued patience and persistence. They do not imply a time to charge ahead in a destructive way.

As information is provided, always assume more can be forthcoming, that a greater supply of data is available if only appropriate questions are asked with adequate encouragement given. When reaching a point seeming to signal interview termination, when all questions seem to have been asked and answered, continue to believe that more information is available. Always assume that there is more available, within reason. Ask "What else is there that you can tell me about what happened?" "What else should I know about this matter?" When asking such questions, at times, nonverbally signal or imply that you may know there really is more data that can be provided. Nonverbals do the implying.

Make no accusation to suggest data is being withheld; only subtly suggest more is expected. Use such implied expectation skillfully, not directly. Subtle use of that tactic probably will not interfere with established rapport. Realize, however, using such a tactic may cause defensiveness and hostility.

Promote development of friendly techniques; use of or threat of use of force is not recommended. Do not use coercion in any form! And, avoid using "Is there anything else?" Always assume there is more data available. Again, within reason, use "What else is there?" Persistence pays!

Chapter Fourteen

INTUITION

Intuition is the power of knowing through the senses without recourse to inference or reasoning. Interviewers possess this ability to some degree, varying in proportion to its exercise. For some, it remains dormant in the subconscious for life because it is never brought into play. Intuition has many commonly used names: gut feeling, hunch, sixth sense, third ear, reading between the lines, quick insight.

Pascal, the French Philosopher, said, "The heart has its reasons which reason knows nothing of." He was referring, it seems, to intuition, a kind of sixth sense by which you know things that you can't exactly explain.

Intuition is spontaneous and valuable in interviewing. It is automatic, not requiring preoccupation or distraction. Keen intuition is accurate and helpful, but difficult to explain. " . . . through an intuitive weighing process, decide which alternative, on balance, seems best. In the course of this intuitive process, the client brings into play his/her own values and sense of appropriate risk avoidance."[10 p. 152]

Use intuition as the primary reaction in interviewing, automatically guiding and benefiting you through various sensitive matters. Although some people disregard intuition and consider its use unscholarly, I consider intuition a valuable asset.

"Intuition: The word has been used by different philosophers to describe a variety of objects of knowledge, belief or understandings, as well as the ways in which such objects are known. In each case, such knowledge is supposed to be in some way or other independent of inference, justification or theory."[33 p. 321]

It is vital to acquire a careful balance of the scientific and intuitive in interviewing to avoid rigid procedures in most interpersonal communication; thus, use spontaneous actions and reactions rather than rigid rules. I recommend using moment-to-moment changes and diagnoses with confidence and ease; they are subtle, complex, and often confusing. Develop reasonable intelligence, self-awareness, sensitivity toward others, and intuition to cope with spontaneity prevalent in interviews.

151

Develop vision to perceive undefined and spontaneous happenings. In the year 500 B.C., the Greek philosopher Heraclitus proclaimed the following axiom, "If you expect not the unexpected, ye shall not find the truth." Since seeking truth is your primary objective or responsibility, expect the unexpected.

Generally speaking, most people do possess a remarkable sensitivity to other people, but they are not keenly aware of it. Edward Sapir (1884–1939), an American anthropologist who won his fame as the man who laid the foundation for modern linguistics, wrote: "We respond to gestures with an extreme alertness and, one might say, in accordance with an elaborate code that is written nowhere, known by none, and understood by all."

Those seemingly insignificant messages may assist you in developing needed information in determining the truth. Observe and assess interviewees to include:

- What they say both verbally and nonverbally
- How they say what they say
- What they fail to say

Bodily tension, flushing, excitability, frustration, evasiveness, and dejection can either supplement or belie interviewee words. Your awareness of such behavior will assist you in detecting deception or, more clearly, seeing emerging truth.

Kinesicists limit themselves to nonverbal behavioral studies and do not speculate about feelings because they do not believe feelings can be measured scientifically. They contend that the certainty of identifying feelings is nebulous. You, as the perceptive forensic interviewer, should sense interviewee feelings by reflecting on perceived actions. Trust yourself to expect and understand what you see and sense.

It is essential to turn-on and tune-in to verbal and nonverbal communication which signifies active participation. Turning-on here means getting involved by drawing upon your knowledge and the storehouse of experiences in your subconscious. Tuning-in means to concentrate your efforts on accomplishing the goal of interviewing by utilizing your intuition to solve problems and reach solutions. Unrecognized subtleties can influence your judgment. Therefore, concentrate on using your background, knowledge, experience, and sensitized imagination to capture every subtlety or complexity observed and sensed.

Skillfully use your imagination to anticipate various contingencies to conceive of a host of alternatives for effective actions. Imagination and awareness are not unique to professional interviewers; unfortunately, they are special qualities not developed by all. You are fortunate to possess them by nature for it is questionable whether or not they can be taught. Knowledge, imagination, and awareness put to action emerge in the form of intuitive judgments. The seeds of intuitive judgment are probably within you to be discovered, nurtured, sensitized, and enhanced.

The selection of investigative pathways are subjective and dependent upon your intuitive judgment. Thus, be acutely aware of how confidence in judgment, intuition, and empirical evidence play in your role and accomplishments.

Some psychologists believe human actions are based on information picked up by the senses and self-interpreted. This seems to imply a cognitive, thought out, evaluation exclusive of the subconscious, intuition, or conscious evaluation. Applied, this seems to mean the senses are part of an analytical computer that evaluates on-the-spot evidence exclusive of mentally recorded experiences or proven methods. In contrast, I believe intuitive, subtle actions are influential and do impact daily life.

Perception by the senses or mind (exclusive of the reasoning, process) in problem solving is an application of intuition. Senses, rather than facts, are used to direct and execute the interview based upon the immediate situation events, actions, and reactions.

I believe in using intuition freely to utilize on-the-spot opportunities rather than be inhibited by rigid stereotyped methods. At first you may not comprehend the selection of techniques by skilled interviewers because they frequently cannot explain the role of intuition in their interviewing process. Proficient interviewers know that it is effective to exercise confidence in nurturing innate intuitions and act upon them.

Sense the tenseness of victims/witnesses/suspects to deduce spontaneously what words or actions are appropriate to encourage their truthful responses. Your sense of competence is probably the result of cumulative learning, experience, trial, and error. Conscious of it or not, you constantly influence interviewee activities. Therefore, a trust in past experiences has strengthened your intuitive ability to perform. I'm convinced that your total sensing of the situation is more trustworthy than your intellect. Because raw intellectual knowledge cannot be applied arbitrarily in interpersonal encounters, common sense is more effective.

It would be foolhardy to ignore interviewee intuition. They, like you, are human with similar intuitive potential. In fact, it is highly likely that they have been exercising intuition—perhaps to achieve less than positive ends, but nonetheless they may have become skillful in the art.

By nature of their position in an interview, they are keenly alert to your signals, and, for the most part, respond positively or negatively based on what they sense moment by moment. Your every move or gesture, both in your delivery and your reception of their delivery, is under scrutiny. Many interviewees interpret hurried methods and indifference as a sign of insincerity therefore, ask yourself:

- Do you spend whatever time is needed to complete the interview? Do you plan each interview in advance? Do you convey a calm composure?
- Do you intuitively show you care about the interviewee? Don't simply perform a routine job! Do you have a sincere concern about interviewees as human beings? Do you exhibit a sincere interest in interviewees? Do you realize accepting other human beings does not encompass condoning antisocial behavior?
- Do you consciously provide positive signals so that interviewee intuition reads positive actions/reactions that ensure your acceptance and reinforcement? Do you realize that interviewees in their secret, and sometimes bashful way, are searching for a signal from you that it is indeed okay to be open and reveal themselves and the truth?
- Do you maintain positive neutrality to prevent displaying negative signals to interviewees? You may be subconsciously projecting your undesirable traits during interviews. These may trigger hostile interviewee feelings, threaten rapport, and frequently set the stage for interviewees to physically leave in order to escape answering questions.

In most worthwhile endeavors, the success or result is in direct proportion to what you put into it. This applies equally to using intuition. Your hunches or gut feelings cannot bear fruit until you put them into action. Initially, rely on personal confidence to implement intuitions, and be prepared to accept the results for what they are.

Personally work through various steps of Interviewing, accepting generally accepted concepts, but apply effort in developing techniques to capitalize on your intuitive talents. Use intuition positively to read psychological movements, feelings, private logic/rationale, or any other words/signs of interviewees to assist in achieving goals.

Be alert to hints of facts and feelings revealed by a slip of the tongue, but conceal your interest. Subtle behavioral cues, word, gestures, and body language can intuitively direct you. This is not to imply that there is no planned approach. Like so many other things, a good balance is required. Alexander Pope so aptly said, "The proper study of mankind is man." Attaining a mental storehouse of information about human behavior is a must.

Chapter Fifteen

RAPPORT

Rapport is like an electric current or glow of expectancy flowing between interview participants, based upon how they communicate rather than what is said; it requires your practiced effort. It is a feeling of participant closeness nurtured through skillful adaptability; but not suggesting emotional involvement to erode interviewer commitment, persistence, and objectivity. It is a feeling sponsoring empathic interviewer understanding and truthful interviewee compliance. Established, it is a major achievement.

"Rapport: Interpersonal relationship characterized by a spirit of cooperation, confidence and harmony."[19] "Rapport involves building a degree of comfortableness together, of trust in one another, and of basic goodwill that will permit non-defensive interaction."[25 p. 57] "You can build rapport through small talk, a good orientation, and a very warm, friendly manner. Actions that tend to curtail rapport are negative comments, a monologue by the counselor, second-guessing of the client, a condescending attitude and a hurried approach to the interview."[25 p. 201]

" . . . rapport is the good feeling or warmth that exists between people." To achieve rapport: " . . . call attention to ways in which you and the other person are similar. . . . you can call attention to similarities in such subtle ways as by complimenting the person (thus showing that you have similar tastes) or by identifying a common gripe."[25 p. 259]

To develop rapport is to create a feeling within yourself and interviewees of alertness, well-being, and even excitement. Hence, rapport is a psychological closeness.[20]

A marvelous interaction may take place when individuals react in interview situations. Words cannot really describe the tuning in of two minds communicating; they seem to flow with thoughts both emotional and intellectual. There can be an enjoyment, a high, a euphoria, by both parties as they journey, mentally, through vast areas of the unknown. You, as a catalyst, can cause the blending of participant thought and feeling.

Your role is to be a catalyst probing with appropriate questions for facts, anecdotes, and feelings from interviewees.[63] As a catalyst, use pliable characteristics. Stand back from the crowd which has taken on a particular attitude, look at each inquiry with clear thinking as you plan your approach. Look in an unbiased, unemotional way at interviewees before beginning; your preparation constitutes the success of your efforts.

As a catalyst, you are not personally or materially affected by interviews. You are the agent initiating forces to act between yourself and interviewees, encouraging reactions within them to stimulate favorable, if temporary, changes of attitude, and then compliance. Cause an unspoken chemistry to take form; it cannot easily be described, but you certainly can sense it happening.

Be secure in your personal identity. Understand yourself and maintain a sturdy philosophical core in your personality which includes your cultural values. Be able to use self-selected identities without "injuring" the core of your personality.[23 p.27]

Even when interview time is limited, develop a close feeling of rapport wherein a degree of trust and understanding can be fostered.[6 p.216] The more trust and understanding encouraged, the better have been your plans and preparation. Interviewees behave according to their definition of the situation.[52 p.24] Therefore, paint an appropriate picture of yourself, your inquiry, and the specific interview into which they will add necessary data.[7 p.251]

Rapport is a part of a social interchange founded in the introductory segment of interviews when you blend your verbal and nonverbal actions to those of the interviewees.[53] Developing rapport is necessary, but often elusive. "Research has shown that people form their basic impressions of one another during the first few minutes of an interview"[55 pp.8-14] (see Contact Section, Initial Phase).

Mutual confidence and trust are difficult to establish in interviews, and participants are not always partners in seeking the truth; participant goals often differ.[72 p.210] By orienting interviewees as to the objective of your interview, you may encourage them to be less secretive or defensive. The seriousness of your objective is reflected in your thoroughness. Realizing your inquiry has a certain seriousness, they may weigh it more accurately to comply more completely.

Develop a feeling of trustworthiness with interviewees—the more trust, the less reluctance.[6 p.228] Exhibited understanding and appreciation of the speaker's feelings and reactions helps to support further cooperation and build trust. Calm thinking and freedom of communication is vital. Sensing your courteousness and respect, they may become comfortable in complying.

At the beginning of interviews, interviewees may be uneasy in their thoughts and actions. You may notice their distinct sigh of relief signaling harmony and a certain amount of trust as rapport develops. At least, the sigh seems to signal a lessening of distress, and, from that point onward, interviews may take on a more relaxed character. Even truthful interviewees have some anxiety over whether or not you will be fair or unbiased in your methods.[53]

With an internal feeling of rapport, you sense that you are communicating with interviewees, moving mentally and physically together. With that Interactional Synchrony experienced, you may feel uninhibited in asking questions. In the most intimate sort of situation dealing with a sexual assault upon a victim, many interviewers feel restrained. But, if participants have established a rhythm together . . . a rapport . . . then questions can be less restricted and interviewees less resistant to providing data.[20] Establishing rapport will probably not deter from your officially designated task assignment.

With smooth-acting and skillful style you may feel an intensity of internal dissonance causing you distraction.[6p.203] Dissonance is being out of harmony within yourself, provoking any normal citizen to be angry, resentful, and to seek revenge for the victim. Some investigative situations may literally turn your stomach and make you physically sick. However, no matter the circumstances, gain cooperation by treating interviewees with kindness, decency, and human dignity.[52] Consider all interviewees valuable in the brotherhood of mankind.[71]

By studying previous interviewee actions and experiences, you can comprehend more fully their image, quality of self-esteem and how they may attempt either to protect their self-image or to enhance it. They may sense interview potentials, realizing your status, and if their involvement will enhance their self-image and self-esteem. If your inquiry is handled in a "classy," professional way, they may feel honored to cooperate so as to enhance self-image and later be "proud" of compliance with "authorities."[52] Make your inquiry relevant to their here-and-now life and concerns.[6p.199]

Although interviewees often want to comprehend how interviews are relevant and significant to your inquiry, it is not wise to explain your overall objectives or hypothesis.[23p.32] Too much explanation may cause them to become uptight about how their help might harm fellow human beings, detracting from rapport. They may not accept your explanation and only provide limited data which might not be the truth.[6p.216] Hence, too much explanation provides directive powers to interviewees unnecessarily.

Encourage interviewees to provide information even when they have preconceived ideas about their roles in the total situation.[35] By intentionally altering your own verbal and nonverbal communication in a positive manner, you stimulate them to respond cooperatively and truthfully to inquiries.[53] Encourage them to feel emotionally comfortable by cooperating, promote their sense of usefulness; associate cooperation with need fulfillment.[53] Provide acceptable reasons for compliance as part of the basis of their feeling it is worthwhile to cooperate.[53] Justify compliance.

Promote or enhance rapport development by trying to be:

Calm: maintaining a peacefulness, a composure, even-tempered disposition, serenity, patience, an emotional strength, even-balanced approach.

Cool: not cold emotionally, not easily emotionally heated, not volatile, having human warmth, not without kindness, a mid-range, not extreme in emotional display.

Collected: clear thinking, emotionally mature, adult reasoning, seeking a worthwhile objective.

Do not become frustrated, agitated, or excited easily; have about you a calm manner that will not be disturbed. Have a tranquil appearance free of passion and rough actions. When looked upon by those about you, seem not to be tempestuous in your way of doing things; seem peaceful. Your serene being represents a quiet strength understood by almost everyone as a quality to rely on in times of potential tension. That calmness and strength is patience at work.

"Don't lose your cool," is a well-used phrase; it implies not to lose calmness or composure. Control your emotional actions without losing your enthusiasm. Keep your thoughts collected and composed so they are well thought-out before being presented for inspection by interviewees. Use an unruffled style to maintain a clear view of your goal.

Using charming personality and pleasing manner as tactics may be challenged by some who need to be macho. Skeptics may declare that to use a charming personality as being too ingratiating. In contrast, I have learned that no matter how terrible respondents seem, they need consideration as worthy human beings. Small courtesies and kind words go a long way toward cementing a meaningful friendly relationship.

The use of sarcasm, ridicule, or cynicism create tension that does not help in gaining cooperation.[5 p. 153] I suggest not dealing with interviewees from the critical or prejudiced Parent Ego State (see T.A. Theory), considering them to be naughty children deserving of reprimand. Instead, assist them to rationalize and save face.

> Most people resist being thought of as inferior; therefore, they would be very reluctant to establish rapport with or to be persuaded by anyone who tries, consciously or unconsciously, to make them feel inferior. Therefore, you need to omit phrases that inadvertently talk down to the person.[25 p. 264]

Can you tell if someone has compassion for you or another person? I think so! There is a certain something that takes place that announces loud and clear that you have compassion for another person. That warm glance or gesture, that soft word or sound, notifies there is a special feeling of understanding flowing to those who are hurting. The time spent, your unhurried method used, that consideration and unspoken respect displayed all add up to a closer bond.

Of necessity, negotiate with interviewees so information is obtained without causing them too much emotional "pain."[52 p. 9] Sensing if the cost is too great to cooperate, they can tell if you are striking a bargain for truth which will cost them too much as far as loss of face, loss of self-esteem.[52] When respondents feel they will not totally "lose" in negotiations for truthful data, interviews take on the appearance of a pleasant or at least bearable event (see Self-beliefs, SFP).

Refusal tends to be the most resistant response; most will not resort to violence in their attempt to avoid cooperation.[23 p. 32] Faced with refusal, plan the next canny maneuvers leading toward your next attempts. Display an attitude of understanding and confidence, that, given time, the respondent will be more comfortable in cooperating in the future.[71] When interviewees sense they can leave interview situations if they choose, they often feel trust and faith in you.[6 p. 252] That freedom to leave releases any fears that might hinder compliance. Intimacy, a sense of closeness, is directly related to the amount of cooperation developed, as reflected in the flow of information.[54 p. 226]

Often, several interviews are necessary in order to outline the dynamics of an interviewee's personality.[72 p. 160] Being resourceful, they desire to believe that they decide their course of action. Their compliance may be withheld until the second interview to show that they are in fact masters of their own fate. They may be insulted, lose face, to think that they are thought of as not being able to make decisions. Sensing that they are expected to decide to comply at some future date, interviewees may be approachable under other circumstances after they have had an opportunity to consider your request.[29p.59]

When leaving interviewees at the end of unsuccessful interviews, make no effort to create hard feelings at the last minute. Even though hostile interviewees did not comply with your requests, hold no "grudge," show no disgust, frustration, anger, and do not allow yourself to "vent your spleen," as an authoritarian might. Lay a positive foundation for future interview attempts. Leave them with a positive feeling allowing them to sense they experienced an interaction of meaning, value, and significance. Even unproductive interview experiences can help build self-esteem and feelings of well-being.[6p.66]

If information is potentially available and important, your continued effort to learn of it is still worthy of future inquiry. Don't allow pride to cause you to blame interviewees exclusively for lack of cooperation and release yourself from blame for failures of techniques. Being perceptive, you realize, to a large extent, the degree of rapport established determines the degree of compliance attained.

Application of rapport applies to most of the interview process and carries into the resolution of inconsistencies and also throughout any interrogation.

Chapter Sixteen

LISTENING

Efforts to listen are the core element of showing humanness. Listening exhibits attentiveness expressed by intonation of voice, positioning of the body, facial expression; it involves your total person to reflect your quality of listening. It is all a part of your presentation.

Approximately 5,000 years ago, advice was written regarding listening.[31 p. 49]

An up-to-date translation indicates:

> If thou art one to whom petition is made, be calm as thou listenest to what the petitioner has to say. Do not rebuff him before he has swept out his body or before he has said that for which he came. The petitioner likes attention to his words better than the fulfilling of that for which he came . . . It is not necessary that everything about which he has petitioned should come to pass, but a good hearing is soothing to the heart.[79]

Even today it is wise to be calm; do not rebuff; be attentive to interviewees. "Eventually he may spend less time as he winnows more skillfully the valuable information from the valueless. And yet it is the listening and not the talking that produces the better results."[36]

"Hear" interviewees with total undivided attention, attempt to determine their frame of reference.[23 p. 19] Empathize their attitudes, the roles they are playing, their expressed and demonstrated needs to comprehend and guide your moment-by-moment progress. Through self-discipline, concentration, and dedication become an active, effective listener to hear, so to speak, by using ears, eyes, and total sensing.

Through an open, listening method you may hear a blast of interviewee emotion released while you try to gradually obtain clear expression of facts. Again, deal with feelings and facts, allowing for opinions and feelings. "Listen as though you think interviewees have something worthwhile to offer."[53]

Always be alert for signals of their mental processes, look for clues of motivation and hidden needs. As you listen attentively to what interviewees have to say, continually observe the ways they act. Through mannerisms, gestures, recurrent phrases and modes of expression, interviewees signal their thinking, hidden needs, and possible deception. Be aware that they are also alert to watch for such signals from you; they may alter their compliance based upon how they "read" you. As an active listener, your attention should not be fickle, fragile, or fall apart at the least distraction or promise of pleasure, excitement, or frustration.[53]p. 5 Hence, display signals that you are genuinely, believably involved in each interview.

As an ideal interviewer, listen with nonjudgmental understanding instead of criticizing or admonishing.[29]p. 20 Dr. Eliot Chapple, anthropologist, said, "Finding the perfect listener, gaining that sense of relaxation from being able to talk or not talk when one wants to, is one of the greater pleasures."[20] Be a perfect listener and be alert, courteous, and giving undivided attention while being ready with appropriate questions or comments to show interest in what is said and the subtle message presented. Display expressions of interest, sponsoring continued rapport.[20] A variety of skills is required of interviewers to include patience, and the accuracy of a scientist combined with calculated cunning. Listening is concentrating on what is and is not being said, both verbally and nonverbally; it assists in strategy on the run.[52] A good interviewer is a good listener![23]p. 111 Listening fuels intuition.

"His thoughts were slow, his words were few, and never made to glisten. But he was a joy wherever he went. You should have heard him listen." (Author unknown) Listen by adapting and noting the interviewee's frame of reference; be guided in moment-by-moment inquiry by that "third ear."[23]p. 19 Use every advantage to evaluate the story you hear to make it sensible.[72]p. 147 Evaluating interviewees properly helps determine how hurriedly interviews can be conducted and the direction to take. If rushed, interviewees may sense that you are insincere in your efforts and they may become less compliant.[71]

Expressing attentive listening involves being alive and alert, engaging your body and not merely your words in the communication process. When gesturing, display a total response involvement to what is being said. Kinesicist Professor William Condon's observations indicate that listeners move in time with the beat or rhythm of the speaker. Although there is possibly no awareness of such rhythm, it nevertheless takes place; and, as it does, the speaker and listener blend. Listeners show in subtle ways of moving their bodies that they are "with" the speaker, that they are attentive.[20]

There are two main conditions of listening, the inattentive and the attentive. Inattentive listeners may not even hear what is being said; they superficially signal hearing and responding, but no real thoughts are formulated. Inattentiveness can be sensed because the listener is a bit out of rhythm with what is happening. Sharp, alert, quick responses are missing in fast-moving interviews if inattention prevails. Inattentive listeners display preoccupation and never quite catch up with interviewees; they are out of step with the mood of the discussion, not synchronized.

Flow with the rhythm and ongoing pattern of thought, seeming always to think clearly. Be in synchrony and think on the run without loss of balance. Avoid making superficial comments, while being alert to what is going on moment by moment.[53] Signal that you are paying attention by sharing postures, by standing or sitting close, and, by facing interviewees squarely or at a 45 degree angle. Look at interviewees often, wear an interested or pleased expression and move in heightened synchrony, thereby signaling attentive listening.[20]

People are drawn toward or attracted by those who seem to mirror one another. Friendship is a good example. This attraction may be the natural groundroots of synchrony. For practical purposes, consider synchrony as a type of meshing of gears. You probably know that a perfect meshing of gears is essential to a smooth-running engine. Likewise, a meshing of personalities is key to effective interviewing.

Proficient interviewers are alert to hear concrete and abstract interviewee terms. Concrete, objective explanations paint a clear picture of the event or situation while subjective/emotional terms are cloudy, abstract, and not specific enough, leaving room for opinion and conjecture. Emotionally charged, abstract terms are often misleading. Thus, strive to obtain concrete terms which can be visualized and are not vague generally.[53] Again, allow for subjective/emotional terms blended among sought after facts.

Your attentiveness implies acceptance and encourages interviewees to say more. With attentiveness, ponder, at least momentarily, what is said to show that you are really interested in what is being said. They can sense if you are truly interested by the subtle pauses of reflection, respectfulness, given. The development of rapport is built upon a foundation partly made up of your ability to show you are listening. Your true listening allows interviewees to sense the genuine, unplanned, spontaneous you.

Thus, avoid putting on a show of authority with more interest in yourself and your role than with listening. Rely on your spontaneity, sensitivity and basic common sense; listen better and understand more. Through the use of questioning, accepting, rephrasing, and pausing, you can listen. By rephrasing of words and reflecting feelings and attitudes as a mirror you can signal that you are listening.[53]

Interviewees may not be truly listening receptively just because they are silent and appear to be listening. Be alert not to falsely assume interviewees understand, accept, or consent to your behavior. Test your inquiry techniques for desired effect. Periodically ask questions designed to produce signals related to their listening. A blank unresponsive stare may signal distress, unclear thinking, imbalanced mental process rather than meaningful interviewee listening.

Be determined to avoid idle thinking by concentrating on interviews' specifics; blend into the mood of the data gathering and listen more constructively. Allowing interviewee comments to glide over the surface of your mind is self-defeating.[53] Concentrate! Successful listening is based in goal-achieving rather than tension-relieving.

If you don't concentrate your thinking, you may be easily misled by moderately skilled deceptive interviewees. Even illusive interviewees, who are not really deceptive but only reluctant or hesitant to comply, can mislead you if you don't pay attention. Some interviewees play mental games with authority figures to test sincerity.[53]

Sounds and actions signal participant acceptance. Coupled with alert, concentrated attention, murmur vocal sounds such as "uh-huh," at appropriate times in interviews and also nod your head in an affirmative manner or display facial or nonverbal action to show alertness.[20, 25 p.78] Your face will not crack and break if you flex facial muscles to show expression! If interviewees talk spontaneously, avoid interrupting until there is a significant pause. Encourage their continued recitation by showing interest through careful attention and nonverbal communication such as nodding, indicating the wish to have them continue.[72 p. 154]

Nonverbal aspects of communication such as gestures, mannerisms, and facial expressions are learned throughout life; they symbolize underlying personality traits, subconscious attitudes, intentions and conflicts. Use them. Nonverbal behavior, including head nodding, a curious expression, moving forward in the chair, and smiling, may encourage interviewees to continue speaking. Expressions such as "I see," "Please go on," "Yes," and "Uh-huh" indicate interest and desire to hear more.[72 p. 165]

Such expressions can be negative or positive in character depending on how they are employed. To say "Please go on" might stop the flow of information depending on the intonation given, and the implied message expressed. Misused, they may signal you are biased, not neutral, causing a breakdown in communication.

Because most interviewees have a degree of sensitive, intuitive feeling, they are aware of preoccupied glances or inattention during interviews. A way of turning people off is not to pay attention to their comments, to be thinking of the next question to ask and not devoting yourself to the emotion of the moment.

While interviewees, in the main, think what they are saying is the most important thing happening in the world, they continuously evaluate their listener. Interviews tend to be cause-and-effect situations wherein interviewees expect and appreciate appropriate responses to their comments; but not necessarily an evaluation. They need reassurance, support, and acceptance while expanding thoughts and exposing innermost hidden secrets.

They may hold back a wealth of knowledge and consider the situation a waste of time when faced with inattention. However, their excuses not to comply may not be expressed outwardly. Consequently, you may never realize your inattention stopped the flow of needed information.

How and where you sit and what you do during interviews express your attention to facts, feelings, and opinions. It seems most people are seldom listened to during their lives; they appreciate an opportunity to be expressive.[6p.541] Their opinion is not usually requested; hence, they may hunger for a feeling of importance when approached for their views.

If interviewee information can be obtained without causing emotional discomfort, continued cooperation is more likely. However, if made to feel used, they may become embarrassed and refuse to comply. They may say "No thank you" when asked for future cooperation. I suggest not playing the games: that ain't nothin', me too, and can you top this, or I got ya. Prevent your boredom to be reflected in lack of responsive comments, eye contact lacking emotion of the moment, body posture not being alert, being quiet when you should respond, commenting inappropriately when you should be nodding your head. Their feeling of being used may be based upon sensing your lack of believability.

Through participant role reversal you may be skillfully unseated, becoming the interviewee and possibly providing information. The inexperienced may not see the unseating signals and may all too late discover having given up command of the interview, answering rather than asking questions. The unseating should be embarrassing only if it continues. Proficient interviewers realize the shifting taking place and immediately regain control without making it too obvious or causing conflict.

Most interviews are not normal social encounters in which two people equally exchange ideas and experiences. A majority are heavily weighted so interviewees do most, if not all, of the talking while you act as a catalyst, a persuader, a stimulator of thoughts. Too often, unfortunately, the need to talk is greater than the interviewer's ability to listen. Hence, effectiveness demands you overcome this human failing.[5p.86]

Cordially greet interviewees and help them feel at ease; be an empathic listener. Despite your innocent manner, try your best to encourage them to provide needed information. Such an approach works best immediately after they have a stressful experience. Relaxation of defenses is increased just after a period of tension, just after traumatic neurosis. When there is a feeling of being at ease, there is a natural feeling of intimacy and mood for discussion. Thus, establish ease and relaxation to the degree that interviewees do not feel threatened; but, again, reducing all stress is neither to your advantage, nor possible.

Again, some tension in interviews often helps interviewees think actively and respond productively.[54p.138] As a good listener, seemingly take a back seat and allow them time to talk.[71] As they talk they will probably begin to feel comfortable enough to express sought-after data. It is through expressed emotion at times of tension that interviewees test interviewers to sense their sincerity, compassion, and caring.[29p.50]

I have found that inexperienced interviewers rush from one question to another without waiting for an answer. They fail to sense patience, as necessary or, coupled with active listening.[23p.112] Remove any displayed threat, of actions and appearance that may cause lack of interviewee compliance.[6p.566] Threats cause defensive behavior, reducing their ability to perceive accurately your motives, your values, and emotions.[6p.488] In some situations interviewees are cynical and paranoid in response to you because they might sense some hidden agenda of the inquiry; resistance may be invoked because of those "hidden motives."[6p.490] Listening is an art with broad application, essential in assessing others; both participants are involved in that listening process.[26p.15] Thus, by expression, manner of speech, tone of voice, or verbal content the sender often seems to be evaluating or judging the listener.[6p.489] There is often a schizoid look of detachment when the listener is through listening. The listener's blank, far-away look indicates a lack of attentiveness, general lack of concentration, and disassociation.

There is a close connection between active listening and intuition, according to Mallory: "Probably one of the most powerful actions for implying acceptance of someone is to listen." " . . . good listening takes practice; it's actually a discipline." "Listening doesn't come naturally; it has to be developed."[44 pp.146-151]

One difference between mediocre and first class interviewers is the ability to combine active listening, analyzing and truth-revealing questioning. By staying keenly aware of the important role of active listening in interview situations, you can analyze and encourage in a meaningful way. Through listening, the interviewee frame of reference can be determined and emotional tension reduced. The pervasive effort of active listening can display your recognition of worth and encourage continued cooperation. Therefore, attentively and analytically listen and actively seek information.

Chapter Seventeen

POLYGRAPHY AS AN INVESTIGATIVE TOOL

What is Polygraphy?

Polygraphy is a means by which to detect deception. My training and experience over the past thirty years leads me to believe this means of detecting deception is reasonably accurate as an investigative tool. To my knowledge, a majority of the law enforcement agencies in the United States prefer, in addition to the individual mental capacity of investigators, use of polygraph examinations to any other means in the detection of deception.

Based upon information provided by the American Polygraph Association:

Psychophysiological Aspects

In order to understand the polygraph procedure, one must first have some awareness of its psychophysiologic basis. The autonomic nervous systems which activates the smooth muscles such as the stomach and blood vessels, the glands, and the heart function automatically and involuntarily so that, for the most part, it is beyond the conscious control of the organism. It is composed of two branches, the sympathetic nervous system and the parasympathetic nervous system which operate in opposition to one another. While one facilitates a function, the other inhibits it. The parasympathetic nervous system is dominant most of the time and particularly during periods of rest and tranquility. It enhances functions leading to growth, digestion, and repair. As such, it is essential for survival. In contrast to the parasympathetic nervous systems the sympathetic nervous system is activated during stress situations and serves to prepare the organism to deal with a threat more effectively through the stimulation of a series of physiological changes.

Vasoconstriction takes place in the peripheral blood vessels, causing a decreased flow of blood to the skin, increasing blood pressure, and fostering a reduction in blood loss should an injury occur. Vasodilatation takes place in the skeletal and cardiac muscles so that the increase in blood supplied to these areas can provide more metabolic fuels to these regions. Adrenaline is released into the blood stream to increase sympathetic activity and the liver secretes glycogen, thus increasing the body's blood sugar level. The passages of the lungs dilate, allowing for a greater intake of oxygen, and the contractions of the heart are strengthened, resulting in greater cardiac output. The palms of the hands and the soles of the feet perspire so that locomotion and grasping *will* be facilitated. Because of these physiological changes within the organism, the individual is better able to cope with threats through what has been described as this "flight or fight" reaction. This enables an individual to utilize all of the body's resources to run or fight more effectively.

The emotions that cause these reactions can vary, including *conflict,* anger, and fear. In a polygraph situation, fear is more than likely the major precipitating factor. The subject, afraid that his lie will be detected, and fearing the consequences of that discovery, reacts to the critical questions with sympathetic arousal. Some of the physiological reactions include changes in blood volume, sweat gland activation, heart rate, and respiration. Recorded on the moving chart of the polygraph instrument, these responses can be readily interpreted with a great deal of accuracy.

The Polygraph

The polygraph consists of a minimum of three measures of physiological functioning. Although these may vary on occasion, the basic components are the cardiograph, which monitors changes in blood volume and heart rate; the pneumograph, which provides a measure of respiration as *well* as related movements in the abdominal and thoracic areas; and the galvanometer. The sensors for the latter are usually two dry electrodes affixed to the fingers. The galvanometer records the reduction in resistance to electricity that is related to the increase in perspiration. Such an increase is, in turn, associated with sympathetic arousal. The constant changes in resistance are transmitted to a pen and recorded on a moving chart.

The cardiosphygmograph consists of a blood pressure cuff which is positioned about the arm and connected by means of, rubber tubing to a tambour or amplifier. The changes in air pressure in the cuff associated with alterations in air size which are due to increases and decreases in blood volume are transmitted to the chart through the tambour mechanism or amplifier circuit. The pulse rate is also recorded at the same time and in the same manner.

The breathing pattern and rate are obtained through the use of one or two convoluted rubber tubes placed about the chest or abdomen. As in the case of the cardiograph, the changes in pressure are transmitted through tubes to a tambour or amplifier which directs the sweep of the pens. Thus a continuous measure of these physiological functions is obtained and is *available* for scoring and interpretation.

Ongoing research will modify future instrumentation for polygraphy.

The Polygraphist

The polygraphist, examiner, carries out the examination in four separate phases: data collection, pretest interview, testing, and posttest interview. Among other titles for persons administering detection of deception examinations are: Detection of Deception Examiner, Lie Detector Examiner, Truth Verifier, Polygraph Examiner, and Polygraphist. The most current identifier, Forensic Psychophysiologist, has been adopted by the Department of Defense for their personnel administering detection of deception examinations.

Procedure

A polygraph examination must be voluntary, both legally and from a practical viewpoint. Most polygraphists have a consent form which the examinee must sign before an examination *will* be conducted. The form gives permission to conduct the examination, and often mentions the subject's rights, observation or recording equipment, and other matters of mutual importance. Most people think that the only questions in a polygraph test are those asked during the examination with the instrument in operation. In fact, many more are asked in the pretest interview and in the posttest interview. A polygraphist needs background information on the medical and physical history of the subject, recent use of medicine and drugs, personal identification, and the subject's views and comments on the issues to be covered during the examination.

The examiner carries out the test in four separate segments: data collection, pretest interview, testing, and posttest interview. Prior to meeting the subject, the examiner accumulates all pertinent information related to the individual and the case. He obtains this information through discussions with the attorneys and investigating officers and through reading all available reports.

The pretest interview begins with an explanation of the subject's rights and a signing of forms in which the subject acknowledges that he fully understands those rights. The pretest interview includes a full discussion of the matter or issues to be resolved by the examination including the subject's views.

During the pretest interview the examiner attempts to develop a rapport between himself and the subject to the extent that, regardless of whether the examiner works in the private or the law enforcement realm, the subject will feel confident that the findings will be objective. The polygraphist determines if the individual has the *ability* to understand the questions and answer them with an unequivocal "yes" or "no." He does this by reviewing each question with the subject, and by listening to the explanation the examinee gives as to his understanding of the question. The formulation of questions is vital to the test, and every examiner strives to be certain that the questions are fully understood.

The test will consist of a series of questions which will be asked while the polygraph instrument is in operation. Prior to the testing, the examiner will explain the operation of the instrument, and will explain the sensors as he puts them on the examinee. At a minimum, there *will* be sensors to record breathing, electrodermal responses, heart rate, and mean blood volume. The latter is closely related to changes in blood pressure. The instrument may also record other physiological processes. The examiner will take several recordings while asking the questions, the number of recordings depending on the techniques employed, the examinee's attention span, and the number of issues to be resolved.

Validity

Determining the validity of the polygraph approach has been rather difficult. Research carried out in a laboratory has the weakness of being unable to arouse an emotional state comparable to that which is found in an actual criminal investigation. While validity is a measure of accuracy, reliability refers to consistency. Most specifically, reliability indicates the degree to which different polygraphists will achieve similar results when testing the same examinee.

Who Uses Polygraphy

While exact figures are difficult to determine, several surveys indicate that approximately 20 percent of all major businesses in the United States have used polygraphy. In particular, certain industry figures are much higher. For example, approximately 50 percent of all commercial banks and over 60 percent of all retail operations have used polygraphy in some capacity.

In addition to private business, polygraph examinations are widely used in state and local law enforcement, and almost all federal law enforcement, intelligence, and counterintelligence agencies.

Accuracy of Polygraphy

In the past 20 years, over 100 studies have been conducted on the accuracy of polygraphy. Since many different conditions and factors are involved in the research, and since polygraphy involves a complex process, it is difficult to draw from the data a precise figure for the accuracy of polygraphy in all settings. Nevertheless, the preponderance of available information indicates that when a properly trained polygraphist utilizes an established examination procedure, the accuracy of decisions made by polygraphists is generally in the range of 85 to 95 percent for specific issue investigations.

The Office of Technology Assessment (OTA) Report

The authors of the report, Scientific Validity of Polygraph Testing: A Research Review and Evaluation—A Technical Memorandum (1983), indicated that polygraphy does in fact seem to achieve a significant degree of accuracy. Specifically, the authors indicate that between the 10 field studies they reviewed, the average accuracy rate for correctly identifying innocent examinees (true positives) was 81 percent and the average accuracy rate for correctly identifying guilty examinees (true negatives) was 90 percent.

When the 14 analog studies were averaged out, the report indicates an accuracy rate of 86 percent for correctly identifying innocent examinees, and 90 percent accuracy for the correct identification of the guilty examinees.

Furthermore, these figures include inconclusive results as "errors."

The OTA Report acknowledges that "exclusion of inconclusives would raise the overall accuracy rates calculated." It has been estimated that the elimination of inconclusive test results would increase the average accuracy rates to 90 percent.

It is also interesting to note that in their "base rate" projections, OTA, in this report as well as their March 1987 report (Review of the Defense Department's Polygraph Test and Research Programs), suggests that if 4,000 people are tested, about 600 innocent people should fail the test. Specifically, the OTA says that if 4,000 people are tested for spying, and there are actually only 4 spies in the group, then 599 innocent people would fail because polygraphy is so inaccurate.

The erroneous nature of all of these predictions is exposed, however, when compared to a real-life testing situation.

In their report to the U.S. Congress for 1986, the Department of Defense showed that they had tested nearly 4,000 people in a screening (espionage) context. According to OTA predictions (and the others as well), almost 600 people should have failed their polygraph examination, the overwhelming majority of whom were innocent. In reality, however, only 13 were reported as deceptive, 8 of whom acknowledged their wrongdoing.

Hence, in consideration of the above mentioned American Polygraph Association perspective, while polygraphy is not infallible, research clearly indicates that when administered by competent polygraphists, polygraphy is the most accurate means available to determine truth and deception.

The American Polygraph Association Newsletter, v.21, 1988, offers information to broaden perspectives regarding polygraphy as an investigative tool:

False Positives and False Negatives in Medical Tests

Polygraphy has often been criticized for having high false positive rates, and users have worried about false negative rates. For comparison, Mary Spletter, a freelance medical author summed up the medical profession's assessments of certain medical tests as abstracted from "Testing, 13 Common Medical Tests Yield Mixed Results." Hippocrates, May/June 1987:

AIDS Antibody: The test is made from blood which is exposed to the AIDS virus. A reaction that produces a color indicates that antibodies are present. It is reported as positive or negative. When positive, the test is often repeated and may be checked with a more specific test. For every 1,000 healthy blood donors tested, two to five will show a false positive. Women who have had more than one pregnancy and people with autoimmune diseases, such as lupus, have higher rates of false positive readings. Also, some test kits yield up to 7 percent more false positives than others. False negatives may occur for those recently infected. It takes up to eight weeks for it to show. Also, AIDS patients with certain other illnesses may test negative, even though antibodies are present.

Blood Pressure: The major cause of erroneous readings is faulty measurement technique. But even accurate readings can reflect normal fluctuations. Anxiety, exercise, talking, and foods such as coffee can temporarily raise your blood pressure. Sleep and sudden changes in body position can lower it. Blood pressure is often lower when measured at home.

Chest X-ray: Any X-ray can be dangerous if overused, but for some diseases the benefits outweigh the risks. Not all radiologists and physicians interpret evidence of diseases such as pneumonia, collapsed lungs, size and shape of the heart, bronchitis, and emphysema in the same way. Reliability varies widely with the skill and experience of the doctor, the quality of the radiograph, and the nature and status of the disease.

Chlamydia: The chlamydia organism causes the most common sexually transmitted disease of the 1980s. The three tests use infected cells removed with a cotton swab from the cervix, penis, or other area. Rates of false positives for the three tests range from 10 to 20 percent. Culture is the most accurate, with only 10 percent false positives, but it is the slowest and most expensive. The tests also yield 10 to 30 percent false negatives because of faulty lab methods of failure to collect the organism in the swab.

Cholesterol: The test looks for concentrations of fatty lipids in the blood. The analyzer types out a series of numbers. Exactly what constitutes a normal level is hotly debated, but a total cholesterol count of 150 to 280, with the upper limit extending to 330 in people older than 50, is generally considered acceptable. Good laboratories are accurate within 5 percent, but studies have shown wide deviations in accuracy in other labs. Although it predicts an increased risk of heart disease, cholesterol does not predict heart trouble. Most people who have heart attacks do not have high cholesterol levels. Cholesterol levels increase during winter months, times of anxiety or pain, and pregnancy. Taking male hormones, some tranquilizers, vitamins A and D, or epilepsy medications will raise the levels. Antibiotics, aspirin, high doses of vitamin B, and female hormones may temporarily lower the cholesterol levels.

Blood Count: The most frequent performed lab test, it provides doctors with information about anemia, infection, and other blood conditions. Modern machine blood counts are highly accurate. However, normal values are often based on obsolete standards, such as hemoglobin levels based on young white medical students and nurses, 50 years ago.

Electrocardiogram: An electrocardiogram (EOG) is used to investigate chest pains when a heart attack is suspected. They can be up to 90 percent successful in diagnosing abnormal heart rhythms. However, on occasion, normal EOGs have been recorded in patients suffering from heart disease. The test will detect enlargement of the left side of the heart about 50 percent of the time; it is a little less accurate for the right side. A single EOG alone is not a sensitive detector of blocked coronary arteries.

Mammogram: It is now the standard test against which all other tests for breast cancer are judged. When performed well, it will locate calcifications or suspicious growths but cannot diagnose cancer. Only a surgical biopsy or needle aspiration of cells from the suspicious mass can determine that it is cancer. Mammography successfully detects between 80 and 90 percent of breast abnormalities, including many growths too small to be felt in a self-exam. Errors come from improper positioning of the patient or the X-ray source, or the result may be misinterpreted, most often with young women whose dense tissue makes reading more difficult.

Mononucleosis: The common spot test does not detect the antibodies during the first week after infection. After that, 2 to 3 percent of the tests will give false-positive results. The number of false negatives can be even higher, depending on the patient's age. Ten to 15 percent of infected adults will be shown to be healthy by the test. The false negative rate jumps to 50 percent in children under five years because the test isn't always sensitive enough to find the smaller proportion of antibodies in children's blood.

Occult Blood: The test looks for signs of colon or rectal cancer by detecting invisible blood in stool specimens before other kinds of symptoms appear. Positive results are particularly controversial. For every 1,000 symptom-free people tested, 20 to 60 will receive a positive result. Up to half of these may be false positives. Many of the false positives come from iron supplements, aspirin, rare red meat, turnips, horseradish, and some other foods. Typically, patients with positive results are put on a meat-free diet and then tested again. Once the other false positives and noncancerous blood sources are eliminated, only 5 to 12 percent of the people with positive results truly have cancer. Overall, one-third to one-half of existing cancers are missed.

Pregnancy: The test detects a hormone released by the newly formed placenta. The test accuracy can be close to 95 percent as early as seven to ten days after implantation. False negatives may occur if the embryo is outside the uterus, extopic pregnancy, or from lab errors and tests of diluted urine. False positive and borderline results can occur after undetected early miscarriages.

Pap Smear: Cervical cells are collected with a cotton swab. The smear can yield from 15 to 40 percent false negatives from sampling mistakes and misinterpretation of slides. Douching and tampon use also can cause false-negative readings. In half the cases where the cancer has advanced to an invasive stage, the test can miss it because inflammation and high numbers of dead cells impede the sampling.

Stress: The exercise tolerance or treadmill test is used to detect blocked or narrowed coronary arteries and to monitor various heart conditions. Healthy men with abnormal results had only a 20 percent chance of suffering a cardiac event during the following four years. Getting a normal result is no guarantee of health. By one estimate, 20 to 30 percent of the people whose test results are normal have some kind of heart abnormality."

There is no intention, herein, to detract from the relative value of the above mentioned medical tests. It is reasonable, however, to see the implication of comparing their validity with that of properly administered polygraph examinations.

Detection of Deception in Court

For those misinformed to believe polygraphy evidence is not or has not been admissible in courts of law, the American Polygraph Association reports:

> In the last 35 years, numerous courts have recognized the evidentiary value of polygraphy evidence. Stipulated polygraphy evidence is generally admissible in state courts. In California stipulated polygraphy evidence is admissible under state law. New Mexico and Massachusetts have rules which, under certain conditions, allow polygraphy evidence to be admitted over objection. A majority of the United States Courts of Appeals allow the admissibility of

polygraph examination results into evidence at the discretion of the trial judge, either on stipulation or over objection. However, most federal district judges are conservative in ruling on admissibility. As of June 1987, only the Fifth, Tenth, Eleventh, and District of Columbia circuits prohibitions on the introduction of such evidence. The United States Supreme Court has not ruled on admissibility.

Representative case citations are provided for reference:

Arizona:	State v. Valdex, 91 Ariz. 274, 371 P.2d 894 (1962) State vs. Molina, 117 Ariz. 454, 573 P.2d 528 (App. 1977)
Arkansas:	Holcomb v. State, 594 S.W. 2d22 (1980)
California:	People v. Houser, 85 Cal. App. 2d 686, 193 P. 2d 937 (1948) Robinson v. Wilson, 44 Cal. App. 3d 92, 118 Cal. Rptr. 569 (1974) People vs. Trujillo, 66 Cal. App. 3d 547,136 Cal. Rptr. 672 (1977)
Florida:	Moore v. State, 299 So. 2d 119 (Fla. 3d DCA 1974) Codie v. State, 313 So. 2d 754 (1975)
Georgia:	State v. Chambers, 240 Ga. 76, 239 S.E. 2d 324 (1977) Ross v. State, 245 Ga. 173 (1), 263 S.E. 2d 913 (1980)
Indiana:	Tope v. State, 266 Ind. 239, 362 N.E. 2d 137 (1977) Owens v. State, 373 N.E. 2d 913 (1978)
Iowa:	State v. McNamara, 104 N.W. 2d 568 (1960) State v. Galloway, 167 N.W. 2d 89 (1969) State v. Connor, 241 N.W. 2d 457 (1976)
Kansas:	State v. Lassley, 218 Kan. 758, 545 P. 2d 383 (1976) State v. Roach, 576 P. 2d 1082 (1978)
Massachusetts:	Commonwealth v. a. Juvenile, 365 Mass. 421, 313 N.E. 2d 120 (1974) Commonwealth v. Vitello, 381 N.E. 2d 582 (1978)
Nevada:	Corbett v. State, 584 P. 2d 704 (1978)
New Jersey:	State v. McDavitt, 62 N.J. 36, 297 A. 2d 849 (1972) State v. Baskerville, 73 N.J. 230, 374 A. 2d 441 (1977)
New Mexico:	State v. Dorsey, 88 N.M. 184, 539 P. 2d 204 (1975)
Ohio:	State v. Towns, 35 Ohio App. 2d 237 301

N.E. 2d 700 (1973) State v. Souel, 53
Ohio St. 2d 123, 372 N.E. 2d 1318
(1978)

Oregon: State v. Bennett, 17 Or. App. 197, 521 P.
2d 31 rev. den. (1974)

Utah: State v. Jenkins, 523 P. P. 2d 1232
(1974) State v. Abel, 600 PL. 2d 994
(1979)

Washington: State v. Ross, 7 Wash. App. 62, 497 P. 2d
1343 (1972)

Wyoming: Cullin v. State, 565 P. 2d 445 (1977)

Arrest—Validity of Warrant—Use of Polygraph Results

An arrest warrant is not defective because the issuing magistrate relied on the results of a polygraph examination in determining that probable cause to attest existed, the U.S. Court of Appeals for the Fifth Circuit declared September 19 in a civil rights case. "Polygraph exams, by most accounts correctly detect truth or deception 80 to 90 percent of the time," the court observed. "We, therefore, see no reason to create a *per se* rule barring magistrates, who may already consider information like hearsay, from using their sound discretion to evaluate the results of polygraph exams, in conjunction with other evidence, when determining whether probable cause exists to issue an arrest warrant. Absent an abuse of discretion, a magistrate may consider these results, as well as the other information, when determining whether probable cause exists to issue an arrest warrant." (Bennett v. City of Grand Prairie, CA 5, No. 88-1493, 9/19/89)

Polygraph evidence may be admitted by stipulation or to impeach or corroborate witness testimony. En Banc Ca 11 relaxes rules prohibiting use of polygraph results at trial:

The results of a polygraph examination may be admitted at trial if the parties stipulate in advance to their admission or if the evidence is used to impeach or corroborate witness testimony under Fed.R.Ev. 608, a majority of the En Banc U.S. Court of Appeals for the Eleventh Circuit held September 28. The majority said that significant progress made in the field of polygraph testing compelled relaxation of the court's prior per se ban on such evidence. (U.S. v. Piccinonna, CA 11 En Banc), No. 86-5335, 9/28/89)

In light of the current state of polygraphy—better equipment, more qualified polygraph operators, and widespread use of the polygraph among law enforcement agencies—it is no longer accurate to say that polygraph evidence lacks general acceptance, the majority said. Thus, the threshold admissibility standard of *Frye v. U.S.*, 293 F 1013 (CA DC 1923), is met. The majority stressed, however, that neither of the modifications it made to the prior rule limits the trial court's ability to exclude the evidence under other provisions of the evidence rules.

A stipulation for the admission of polygraph results must address the circumstances of the test and the scope of the results' admissibility, as well as the purpose for which the evidence will be introduced, the majority said. To use polygraph evidence for impeachment or corroboration under Rule 608, the proponent must provide advance notice and a reasonable opportunity for the opposing party to subject the declarant to a polygraph examination by its own polygraph expert. The polygraph operator's testimony will be admissible only after the witness's character for truthfulness has been attacked.

Partially concurring and dissenting, Judge Johnson, joined by Chief Judge Roney and Judges Hilland Clark, agreed that polygraph evidence should be admitted if the parties stipulate, but he disputed the majority's assertion that the polygraph has gained acceptance in the scientific community as a reliable instrument for detecting lies.

Courts of Appeals

The following case is brought to your attention to, again, point up the reality that polygraphy is a viable investigative tool. It is not so much that the opinion of the polygraphist is admitted into courts as evidence, but that proper use of polygraphy can help society.

The case review, following, represents vital elements related to a confession being admitted into courts as evidence. During an inquiry, successful investigators always consider the totality of the investigative circumstances; if they don't, you can be sure a Court of Appeals will. If the rules are not followed during the inquiry, you probably won't get the confession into court as evidence. Each step of the interview process leading up to and including the interrogation has a bearing upon the total of the circumstances that might be reviewed by the court. There is an interrelationship of all segments to make up the total.

Although the case reviewed pertains to a confession obtained during the process of a polygraph examination, it is, none the less, a confession legally obtained. The fact that the confession was obtained during a polygraph examination only introduces more for the court to review, more elements to consider in the totality of the circumstances.

Chapter Eighteen

POLYGRAPHY IN COURTS OF APPEALS

State of Minnesota in Courts of Appeals — C5-86-1237
Cite as 403 N.W.2 281 (Minn.App. 1987)
Minnesota Appellate Courts — Filed March 31, 1987
Judge Crippen
Steven Lee Erickson — Appellant
Anoka County, State of Minnesota — Respondent

SYLLABUS

A signed, knowing, and intelligent waiver authorizing disclosure of appellant's statements made during a polygraph examination supports the trial court's decision to admit the statements as evidence. Admissibility does not offend appellant's right to counsel where he consulted with counsel and voluntarily chose to be interviewed alone.

Affirmed.

Considered and decided by Popovich, Chief Judge, Sedgowick, Judge, and Crippen, Judge, with oral argument waived.

opinion

CRIPPEN, Judge (Hon. Lynn Olson, District Court Trial Judge)

This appeal deals with admissibility of incriminating statements made to a polygraph operator. We affirm a decision to admit the statements and we find no other trial court errors.

FACTS

Criminal charges were brought against appellant Steven Lee Erickson following allegations of criminal sexual conduct. Appellant's 13-year-old daughter told authorities that appellant engaged in various forms of sexual conduct with her, including sexual intercourse, between August 1982 and April 1985. Appellant denied the charges.

Anoka County authorities retained private investigator Charles Yeschke to examine appellant by administering a polygraph test. Appellant voluntarily appeared at the Anoka County Courthouse on December 11, 1985, with his attorney, Joseph Marvin. The investigator met with Marvin and explained the testing procedures. Marvin did not object to the procedures but told Yeschke that appellant had difficulty reading and writing. Particularly, Marvin did not object about Yeschke's policy to keep counsel out of the room during the test.

Yeschke gave Marvin a waiver form that Marvin was to review with appellant before appellant would be asked to sign it. The signed form would authorize Yeschke to report to Anoka County authorities on any statements appellant made to Yeschke. Appellant signed the form, and Yeschke administered the polygraph examination.

During the course of the exam appellant made several incriminating statements, declaring that he touched the bare breast and bare vagina of his daughter on several occasions during the past three years, but not sexually. Following the exam itself, Yeschke reviewed the results with appellant. "I sat in front of [appellant], explaining to him that the results indicate that he is not truthful with me***. He assured me that there was nothing more than touching her—[her] breasts and vagina over the clothing***."

Yeschke assisted appellant to prepare a written statement so that appellant would know what Yeschke was reporting to the authorities. The statement was prepared and written by Yeschke, based on appellant's declarations, and it was reviewed and signed by appellant. The statement read as follows:

Dear Investigator:

During the past three years I have needed to be close to [my daughter] as her father. On many occasions I did hug and kiss [her] as well as touch her breasts and vagina. When I touched her breasts and vagina it was in a loving way and not a sexual way. I did not gain any sexual pleasure from touching her breasts and vagina. I only wanted to show my love and concern for her. It was a loving touching only and I did not intend to have sex with [her].

I had no other sexual type contact with [my daughter] in the past three years other than kissing [her] on the breast over her clothing. This statement has been read to me by Mr. Yeschke and I understand it. Mr. Yeschke has treated me fairly today, no one has promised me anything or threatened me in any way to make this statement."

The above is true.

Signed: Steven L. Erickson

The omnibus hearing judge ruled that appellant's oral statements and the signee letter were voluntarily given and not in violation of appellant's right to counsel. This ruling was confirmed by the trial judge and the evidence was admitted at trial.

Appellant was convicted of six alternate counts of criminal sexual conduct in the first and second degrees. He was adjudicated guilty of one count of criminal sexual conduct in the first degree, Minn.Stat. SS 609.342, subd. 1(a) (Supp. 1985), and was sentenced to 45 months in prison. On appeal he raises a number of issues to support the contention that he was denied a fair trial.

ISSUES

1. Did the trial court err in admitting statements made by appellant during a polygraph examination?
2. Was appellant otherwise deprived of a fair trial?

ANALYSIS

1. Polygraph test results are "almost universally held" inadmissible. *State v. Anderson,* 261 Minn. 431, 437, 113 N.W.2d 4, 8 (1962) (citing *State v. Kolander,* 236 Minn. 209, 52 N.W.2d 458 (1952)). The "refusal or willingness of a defendant to take the test is also inadmissible." Anderson, 261 Minn. at 437, 113 N.W.2d at 8. *See* Kolander, 236 Minn. at 222, 52 N.W.2d at 465–66 (new trial required when court admitted evidence of defendant's refusal to take polygraph).

In Kolander, the Minnesota Supreme Court explained the basis for the rule: "the lie-detector has not yet attained such scientific and psychological accuracy, nor its operators such sureness of interpretation of results shown therefrom, as to justify submission thereof to a jury***." *Kolander,* 236 Minn. at 221, 52 N.W.2d at 465. In more recent decisions, the Supreme Court has consistently refused to reconsider the "long-established" rule. *State v. Michaeloff,* 324 N.W.2d 12, 15 (1976); *State v. Goblirsch,* 309 Minn. 401, 407, 246 N.W.2d 12, 15 (1976); *State v. Perry,* 274 MN, 1, 12–13, 142 N.W.2d 573, 580 (1966).

The polygraph is, however, used as an interrogation or investigatory tool by law enforcement authorities, and "may frequently lead to confessions or the discovery of facts which may ultimately lead to the solution of many crimes***." *Kolander,* 236 Minn. at 221, 52 N.W.2s at 465. A majority of the states have "held that admissions made by an accused during the course of a polygraph examination are admissible where found to be voluntarily made." *State v. Blosser*, 221 Kan. 59, 61–62, 558 p.2d 105, 107–08 (1976) (finding only a single exception to the majority rule). *See also Wyrick v. Fields*, 459 U.S. 42, 48 n.* (1982) (although the results of a polygraph examination might not have been admissible evidence under Missouri state law, statements "make in response to questioning during the course of the polygraph examination surely would have been").

The majority rule applies the constitutional requirement for all criminal cases that the "prosecution must demonstrate *** that (the accused's) confession was voluntary." *United States v. Little Bear*, 583 F.2d 411, 413 (8th Cir, 1978) (citing *Lego v. Twomey*, 404 U.S. 477, 489 (1972)). *See also State v. Orscanin*, 283 N.W.2d 897, 899 (Minn.), *cert. denied*, 444 U.S. 970 (1979). In determining voluntariness, the court must consider the totality of relevant circumstances. *Id.* A waiver permitting the disclosure and use of such statements must also be shown to be knowing, intelligent, and voluntary. State v. Linder, 268 N.W.2d 734, 735 (Minn. 1978) (determination of the voluntariness of a waiver involves "the same kind of inquiry basically that is made to determine whether a statement is 'voluntary' within the meaning of traditional voluntariness requirement").

The omnibus hearing court found Yeschke was acting as an agent of the State when he administered the polygraph examination. The issue of voluntariness has not come before the Minnesota Supreme Court in the context of statements made to a polygraph examiner who was not a police officer or investigator. The Supreme Court has, however, reviewed a trial court's determination that a defendant's confession to police officers after being told he failed a polygraph examination was voluntary under the totality of the circumstances. *See State v. Jungbauer*, 348 N.W.2d 344, 346 (inn. 1984).

In *Jungbauer*, the Supreme Court criticized a promise made to the defendant by the police that if he confessed they would release him on his own recognizance and use a summons rather than an arrest warrant to bring him in after he was formally charged. *Id.* at 346. The court nevertheless upheld the trial court's determination, citing the absence of misrepresentation by the police as the reliability or admissibility of the test results, the lack of prolonged interrogation, the fact that the promise was not the sort of promise that might tempt an innocent person to confess, and the defendant's previous exercise of his right to silence. *Id.* at 346–47 (the making of a promise does not automatically render any confession involuntary; rather, on voluntariness).

This court has had one previous opportunity to consider the voluntariness of statements made to a polygraph examiner who was not a police officer or investigator. *See State v. Davis*, 381 N.W.2d 86 (Minn. Ct. App. 1986). In *Davis*, the issue was "largely one of relative credibility of Davis and [the polygraph examiner]," and the trial court "believed Davis' version of what occurred***." *Id*. at 88. The trial court in *Davis* found the examiner had exceeded his authority when he administered the test, had attempted to convince the defendant that the polygraph test is foolproof, that the written statement he prepared was a result of impermissible and reprehensible remarks, and that the statement was not in the defendant's own words. *Id*. Giving deference the trial court's latitude in credibility determinations, this court found the "trial court had adequate evidence to determine, based on the totality of the circumstances, that the confession was not voluntary." *Id*.

The procedure used by the polygraph operator in *Davis* was similar to that employed here, including the use of a signed consent form and the preparation by the examiner of a written statement for the examinee to sign. However, unlike *Davis*, appellant had an attorney who advised him and who discussed the procedure with Yeschke before the examination began. The omnibus hearing court found appellant's attorney presented no objections, question, or limitations to Yeschke other than to caution him that appellant had difficulty reading and writing. The attorney also reviewed the waiver form with appellant before appellant entered the examination room.

It is equally significant that appellant does not claim Yeschke made any promises, threats, or misrepresentations to him such as those alleged in *Davis*. Rather, appellant argues Yeschke employed "psychologically coercive" tactics during the polygraph examination. After considering and making findings on all the relevant circumstances, the omnibus hearing court rejected this view of the facts. *See Linder*, 268 N.W.2d at 735 (trial court must proceed under a totality of the circumstance approach).

Appellant is 35 years old, has an eighth grade education, and is of sufficient intelligence, maturity, and experience to understand his rights. Yeschke testified appellant understood the procedure, his rights, and the statements he made. No police officers were present. The interview was conducted in a conference room. Appellant's attorney made no objection to his exclusion from the examination room. No weapons were displayed. Yeschke did not misrepresent the reliability of the polygraph machine or imply the test results were admissible. Appellant's difficulty in reading and writing was taken into account by Yeschke as he read the waiver form slowly and clearly. Although Yeschke prepared the letter, he reviewed it several times with appellant.

The omnibus hearing court concluded appellant's statements were voluntarily given. *See Orscanin,* 283 N.W.2d at 899. The record supports the conclusion that appellant understood his rights, spoke voluntarily with Yeschke, signed the waiver, and understood its implications. *See Little Bear,* 583 F.2d at 413–14 (despite the "often coercive impact of a lie detector test" and the defendant's lack of sophistication, the trial court committed no error in denying the motion to suppress statements made to a polygraph operator when she not only signed a waiver but also understood what it meant). Thus, the omnibus court did not err in ruling that appellant's admissions to Yeschke were given voluntarily.

Appellant also asserts his statements were obtained in violation of his right to counsel. The trial court found appellant waived his right to have counsel present during the polygraph exam questioning.

There is no question that appellant's right to counsel had attached. *Brewer v. Williams,* 430 U.S. 387, 401 (1977). The sixth amendment prohibits the government from eliciting incriminating statements unless a valid waiver is obtained, *State v Kivimaki,* 345 N.W.2d 759, 763 (Minn. 1984).

Appellant and his attorney voluntarily appeared for a polygraph examination. Yeschke explained to Marvin that the examination consisted of four parts: the preliminary interview, the review of the questions, the test itself, and a review of the results with the examinee. Yeschke asked Marvin to review a waiver form with appellant prior to the examination. Marvin knew that no attorneys would be allowed in the room during the polygraph examination. Marvin had no objections to any of the procedures used. Appellant voluntarily entered the examination room with Yeschke.

We conclude the omnibus hearing court did not clearly err in determining that appellant voluntarily, knowingly, and intelligently waived his right to counsel and thus properly admitted the statements at trial.

2. We have examined but find no merit in five additional claims of trial court error.

a. Prior to trial the court held an in-camera hearing regarding the State's request to introduce *Spreigl* evidence that appellant sexually assaulted his younger daughter at his apartment during a visitation two years before trial. The trial court gave a cautionary instruction before the witness testified and in its final instruction. The daughter testified that when she was 10 years old and visiting appellant, he asked her to go into his bedroom. There he touched her breasts and massaged her vaginal area, under her underwear. Appellant stopped when someone knocked at the door.

The trial court's decision admitting *Spreigl* evidence will not be reversed absent an abuse of discretion. *State v. Ture*, 353 N.W.2d 502, 515 (Minn. 1984). The evidence must be relevant, its probative value should outweigh the potential for unfair prejudice, and the dant's participation in the prior offense should be clear and convincing. *State v. Filippi*, 335 N.W.2d 739, (Minn. 1983).

Here the incident was relevant because the evidence was not remote and showed a similar scheme in terms of location and modus operandi. The evidence was clear and convincing based on the daughter's testimony, and was highly probative. We find no abuse of discretion in admitting the *Spreigl* evidence.

b. Before trial the court ruled that no reference could be made to the polygraph examination. In his direct examination, appellant unresponsively answered his own counsel's question by stating, "I volunteered for the polygraph to say the truth." Appellant's motion for a mistrial during recess was denied and defense counsel refused the trial court's request to give the jury a cautionary instruction.

We find no prejudice in appellant's unresponsive comment that he volunteered to take a polygraph. His remark did not indicate that he took a polygraph test. There was no error in denying appellant's request for a mistrial.

c. Appellant claims the evidence is insufficient to support the convictions. Based on a review of the record we conclude otherwise. The victim's testimony in this case was clear and consistent and her version of the events was corroborated by several witnesses. Appellant's incriminating statements to the polygraph examiner support the verdict.

d. In its oral instructions the trial court mentioned the victim's testimony need not be corroborated. This statement is true, Minn. Stat. 609.347, subd. 1 (1984), but it should not have been included in the instructions. *State v. Williams*, 363 N.W.2d 911, 914 (Minn. Ct. App. 1985), *pet, for rev. denied,* (May 1, 1985). Defense counsel did not object to the instruction. In the written copy of instructions, the court deleted the reference to corroboration. Failure to object forfeits this issue for appeal purposes. In addition, when viewed as a whole, the instructions were not prejudicial. *See id.*

e. Appellant contends that several portions of the prosecutor's closing argument were improper. Defense counsel did not raise this issue at trial and this subject is waived on appeal. *State v. Parker,* 353 N.W.2d 122, 127 9 (Minn. 1984).

DECISION

Appellant was convicted in a fairly conducted trial proceeding and his conviction must be affirmed.

Affirmed.

Whether or not polygraphy is used as an investigative tool during the investigative process to assist in the detection of deception: is left to your discretion. In my view, there is a time and place for the use of polygraphy in our judicial system. *Polygraphy* is just one more tool in uncovering truth; not perfect, but, useful.

The case reviewed, following, is molded around the Polyphasic Flow Chart, considered earlier in this writing (see Primary Phase, Semi-structured Approach). It represents thousands of other such interviews conducted by this presenter over the past thirty years. The interaction of participants is provided based upon notes and memory. Precise dialogue is attempted. As you contemplate the process used in this review, consider this case typical of theft, embezzlement, and fraud type investigations.

Chapter Nineteen

A CASE REVIEW

The Alien Connection

Many years ago, Glen Dornfeld, a former FBI Agent, friend of mine, called to find out if I would be interested in conducting an internal theft investigation for a company he had worked for in the past. He said he didn't have time to handle the case himself. I agreed to work on it and we arranged to meet at the corporate offices of the victim company. The company president, Glen, and I talked over the details of the loss and set the stage for my entry into the investigation. Before talking to any of the company employees I needed to find out who the players were and as much about the circumstances as I could surrounding the alleged theft.

What follows pertains to the Precontact and Strategy Sections—Initial Phase. It is information stemming from the preliminary discussion with the company president and Glen. They didn't tell me how to conduct the inquiry, but they did provide data necessary for me to handle the case in a logical fashion. As I have outlined previously, I look at each investigation as related to a scientific process having six phases as illustrated in the Polyphasic Flow Chart, previously discussed.

Investigative Day One

Preliminary Inquiry data, evidence collection:

Investigative Problem: Determine if a diamond ring was stolen, who stole it and attempt it's recovery. Company representatives were convinced the ring had been stolen.

Crime Profile (assuming a crime committed): A female customer brought her diamond ring to a reputable jeweler to be cleaned and adjusted. It was handled according to established policy. The ring, containing a 2.6 carat diamond, had an appraised wholesale value of $21,000 and held much sentimental value with the customer. All went well in the routine handling of the diamond ring until it was returned to the jeweler by the subcontractor, jobber, that completed the work. The ring did reach the jeweler's shop and was specifically handled by employees, then it mysteriously disappeared. A logical search for the ring was fruitless.

Law enforcement authorities said the loss was probably intercompany error or employee theft.

Interviewee Profile (as provided by the president of the company):

1. Carl — Born in Manila. Not a United States citizen at the time of the inquiry. Some difficulty getting along with other employees. Considered to have possibly stolen petty cash during his employment; not substantiated.

2. Brian, 3. Judy,

4. Hugh — Employed with the company for eleven years before the ring disappeared. Exhibited signs of lethargy and passiveness regarding sales about the time of disappearance of ring. Received a recent demotion within the company.

5. Marge, 6. May, 7. Babs,

8. Patty — Worked in repair area part time — was working at the time of ring disappearance. At the time of the missing ring, she was a high school student with the daughter of the woman customer who brought the ring in for repair, cleaning and adjusting. During her interview by company security people it was learned she "found" one man's ring (value — $750.), one pair of woman's earrings and key rings in a drawer at home. She returned those items to the company.

9. Bob, 10. Peggy, 11. Pat, 12. Ann, 13. Anna, 14. George,

15. Doug — Worked the repair area from which the ring disappeared. Worked less than one year with company.

16. Patricia, 17. Nata, 18. Pattie, 19. Tom, 20. Laura, 21. Lora, 22. Liz,

23. Bev — Worked the repair area. Handled the missing ring. Within the year before the ring disappearance she was unhappy with pay received. Had illness in her family about the time of disappearance. With the company about six years.

24. Annie, 25. Shar, 26. Mary Ann, 27. Lynn, 28. Jean, 29. Mel, 30. Leo, 31. Nancy, 32. Marie, 33. Jim, 34. Terry

35. Essie — Had clerical duties. Generally projects a negative attitude, dissatisfied with salary and promotion potential within company. Had recent personal medical problems.

Possible motivation: (reflected in life style; habits, hobbies, stressors)

The interviewees had little or no social interaction with each other outside of work; therefore, that angle of evaluating them was not available. They did their work and went their separate ways.

Initial Phase—Strategic Planning Section

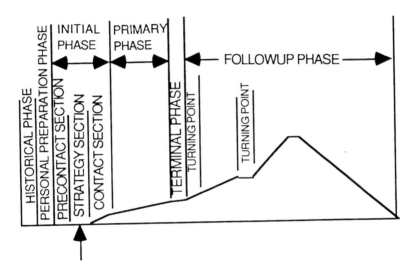

Environmental Setting: So as not to disrupt attention to business, most of the interviews were conducted at the company in a small office space in which two chairs could barely fit. The space was so cramped that I couldn't move my chair into various locations. The proximics of that situation only permitted the use of the Moderate Location. As illustrated, the office space was triangular, about three and a half feet by six feet. With a narrow folding door leading out into the store showroom area.

Also, in the Strategic Planning Section—Initial Phase I had to determine where best to interview people to gain their greatest compliance. In this case an office at the store worked adequately. More ideally, a spot away from the hustle of the store would have been better. What I used worked, fortunately. Transporting employees any distance to some other site would have disrupted the work flow with minimal gain. The key factor in any interview is privacy and the site used allowed that.

That space limitation emphasized that it is not vital to be able to move closer to the interviewee than the Moderate Location and that beginning the interview in the Conversation Location is not critical.

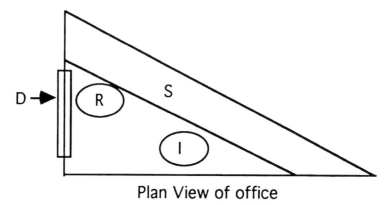

Plan View of office

D=door to the small office
R=chair where interviewees sat
I=chair where interviewer sat
S=shelf (desk), work area

Based upon what the president of the victim company told me in this matter, I thought about the interviewees and calculated how likely it would be for me to gain their compliance:

	T	A	N	P	V	B	%T.I.C.
Bev	7	6	5	6	7	4	75.6%
Carl	4	3	5	4	4	5	69.6%
Gene	5	4	5	4	5	4	71.0%
Patty	6	5	6	4	4	5	73.0%
Doug	5	5	5	5	5	5	72.6%
Essie	5	4	4	5	5	4	71.0%

Initial Phase—Contact Section

From the first contact with every interviewee during the investigation, I tried to project confidence and positive expectancy that the problem could be solved. Although no promises could be made to the management of the company, I tried to express enthusiasm and quiet confidence.

All employees knew I would probably conduct interviews with each of them. The victim store manager coordinated and I scheduled interviews so as not to disrupt store business. As interviewees completed their interview, they were asked to notify the manager who would send in the next available interviewee.

For interviews conducted outside the store with employees and others, I telephoned individuals to schedule times when each would be available. When arranging interviews with the five individuals having had access to the ring, but who were not regular employees at the store, personal introductions were made as the situation directed.

Greeting:

During the first few minutes of each interview I tried to project an image of being calm, friendly, human, and so forth.

Seating:

When possible, I sat about four feet from each interviewee during the interviews.

Objectives Stated:

I told each interviewee that I was trying to determine what happened to the missing diamond ring and that I was trying to recover it. Interviewees were asked to share any information which might assist in finding the missing ring and provide pieces to the investigative puzzle permitting me to see more clearly the picture made by the pieces to determine what had happened to the ring. I tried to convey that I considered their information important.

Investigative Time Expended:

In total, I spent sixteen days during a two months span of time on this investigation. The first day of my involvement in the inquiry was spent discussing with upper management of the company the known circumstances surrounding the missing diamond ring. Employee, #31, Nancy, was assumed to be on vacation and not in anyway connected with the theft; therefore, she was not interviewed.

Day Two (one day after Day one): Twelve interviews at the store site.

(i) = Interview (e) = Polygraph Examination

Id Number	Interviewee	Age	%T.I.C.	Time of Interaction
32	Marie	31	76.0	8:40 a.m.–10:00 a.m.(i)
3	Judy	29	76.0	10:02 a.m.–10:26 a.m.(i)
28	Jean	60	76.0	10:32 a.m.–10:47 a.m.(i)
24	Annie	61	76.0	11:05 a.m.–11:22 a.m.(i)
35	Essie	48	71.0	11:26 a.m.–11:45 a.m.(i)

Id Number	Interviewee	Age	%TIC	Time of Interaction
10	Peggy	54	76.0	1:03 p.m.–1:44 p.m.(i)
26	Mary Ann	40	76.0	1:47 p.m.–2:18 p.m.(i)
33	Jim	23	76.0	2:23 p.m.–2:49 p.m.(i)
4	Hugh	51	76.0	2:58 p.m.–3:14 p.m.(i)
21	Lor	29	76.0	3:17 p.m.–3:33 p.m.(i)
6	May	57	76.0	3:33 p.m.–3:54 p.m.(i)
22	Liz	25	76.0	3:56 p.m.–4:45 p.m.(i)

Semi-structured Approach

Marie (Manager of the victim store) (Day of birth—January 3rd)

She told me that the diamond ring was last seen between 3:10 p.m. and 5:10 p.m. the day before it was determined missing. At about 5:10 p.m. the owner of the ring telephoned to check if the ring had been returned to the store after it was put into a new mounting. It was Jean who handled the ring packet said to have contained the ring and she felt the packet to determine if the ring was there. She reported to the customer by telephone that the customer's diamond ring was in fact at the store and could be picked up the next day. The customer came in the next day to recover her newly mounted diamond ring but it was not to be found.

Interaction with Marie:

> You?
> "No."
> Who?
> "Patty."
> "What did she do or say to cause you to consider she might be involved in the missing diamond?"
> "Ten days before the diamond ring was determined missing the store sustained the loss of a new man's ring valued at about $750. We learned that Patty had 'accidentally' taken that man's ring home and put it in a kitchen drawer. She also brought back earrings which she had worn without permission and left at home. Patty realizes she may be under suspicion regarding the missing diamond ring."
> "Who else might you consider as being involved in this matter of the diamond ring?"
> "Babs, Mary Ann, Bev, Doug, Carl, Ann, and Patty." (No specifics were provided regarding those named; it was just a feeling she had regarding them.)

Judy (Day of birth—January 22nd)

You?
"No."
Who? "No idea! Kitty money at the store was taken by some one working at nights and other things were missing as well. Carl probably took the kitty money, I think."
Trust? "Part time people; Marie and Essie are trustworthy."
Stolen?
I believe there's about 40% chance that the diamond ring may be lost. It was in a ripped envelope and could have fallen out. Bev noticed the torn envelope as she presented it to the customer when the loss was determined.
F.P.?
"No." The ring was checked in from repair and sized by Bev the night before the loss was determined. After the ring was sized it was put into a box for the night people to file according to customer's name. It was probably Carl who filed the ring that night. After being sized, it would have been placed in an envelope and stapled shut.
Happen to doer?
"Court punishment! There were many things on the table where Bev sized the ring. Silver was being polished on that same table by Judy and Anna in the back room. That all added to the possible confusion of time."

As she left the interview situation, I asked her to think about what we had discussed and to notify me of any information she recalls; I gave her my calling card.

Jean (Day of birth—October 1st)

You?
"No."
Who?
"No idea."
Suspect?
"No, none of the regular people, can't judge the part time people."
Happen to doer?
"Terminate, it is a serious matter, justice is justice."

Toward the end of the interaction, I asked her to think of how security at the store can be improved and where changes could be made. As she left the interview site, she commented that she questions the use of part time people in dealing with customer's jewelry items.

She pointed to the part time employees, not named, as a possible suspects in the theft. Her depth of consideration of the questions and other verbal and nonverbal signals implied her truthfulness.

I believe that 90 percent of any communication is based upon paralinguistics such as pauses, tone, silences, stance, and so forth. They happen in about one one-hundredth of a second. Too fast, generally, for me to report to you in words. I sense them as on-going ingredients of the interview. They are stronger and more meaningful than words. Those nonverbal elements of the interview are there, like it or not.

Annie (Day of birth — January 29th)

> You?
> "No."
> Who?
> "Wouldn't know."
> Suspect?
> "Hate to accuse anyone. Patty sat and smoked while Bev worked in the back of the store the day before the loss of the ring. Bev was cleaning silver on that table back there and Bev said she checked it in. Someone else files it away, whether it was a part-timer or not. Carl and someone else also file things away."
> Trust?
> "Marie and Essie are honest."
> Happen to doer?
> "The company should not keep them."
> Jail?
> "I think so, they must be sick."

When she was about to leave at the end of the interview, I asked for her view on how security at the store could be improved to which she responded: "The delivery drivers have free access to the area where the table is located upon which the shining and sizing are done; such should be changed." I gave her my calling card as she left and asked her to contact me if she thought of any further information regarding the missing ring. Her reluctance to accuse anyone in this matter obviously changed to allow her to mention access by delivery drivers. She appeared clear thinking and smooth flowing in the interaction, helping to signal truthfulness to me.

Essie (Day of birth — July 11th)

You?

"No."

Who?

"No idea; the customer said 'the rings not there.' From where the customer was standing she, customer, could not see clearly if the ring was there or not. The customer's reaction was too quick." (Spoken as though she suspected the customer was in some way involved in causing the ring loss).

Trust?

"All the sales people! The edge of the envelope was split, but that happens sometimes. Bev checked the area where the repair jobs are kept. At that time had not been determined to be missing (stolen). I can't recall any other missing repair jobs."

Suspect?

"Patty had that man's ring at home which causes suspicion on her by most employees; we all spent hours looking for it."

Stolen?

"It's gone, it was large and not easily overlooked."

Happen to doer?

"Lose his job and be prosecuted."

I provided my calling card to the interviewee and asked her to think about this matter.

Peggy (Day of birth — August 13th)

You?

"No, nothing from here."

Who?

"I don't think it is stolen, I think it is lost. Repair was running crazy. Bev's face was bright red when she asked me to help look for any loose rings. We searched the drawers. The customer said 'look in that envelope again.' I said there's a hole in the envelope; it was a new ring in plastic. Bev said she must have put her hand in the package to rip it. Why would she put that new setting in a ripped packet?" She wondered out loud. "I'm a detective type," she declared. She went on to think out loud: "That drawer is not locked. We have honest customers. New people are being blamed for thefts. There are two new people. Patty is a suspect; Patty is a compulsive buyer and she has given conflicting stories about various things; she wanted to be mysterious about things. I saw the old setting in a plastic container in the envelope which had a split edge with a hole in it." Bev said she sized it and then couldn't recall what happened to it."

I provided her with my calling card as she was about to leave. I asked her to think about this situation and if she has anything more to discuss, please contact me.

Mary Ann (Day of birth—October 4th)

You?
"No."
Who?
"None."
Suspect?
"No one."
Trust?
"Jean."
Think?
"No."
Approach?
"No."
Happen to doer?
"Don't know."
Jail or what?
"Don't know."
She points to Patty as a suspect.

Calling card given with request to think of how to improve security at the store, and so forth.

Jim (Day of birth—February 21st)

You?
"No."
Who?
"Don't know."
Stolen?
"Probably stolen. I took the ring in as a repair item and saw it when it came back and at the time of the resizing. The first time I saw it the envelope was ripped; I stapled it a couple of times."
Say you did it?

"Well, I have a total in debts of $6000 and I'm newly married."

Think?

"No (laughingly provided); I accidentally had a job (piece of jewelry) in my pocket one time and brought it back after going one block. I have a strict up bringing."

Approach?

"Not at all, no."

Happen to doer?

"Treated as a criminal as the law states. Carl wanted to take a ring on credit but his credit rating was not good and Marie would not okay the credit. That ring was valued at about $2000. Patty should be a suspect because I heard she took a man's ring home and left it. Employment is only a passing thing to her. I have too much invested in jewelry training to lose it on the theft of a ring."

I gave him my calling card and asked him to think about how to improve security at the store, and so forth.

Hugh (Day of birth—March 17th)

You?

"No."

Who?

"No."

Suspect?

"Customer pulled a double claim, a check switch or an inexperienced employee gave it out. The customer doesn't seem to be upset enough about its loss; fraud or theft, not lost."

Happen to doer?

"Prosecuted; company should prosecute and not let them off easy!!"

Think?

"No, it doesn't look good after a while." (Referring to the shine and appeal of jewels, and so forth).

Approach?

"No."

"Anything anyone has done or said that might cause you to think they may have been involved in taking that ring?"

(Doesn't want to speculate on suspect, seems uneasy about naming suspect, discomfort sensed.)

Calling card provided with request to think over store situation and comment later on improving security. To which he responded: It's a dog's dinner in the way those jobs (repairs) are handled back there (showing his disapproval).

   Lor (Day of birth — April 9th)

> You?
> "No."
> Who?
> "Don't know if it is stolen; if it was stolen it was probably to cause problems at the store rather than to get the diamond."
> Suspect?
> "Carl and Mrs. C. are both new in the repair department, they're potential suspects."
> Think?
> "Not really, not tempted."
> Approach?
> "No."
> Happen to doer?
> "Prosecute!"
> Any reason for any one to say they think you did it?
> "Not that I can think of."
> F.P.?
> "Didn't handle the ring at all."
> "Anyone come to mind that you to feel somewhat uneasy because of what they have done or said; I'm not asking you to point fingers or anything?"
> "Carl has put a few things on hold in the past, but can't say he took the ring."

Provided calling card and request to think on this matter regarding improving security at store.

   May (Day of birth — June 6th)

> You?
> "No."
> Who?
> "Lost not stolen."
> "Anyone that makes you uneasy because of what they have said or done?"
> "I don't dislike anyone."
> Trust?
> "Peggy."

Suspect?
"Trusts everyone."
Think?
"No."
Approach?
"No."
Happen to doer?
"Terminate from job."
How about jail?
"You mean sentence? Well, it is no joke!!"
Suspect (Asked again because sensed hesitation on first asking)?
"I like everyone here!"

Calling card given, and so forth regarding security.

Liz (Day of birth—June 13th)

You?
"No."
Who?
"Truly no idea."
Suspect?
"Because I work here I couldn't comment. Patty disappoints people, she is irresponsible at times, she has no need to steal the ring; but she may be seeking attention or some form of retaliation. It would be disappointing if she did steal it. (Interviewee seemed personally attached to Patty and may have been siding with her in this matter.)

Day Three (the day following Day two): Five interviews—store site.

(i) = Interview (e) = Polygraph Examination

Id Number	Interviewee	Age	%TIC	Time of Interaction
23	Bev	47	75.6	9:14 a.m.–10:39 a.m.(i)
15	Doug	19	72.6	11:05 a.m.–11:55 a.m.(i)
27	Lynn	26	76.0	11:55 a.m.–12:00 a.m.(i)
8	Patty	17	73.0	1:40 p.m.–2:14 p.m.(i)
5	Marge	61	76.0	2:56 p.m.–3:04 p.m.(i)

Bev (Day of birth—November 23rd)

You?
"No."
Who?
"No idea."

"How was the job (ring resetting) handled when it was returned to the store?"

"The job came back between 1 and 3 of the day before it was determined to be missing. It was sized and should have been filed with other such jobs. There was a big promotion going on in the store the day the theft was discovered. Carl should have been called and should have voluntarily come in to help locate the ring. Why the customer's merchandise (she mused). Everyone except Carl has access to the majority of the store merchandise. "Was it professionals that stole it?" She thought out loud.

Happen to doer?

"Even if it is a customer, it is "grany" larceny, isn't it? She pronounced.

Prosecution?

"Yes! Managers from other stores had access to jobs (jewelry at the victim store)."

She stated that as she dealt with the customer whose ring was missing, she told herself "It's in the tray Bev, it's in the tray!" The ring could not be found. Essie worked beside Bev that day of the loss. Essie telephoned Carl to ask him if he knew anything about the ring and he became angry with her for calling him about the ring. She realized that she was one of the main players in this drama of the missing ring. She displayed more than a little concern that someone might consider her the one who stole the ring. Bev also talked to Carl and he gave the impression that he always handled things properly.

As though to herself, she declared that Patty had access to everything in the store so why would she take a customer's ring? She further mused: "I wonder about Patty because she did take that man's ring." And further: "Carl may have been too proud to say he made a mistake in giving out jobs to a customer. I wanted to look under the safe where I previously found a man's missing ring and where I found my earring I dropped on one occasion. I was worried that if I did find it (missing diamond) people would suspect me of the theft."

Doug (Day of birth—January 8th)

You?
"No."
Who?
"No."
Suspect?

"When the kitty money (petty cash) was set up by Pat, it appeared that Carl was the one that took some money. Then there's Patty who had that other ring at home in her kitchen drawer. Carl has a full-time job in addition to working for the (victim) store and he has several children. Patty may have taken diamond ring."

Stolen?

"We looked for days, I assume it's stolen. Bev had commented to him how big the diamond ring was. He has cleaned larger diamonds, however."

Think?

"No."

Happen to doer?

(pause) "What do you mean (spoken as though to self), definitely court."

Jail?

"Either that or great fine to teach him a lesson. I'm against crooks."

"What else comes to mind about Patty and Carl?"

"She is unhappy and she has her own style. He didn't seem secure at first, he says what he wants whether it's right or wrong. He tries to cover-up by being definite in what he says. Patty said that she only slipped that men's ring in the drawer accidentally . . . it was in her kitchen drawer."

Approach?

"No."

Calling card given to Doug, and so forth. As he was about to leave, he declared the security is not good in victim store because shoplifting last year was high. Also, Carl could have given out the diamond ring to some other customer by mistake.

Lynn (Day of birth—December 17th)

You?

"No."

Who?

"No."

Suspect?

"None, works in the office only."

Stolen?

"Misplaced, I hope."

Happen to doer?

"Dismissed and prosecuted."
Think?
"No, I've been here (designated number of years)."
Approach?
"No."
Borrow?
"No. I don't know any details about the missing diamond ring."

Patty (Day of birth—March 10th)

You?
"No."
Who?
"No idea."
Suspect?
"Someone in repair. Maybe Carl or Bev."
Trust?
"Lor."
"Tell me about the men's ring you brought back to the store."
"I returned the man's ring about a week after the diamond ring was determined missing. I accidentally put it in the kitchen drawer. I wanted to buy it for my father; but I couldn't afford it."
Borrow?
"No, its a rule in our family that no one steals."
Approach?
"Only in joking way by friends. I would like to take a polygraph examination."

Marge (Day of birth—January 9th)

You?
"No, wasn't here."
Who?
"Who would want it?!"
Suspect?
"Don't know."
"Trust?
"Essie, Annie, Jean and Bev. I trust them all."
Happen to doer?
"Don't know, I don't know the law. Didn't work at the time of the loss."

Day Four (the day after Day three): Six interviews—store site.

(i) = Interview (e) = Polygraph Examination

Id Number	Interviewee	Age	%TIC	Time of Interaction
20	Laura	62	76.0	9:46 a.m.–9:58 a.m.(i)
1	Carl	36	69.6	6:47 p.m.–7:15 p.m.(i)
7	Babs	25	76.0	7:23 p.m.–7:35 p.m.(i)
13	Anna	18	76.0	7:43 p.m.–7:54 p.m.(i)
30	Leo	38	76.0	7:55 p.m.–8:09 p.m.(i)
12	Ann	23	76.0	8:12 p.m.–8:40 p.m.(i)

Laura (Day of birth—August 2nd)

You?
"No."
Who?
"No idea."
Suspect?
"No idea."
Borrow?
"No."
Think?
"No."
Approach?
"No."
Stolen?
"Not by anyone working here; I would trust everyone!"
Trust?
"Marge and Mary Ann."
Happen to doer?
"Pay back if it was done for money. If it was done because that person is sick then determine the motive (provided in a helping attitude). I feel remote from the loss, like reading a story in a newspaper.

Carl (Day of birth—November 8th)

You?
"Why do you ask that question, I would not sell my career over that (Shifts in chair, never denied)."
Who?
"During that evening there was commotion because of sales promotions where the back of the store was open to a lot of people."

Rather confusing?

"Yes. I'm not supposed to open those finished jobs. There were so many people there and the jobs were on the tray. I could not devote my time 100 percent to the counter and to filing the jobs. There has been lack in the systems (as though to show weaken and opportunity, open to the world). I'm willing to face any inquiry."

"Someone from repair area steal ring?"

"No, not likely, it was probably someone from some other area; but, I'm not wiping out that possibility. Considers it an 85 percent chance the loss was in the tray because of the torn envelope. I would not jeopardize my job for that ring; I didn't realize it was so expensive.

Calling card provided, and so forth. As he was about to leave the interview site, Carl declared: "I could work a couple of years and make that much, so why would I take it."

Babs (Day of birth — February 11th)

You?
"No."
Who?
"No one."
Suspect?
"None."
Stolen?
"The store has bad security, anyone emptying the trash could have taken it especially in repair!"
Trust?
"Hugh and Lor."
Not trust?
"Maybe the new people, no one specifically."
Approach?
"No."
Think?
"No, I buy a lot."
Stolen?
"It could be stolen, but probably not by anyone in the store (employees)."
Happen to doer?
"Prosecuted because it's not fair to everyone else."

Handled the ring?

"No."

Calling card provided, and so forth.

Anna (Day of birth—November 14th)

You?

"No."

Who?

"No one."

Suspect?

"Wouldn't consider anyone that would."

Trust?

"Jean and Annie."

Approach?

"No."

Borrow?

"No."

Think?

"No."

Stolen?

"It had to be stolen by someone from inside."

Happen to doer?

"Prosecute as though someone from outside did it!"

Calling card provided, and so forth.

Leo (Day of birth—September 24th)

He was the cleaning man at the store. He cleaned the night before the loss was discovered. He did not notice any unusual confusion going on that night.

Did you check the vacuum you used that night to see if the ring might have gotten stuck in it?

"No."

Think?

"No."

He and Marie subsequently checked the vacuum with negative results.

Ann (Day of birth—November 7th)

She declared the store had a funny filing system.

You?

"No."

"No idea."

Stolen?

"Carelessness, not stolen."

Suspect?

"No one."

Trust?

"Marie and Jean."

Approach?

"No."

Think?

"No."

Borrow?

"No, I've worked for everything I have and it feels good knowing I've earned it."

Happen to doer?

"Whatever the law says! It is stealing!" (Please notice contradiction in her previous comment when she responded: "loss is mostly carelessness.") Further, she complained of the store's accountability system maintained by the store regarding merchandise.

Calling card provided, and so forth. The "so forth," here, is "If you think of anything to help solve this thing, please call me. We need to get this resolved. Thank you for your cooperation. Have a good day.

Day Five (two days after Day four):

(i) = Interview (e) = Polygraph Examination

Id Number	Interviewee	Age	%TIC	Time of Interaction
18	Pattie	26	76.0	2:29 p.m.–2:50 p.m.(i)
25	Shar	36	76.0	2:53 p.m.–3:05 p.m.(i)
2	Brian	27	76.0	3:35 p.m.–4:00 p.m.(i)

Pattie (Day of birth—October 11th)

You?

"No."

Who?

"No."

Suspect?

"Carl."

Stolen?

"Yes."

Approach?

"No." Mentioned Carl and how he talks about investment of tax money.

Happen to doer?

"As the law would predetermine. It is not in my hands."

Calling card provided, and so forth. She commented on the carelessness of money handling by employees at the store and how someone put the money in the wrong register slot almost causing her to give out improper change.

Shar (Day of birth—September 27th)

You?

"No."

Who?

"No."

Suspect?

"None."

Stolen?

"Don't know."

Think?

No, I couldn't wear it."

Approach?

"No."

Happen to doer?

"Fired and give ring back."

Suspect?

"No, it probably was someone who knows the value, probably one of the old ladies that works here."

Trust?

"Marie."

Calling card provided, and so forth.

Brian (Day of birth—March 15th)

You?

"No."

Who?

"No."

Suspect?

"No, not even gossip."

Stolen?

"Don't know, I would hope lost, its rare if it is lost around here."

Think?

"No."

Approach?

"No."

Happen to doer?—

(thoughtful pause) "If it is proven to be theft then prosecute; if an accident, then something less than prosecution; it all depends on the circumstances."

He commented that he appreciated the formulation of my questions. Calling card provided, and so forth.

Day Six (one day after Day five):

(i) = Interview (e) = Polygraph Examination

Id Number	Interviewee	Age	%TIC	Time of Interaction
32	Marie	31	76.0	9:14 a.m.–10:03 a.m.(e)
11	Pat	50(?)	76.0	5:07 p.m.–5:35 p.m.(i)

Marie

After the polygraph examination objective and overview of the procedures were discussed, I formulated examination questions with the examinee. I conducted the polygraph examination and it was my diagnostic opinion that Marie's denials were apparently verified regarding whether or not she stole the diamond ring. During her examination, she declared she worried Carl might be involved in the theft. Carl is not a citizen of the United States, she declared. She added things up in her mind about the ring loss and expressed that she is a forgiving type person. Results of Marie's examination were verified by subsequent events of the investigation, specifically the return of the diamond by Carl.

Pat

You?

"Did not have access to the missing ring!"

Trust?

"Bev."

Suspect?

"Can't point out anyone. I feel impatient when I think anyone would steal anything; I wouldn't enjoy the thing. It is unusual that mistakes are made in the store, such as putting things in the wrong envelope. Giving it out to a customer by mistake is remote. I'd hate to point the finger at anyone!! This all makes me darn uncomfortable."

Calling card provided, and so forth.

Day Seven (one day after Day six):

Nata was interviewed at the store site, Mel and Patricia were interviewed at a sister store while Bob and Terry were interviewed at their individual residences.

(i) = Interview (e) = Polygraph Examination

Id Number	Interviewee	Age	%TIC	Time of Interaction
34	Terry	17	76.0	8:27 a.m.–8:52 a.m.(i)
29	Mel	32	76.0	9:50 a.m.–10:05 a.m.(i)
16	Patricia	50	76.0	10:08 a.m.–10:30 a.m.(i)
9	Bob	27	76.0	2:23 p.m.–2:46 p.m.(i)
17	Nata	54	76.0	3:25 p.m.–3:40 p.m.(i)

Terry (Day of birth—April 21st)

You?
"No."
Who?
"I think it was an inside job."
Suspect?
"Only see three people in deliveries and has no suspicion of them. Made the delivery of the diamond ring between 1 and 4 the day before it was discovered missing."
Reason anyone would say you stole it?
"No, I don't think so."
Think?
"No, because it would be like stealing from my brother." (He works for older brother who is the jobber).
Happen to doer?
"Prosecute and pay back. It's grand theft, isn't it?"
Who do you think would steal it?
"Someone poor that wants it but can't afford it."

Mel (Day of birth—November 26th)

He drove a van with promotional supplies to the victim store about 6:30 p.m. of the evening before the loss was discovered. The store was not overly busy, nothing seemed out of place; there was a lot of waste paper around. Bob, Marie, and Patty helped him unload and unpack the supplies; he was home about 9:30 p.m.

> You?
> "No. The envelope that had contained the missing ring was found intact and should have been filed."
> Suspect?
> "I don't think it is stolen. If it was stolen it would have happened between its check-in and filing. There are too many variables. We can't be complacent! If experienced people were handling giving out the merchandise, then the ring was not given out. It was not likely given out because a customer would probably have questioned it."

He made comments that indicated he does not hold Patty in high regard.

Patricia (Day of birth—September 10th)

This interviewee took part in setting up the promotional materials the evening of the day before the loss of the diamond ring was discovered.

> You?
> "No; display people have stolen in the past however." She was surprised that customers' goods were stolen. "There is an employee with a foreign accent working at the (victim) store; Patty may have a relative who has a jewelry store. Pat (#11) may have some financial problems."
> Stolen?
> "If not stolen then it was placed in the wrong envelope."

Bob (Day of birth—August 26th)

> You?
> "That's a low-blow question!" That response from the interviewee seemed to be based upon the interviewee's sensitive feeling and drew my reply: "If I don't ask it how can I find out who did take the ring, assuming it is stolen." That reply seemed to smooth interviewee feelings by indicating that no accusation was intended and that everyone is being asked the same basic questions.
> Who?
> "No."
> Suspect?
> "No; I know the people at (a sister store) more than those at (the

victim store). I went to the (victim) store as a sales representative to help promote some produce and arrived about 6:30 p.m. the night before the loss was discovered and left that night at about 9:00 p.m. I was at (the victim store) the next three days to assist in the promotion and noticed no unusual commotion on the day of (the loss discovery) other than the search for the missing ring."
F.P? (Would there be any reason for your fingerprints to be on the envelope that contained the missing ring?)
"No." (Some hesitation noticed in the interviewee's response regarding touching any of the repair jobs.) I watched as they searched through the envelopes for the ring. "The theft is not worth it." "I only put the stuff in and went home!" (Interviewee referring to the evening before the loss was discovered.)

Nata (Day of birth—February 8th)
A few rings and other items were missing when she first started. When new people start it seems that some items are missing. Maybe the older employees are using the opportunity of the new employees to steal and make it look like the new ones have done it. It would seem strange that anyone in the display department for promotions would have knowledge of which envelope has what job; can't think display people did it.

> You?
> "I have no reason to take the ring." (Family wealth implied in comments.)
> Stolen?
> "The day of the loss I saw the customer waiting for Bev to search envelopes. I assumed the ring was lost not stolen."
> Suspect?
> (Patty was pointed out as a potential, but not specifically.) "Jim and Lor go into the envelopes from time to time. I put merchandise in my pocket until someone can write up my personal purchase but not for any other reason."

Much of the above information is based upon an outpouring of verbal comment (Emotional Dumping Process) from the interviewee; she seemed to have stored energy waiting to be released.

Day Eight (one day after Day seven):

Although Tom was a Jobber for the victim store he was available for interview at the victim store.

(i) = Interview (e) = Polygraph Examination

Id Number	Interviewee	Age	%TIC	Time of Interaction
19	Tom	26	76.0	3:06 p.m.–3:23 p.m.(i)

Tom (Day of birth — December 6th)
As a Jobber he didn't realize his company worked on the missing ring.

> You?
> "No; I'm bonded."
> Who?
> "Do I know who!?" (Spoken as though he did know but in a joking way.) "No!" (He finally said in a serious way, no longer playful.) "Delivery people do have access to the job area."
> Think?
> "No. I like my job, I wouldn't do anything to jeopardize my employment."

Day Nine (one day after Day eight):

George was also a Jobber for the victim store and was available for interview at the store.

(i) = Interview (e) = Polygraph Examination

Id Number	Interviewee	Age	%TIC	Time of Interaction
14	George	55	76.0	11:38 a.m.–12:25 p.m.(i)

George (Day of birth — March 18th)
As a Jobber he did not have access to the missing job once it was returned to the victim store.

> Who?
> "No."
> Suspect?
> "No."
> Trust?
> "Can't say, Marie and Bev are pleasant."
> How do you think it happened?
> "The summer humidity causes the envelopes to split and staples and tape have been used on most of them. There is not much space in them and its frustrating to deal with them. I've tried to tell (the victim store) to change the design of the envelopes. My first thought was that it was because of the envelope that the loss took place, that the envelope caused the loss."

Day Ten (twelve days after Day nine):

This day I told the company president that I believed Carl probably stole the diamond ring. When I announced to the president of the company that Carl was probably the one that stole the ring, it was agreed that a letter would be drawn up over the signature of the president declaring no prosecution to be sought for anyone returning the ring. Only the recovery of the ring was important, the letter would indicate, and no questions to be asked when the ring is returned.

Also, on this day I began contact with the United States Immigration and Naturalization Service (INS) to determine if deportation was a possibility for a guy like Carl. Immigration and Naturalization Service intervention was out of the question, I learned.

After this point in time, my effort, more specifically, was to find a way to approach Carl so as to encourage him to return the missing ring. I implied to Carl that it was to his advantage to give up the ring rather than face deportation or jail. Let us keep in mind, as did Carl, the reality of his family of several children and their new home in America. I never directly told Carl I thought he stole the ring.

Day Eleven (three days after Day ten):

(i) = Interview (e) = Polygraph Examination

Id Number	Interviewee	Age	%TIC	Time of Interaction
1	Carl	36	69.6	10:00 a.m.–12:00 p.m.(i)

Carl (second interview)

This interaction took place in the public waiting room of Carl's full-time employment. After much thought over the three days from the point of seeking more investigative time from the company president, I called on Carl at his primary job to *chat*. That action did not make Carl happy.

The proximics of this interaction were that he and I sat about in the Moderate Location in chairs prelocated by someone not involved in this investigation. On that occasion I asked what he thought happened to the ring and he declared that it might have been given out to some customer by mistake or it might have been swept up and gone forever or as mistake happened because of the confusion the night before because of the promotional set up.

"Then we have poor controls" (voice cracked). There is a lot of temptation there. I could work and make that much in a couple of

years. I wouldn't jeopardize my position by taking that ring."
(provided as though to convince me that his involvement in such a
theft is obviously not logical).
When the missing petty cash was mentioned, Carl declared:
"Day people took it, if I used petty cash I ask for permission."

Although Carl talked politely in the public waiting room with me, he
was uneasy over the experience and did not like the chat. Carl specifically mentioned how the ring could have been missing because of a
mistake by an employee in that a customer could have received the ring
by mistake and may return it when the mistake is realized (shades of the
scenario I mentioned to him at his home.)

> Does your full-time employment know you are working for the
> [victim] store?
> "No."
> Will he grant permission for the INS to provide his immigration
> records for my review?
> "No."

Without being asked of it, Carl declared that he found a missing
emerald ring at the store valued at $3000 which he provided to Bev. In
mentioning the ring he found, he was inconsistent as to how and where
he found it. (He commented on the find as though to convince me of his
loyalty to the victim store and how he was not tempted to steal it.)

After speaking with me the first time, Carl declared, he searched his
clothes at home for the missing ring. He had gone home, had dinner
then searched for the ring. It was not discussed if he found the ring. That
question of whether he found the ring or not I overlooked.

Day Twelve (three days after Day eleven):

I interviewed Bev at her residence to avoid other employees noticing
the second contact. The purpose of the second interview was to gain
greater insight regarding the circumstances surrounding the missing
ring, I told Bev.

Id Number	Interviewee	Age	%TIC	Time of Interaction
23	Bev	47	81.2	8:00 p.m.–9:20 p.m.(i)

Bev (second interview)

After much thought, I visited Bev three days later and explained to
her that I was trying to better comprehend the circumstances surround-

ing the disappearance of the ring and what she knew of Carl's response to it being missing. My interest in Carl as the probable thief was not announced to Bev; she may have thought she was under special consideration as the thief.

On this occasion I intended to verify the comment made by Carl regarding his return of the emerald ring he had found and given to Bev. Without revealing to Bev the purpose of the inquiry, I asked her about the emerald ring find by Carl and she did not recall specifically the emerald ring being mentioned to her by Carl.

Although other discussion was undertaken at this meeting, I reached my goal without announcing the potential importance of verifying the claim of Carl that he found a sought-after missing emerald ring. She appeared upset over the loss of the diamond ring and that she may have handled it in a careless manner causing it to be too easy for someone to steal. (It could not be revealed to her that Carl was the prime suspect in the matter even though such knowledge may have eased her bad feelings. Compassion is important when used properly.)

Day Thirteen (seven days after Day twelve):

This day was the second contact with INS to finally determine that official authorities could not take part in this matter based upon available data. With the letter from the victim company president in hand, I again went to the INS offices to confirm what might be done in this situation. The letter was not shown to INS. I never mentioned a suspect's name or the victim company. Little to nothing could be done to deport the unnamed alien without having two proven felony charges against him. Copies of the INS regulations regarding deportation were obtained just in case they might come in handy for my canny maneuvers.

Day Fourteen (three days after Day thirteen):

I interviewed Carl at his residence. On this occasion he read the letter from the company and I gave him a copy of the deportation regulations.

Id Number	Interviewee	Age	%TIC	Time of Interaction
1	Carl	36	69.6	7:30 p.m.–9:00 p.m.(i)

Carl (third interaction)

Several of his children and wife peeked in at us several times from the adjoining room. Each time he asked them politely to allow us to talk. He didn't know in advance that I was coming to talk to him at his house. I do that sort of thing on occasions when I want to show someone I'm not afraid to inject myself into their space. It helps to get their attention.

He agreed, for the second time, to check his clothes for the ring. I showed him the company letter referring to no prosecution. He read it. I talked at length to make it clear to Carl how the company did not want prosecution in this matter, only recovery of the ring. I told Carl that my presentation to him was to be the same made to most employees in an effort to encourage cooperation. I reminded him of the five hundred dollar reward offered by the company for the ring's recovery.

I asked Carl, at his residence, to think about the situation and to please search his clothing to determine if he could have possibly carried the ring home by mistake. I asked him to think of how the ring might have been misplaced or how a customer might have gotten the ring accidentally. As I was about to leave I produced the deportation regulations and asked if Carl had ever read them. Carl said no and I suggested he might have some interest in them. I left the regulations with Carl as a passing gesture which carried significant meaning known only to Carl. I hoped.

During the conversation, Carl declared that he thought by now the ring would have been returned by a customer who came in when it was busy and just return the ring without giving a name, just hands it over and leaves at a busy time. (During the several interactions I had with Carl, I provided the suggestion or possibility that the ring may have been given out by mistake and the person having it might return it in the near future.) I'm sure he knew the game I played. Neither he nor I openly revealed what we knew.

Day Fifteen (day after Day fourteen):

Interaction with Carl took place both over the telephone and at the victim store site.

Id Number	Interviewee	Age	%TIC	Time of Interaction
1	Carl	36	69.6	8:45 p.m.–10:00 p.m.(i)

Carl (fourth interaction)

This evening, I telephoned Carl as he worked at the victim store. I asked if he had thought about the conversation we had the evening before and if he might have located the ring in his clothing. Carl became angry and told me not to bother him anymore and if I did, he would contact his attorney. With that, Carl hung up the telephone. (This was a point of calculated risk and a time for quick, clear thinking.)

To meet the challenge of Carl hanging up, I immediately went to the victim store to personally speak with Carl and politely, but firmly, seek further cooperation. It proved to be appropriate action.

When I approached him at the victim store, Carl declared: "You keep asking the same questions!" "I'm not dumb, my answers have been consistent each time I talk to you!" "I could make as much as the ring is worth in a couple of years! Why would I jeopardize my position for it?" "I am integrity from my toes to my head." As a diversion question to lessen the force of Carl's verbal attack upon me, I asked Carl about the emerald ring that he had found and returned to the company. Carl responded in a vague way and returned to his verbal attack. "I will be ready for you if you call me at work!" (Carl referring to his primary job) "If you call me, I'll tell my attorney!" To which I responded: "Good, give me his name so I can explain this to him." Carl retorted: "No, his name is personal!" I tried three times to obtain the attorney's name with no success. (It seemed as though Carl was bluffing.) Carl declared: "If you have anything against me, do what you have to do."

I mentioned to Carl that I telephoned Carl's wife at her employment and left my name and number for her to call back. Then I asked Carl if she had told him about my call. Carl responded: "These are hectic times, I didn't have time to talk to her." I then asked Carl: "Can your educational background stand checking? Isn't that the basis of you being in the United States?" Carl responded: "I didn't mean to be angry with you." I commented: "I just want the ring back!" I provided a calling card to Carl suggesting he give the card to his attorney to have the attorney contact me regarding this matter. At that point I left Carl at the victim store saying I would stay in touch. (The challenge seemed to be met but I still had no real evidence to prove that Carl was the one who stole the ring.) I'm sure he knew I knew. Never once did I say directly to him that I considered him the one who stole the diamond ring.

Day Sixteen (three days after Day fifteen):

Again, interaction with Carl took place both over the telephone and at the victim store site.

Id Number	Interviewee	Age	%TIC	Time of Interaction
1	Carl	36	69.6	6:00 p.m.–9:30 p.m.(i)

Carl (fifth interaction)

Carl telephoned me to report that he had received an envelope from an elderly couple in the parking lot of the shopping center near the victim store and he wondered if I would be interested in coming to the store to open the envelope with the manager and him. What do you think I responded. Carl said that an elderly couple had obtained it by mistake from an employee at the victim company. The couple, claimed Carl, had been out of town and this was the first opportunity they had to return the diamond.

Carl (sixth interaction)

After Carl's call, a quiet surge of joy and exhilaration swept over me as I heard Carl's voice speak the long-awaited words. It seemed that the seed of courage, trepidation most likely, I so tenderly planted took root within Carl and finally bloomed. I hoped my clear thinking, persistent, and calm resolve paid off.

It was about 9:15 p.m. When I arrived at the victim store after Carl's phone call, I didn't quite know what to expect. I was almost certain the caper was to end that night judging by the sound of Carl's voice on the phone. I found Marie, the manager, waiting near the entrance as though not breathing, just waiting and hoping, but not hoping too much for she might be disappointed. She seemed in a daze as she bent, leaned on a showcase with her elbows, face in her hands. I talked to her immediately upon arriving. Carl had, prior to my arrival, advised her of his recent possession of the envelope and his phone call to me and that I was on my way to the store to join him and her in the envelope opening.

Carl, the store manager, and I sat in the manager's office while I opened the white envelope Carl handed me. In the envelope, I found a wadded ball of masking tape and a typed note which read:

> On November a young tall guy in your repair dept. gave this ring to my wife by mistake. We tryed to sell it but we couldn't because people are asking the papers about it. Now we are returning the ring. We hope you don't fire the guy. Sorry we remove the stone from the ring.

Buried in the masking tape was a 2.6 carat diamond, wrapped tightly to about the size of a nickel. Once the masking tape was unwrapped, the diamond inside was presented to the manager to check. She declared it to be a diamond of the shape and size equal to that of the missing diamond.

To unwrap that masking tape without using one's teeth was a challenge of challenges. The unwrapping was accomplished with calm reserve... WOW!... expected of a professional investigator who is about to jump for joy at reaching such a monumental success. The diamond, by the way, was not in its setting. The setting was not returned with the diamond.

After the manager checked the gem and verified it to be a diamond of the size of the missing one, Carl asked me if he could get the reward pertaining to the recovery of the diamond. I suggested he contact me in a couple of days to see if the reward was still available.

This was the last day of Carl's employment at that company.

Carl (seventh interaction)

As you might guess, Carl did call to ask me if the reward was still offered. I suggested he contact the company about it. Was he stupid or did he think I was stupid? You might ask if Carl is still working among us! Yes! Many, like him, are! Do I think he has learned a lesson from all of this and mended his ways? No! I think he's smarter now and may not get caught the next time. For him, I deduce, there will be many next times.

Conclusion

The case review, above, regarding the diamond ring theft is intended to depict how an investigator might apply some of the tactics suggested in this writing. While interrogations occasionally take place, few, if any, investigations are conducted without interviews. No doubt, there is much left to be said about the art and science of interviewing and interrogating.

It is vital to appreciate your talents, accomplishments, experience, and whatever else makes you a unique human being as you envision your worthwhile place the future. Be committed to a specific purpose in life as you contribute to those around you. Service to your fellow man is essential as you turn your dreams into reality. Belief in yourself is the starting point of success.

Strategies suggested in this presentation can work for you too.

Soli Deo Gloria

REFERENCES

Books

1 Adorno, T. W., Frenkel-Brunswik, Else, Levinson, Daniel F., and Nevitt, R.: *The Authoritarian Personality.* New York, Sanford, Harper & Brothers, 1950.

2 *American Psychioric Association: Diagnostic and Statistical Manual of Mental Disorders,* 3rd ed. Washington D.C., APA, 1980, 366.

3. Aubry, Arthur S., Jr., and Caputo, Rudolph R.: *Criminal Interrogation.* Springfield, Charles C Thomas, 1980.

4 Banaka, William H.: *Training in Depth Interviewing.* New York, Harper & Row, 1971, 100.

5. Benjamin Alfred: *The Helping Interview.* Boston, Houghton-Mifflin, 1974.

6 Bennis, W. G., Berlew, D. E., Schein, E. H. and Steel, F. I. (Eds.): *Interpersonal Dynamics, Essays and Readings on Human Interaction,* 3rd ed. Homewood, Dorsey Press, 1973.

7 Berg, Irwin A., and Bass, Bernard M. (Eds.): *Conformity and Deviation.* New York, Harper & Brothers, 1961.

8 Berne, Eric: *Games People Play.* New York, Grove, 1974.

9 Berne, Eric, M.D.: *Intuition and Ego States.* San Francisco, TA Press, 1977.

10 Binder, D. A., and Price, S. C.: *Legal Interviewing and Counseling.* St. Paul, West, 1977.

11 Birdwhistell, R. L.: *Kinesics and Context: Essays on Body Communication.* Philadelphia, University of Pennsylvania Press, 1970.

12 Boorstin, Daniel: *The Image.* New York, Atheneum, 1972, 9–12.

13 Bowers, David A.: *Systems of Organization.* Ann Arbor, University of Michigan Press, 1976.

14 Brady, John: *The Craft of Interviewing.* New York, Vantage Books, 1977, 37.

15 Bynum, W. F., Browne, E. J., and Porter, Roy: *Dictionary of The History of Science.* Princeton, Princeton University Press.

16 Cameron, Norman, and Margaret, Ann: *Behavior Pathology.* Boston, Riverside Press, 1951, 206–208.

17 Cavanagh, Michael E.: *How to Handle Your Anger,* 4th ed. U.S. Dept. of Labor, Employment and Training Administration, 1979.

18 Cleckley, Hervey M.: *The Mask of Sanity: An Attempt to Clarify Some Issues About The So-called Sociopathic Personality,* 5th ed. St. Louis, Mosby, 1976.

19 Coleman, James C.: *Abnormal Psychology and Modern Life,* 5th ed. Glenview, Scott, Foresman, 1976, 507–509, 750.

20 Davis, Flora: *Inside Intuition.* New York, New American Library, Times Mirror, 1975.

21 Dello, E. L.: *Methods of Science.* New York, Universe Books, 1970, 13–26.

22 Dewey, John: *Human Nature and Conduct.* New York, Modern Library, 1957.

23 Dexter, Lewis Anthony: *Elite and Specialized Interviewing.* Evanston, Northwestern University Press, 1970.

24 Dougherty, George S.: *The Criminal as a Human Being.* New York, Appleton, 1924.

25 Downs, Cal W., Smeyak, G. Paul, and Martin, Ernest: *Professional Interviewing.* New York, Harper & Row, 1980.

26 Drake, John D.: *Interviewing for Managers — Sizing Up People.* New York, American Management Association, 1972.

27 Egler, Frank E.: *The Way of Science.* New York, Hafner, 1970.

28 Freeman, H., and Weihofen, H.: *Clinical Law Timing-Interviewing and Counseling.* St. Paul, West, 1972.

29 Garrett, Annette: *Interviewing — Its Principles and Methods.* New York, Family Service Association of America, 1972.

30 Gorden, Raymond L.: *Interviewing Strategy, Techniques, and Tactics.* Homewood, Dorsey Press, 1969, 84, 188.

31 Gunn, Battiscombe: *The Instruction of PTAH-HOTEP and The Instruction of KE'GEMNI — The Oldest Books in the World.* W. London, John Murray, 1918, 49.

32 Hall, E. T.: *The Hidden Dimension.* New York, Doubleday, 1966.

33 Harre, Ron, and Lamb, Roger (Eds.): *The Encyclopedic Dictionary of Psychology.* Cambridge, MIT Press, 1983.

34 Inbau, Fred; Reid, John; and Buckley, Joseph: *Criminal Interrogation and confessions,* 3rd Ed. Baltimore, Williams & Wilkins, 1986.

35 Kahn, Robert L., and Cannell, Charles F.: *The Dynamics of Interviewing: Theory, Technique, and Cases.* New York, Wiley, 1957.

36 Keefe, William F.: *Listen Management.* New York, McGraw-Hill, 1971, 24.

37 Kleinmuntz, Benjamin: *Essentials of Abnormal Psychology.* New York, Harper & Row, 1974.

38 Knapp, Mark: *Non-Verbal Communication.* New York, Holt, Rinehart and Winston. 1972.

39 Kubler-Ross, Elizabeth: *On Death and Dying.* New York, MacMillan, 1969.

40 Levere, Trevor H.: Science. *Collier's Encyclopedia.* New York, MacMillan Educational Company, Volume 20, pp. 498A–499.

41 *The Living Bible* — paraphrased. Tyndale House Publishers, 23rd Printing, 1973, p. 283.

42 *The Random House Dictionary of English Language,* Random House, New York, 1966.

43 Lopez, Felix: *Personnel Interviewing.* New York, McGraw-Hill, 1975.

44 Mallory, James D., Jr.: *The Kink and I.* Wheaton, Victor, 1977.

45 Maltz, Maxwell: *Psycho-cybernetics.* Englewood Cliffs, Prentice-Hall, 1960.

46 Maslow, Abraham H.: *Motivation and Personality.* New York, Harper, 1954, 80–106.

47 McClelland, David: *Motivational Management.* Boston, The Forum Corporation of North America, 1976.

48 McCormick, Charles T.: *Evidence, Hornbook Series.* St. Paul, West, 1954.

49 McGregor, Douglas: *The Human Side of Enterprise.* New York, McGraw-Hill, 1960.

50 Menninger, William C.: *What Makes an Effective Man, Personnel Series No. 152.* New York, American Management Association, 1953, 26.

51 Minnick, Wayne C.: *The Art of Persuasion.* Boston, Houghton Mifflin Company, 1985.

52 Nierenberg, Gerard I.: *The Art of Negotiating.* New York, Cornerstone Library, 1968.

53 Nirenberg, Jesse S.: *Getting Through to People.* Englewood Cliffs, Prentice-Hall, 1963.

54 OSS Assessment Staff: *Assessment of Men, Selection of Personnel for the Office of Strategic Services.* New York, Rinehart, 1948.

55 Quinn, L., and Zunin, N.: *Contact: The First Four Minutes.* Los Angeles, Nash, 1972, 8–14.

56 Reusch, J. et al: *Non-Verbal Communication.* Berkeley, University of California Press, 1954, 4.

57 Rogers, Carl R.: *Counseling and Psychotherapy.* Boston, Houghton Mifflin, 1942, 131–151.

58 Royal, Robert F., and Schutt, Steven R.: *The Gentle Art of Interviewing and Interrogation.* Englewood Cliffs, Prentice Hall, 1976.

59 Schultz, William C.: *The Interpersonal Underworld.* Palo Alto, Science and Behavior Books, 1966.

60 Scientific methods. *McGraw-Hill Encyclopedia of Science & Technology,* 5th ed. McGraw-Hill, pp. 110–113.

61 Selye, Hans: *Stress Without Distress.* New York, American Library, 1975.

62 Shaw, George Bernard: Pygmalion, a play, 1912.

63 Sherwood, Hugh: *The Journalistic Interview.* New York, Harper & Row, 1972, 19.

64 Simons, Hebert W.: *Persuasion.* Reading, Addison-Wesley, 1976, 21.

65 Sipe, H. Craig: Science. *The World Book Encyclopedia.* Volume 17, World Book, pp. 162–172.

66 Stewart, Charles J., and Cash, William B.: *Interviewing.* Dubuque, William C. Brown, 1978.

67 Stewart, Charles J., and Cash, William B.: *Interviewing: Principles and Practices.* Dubuque, William C. Brown, 1974.

68 Totter, Alvin: *Future Shock.* New York, Random House, 1970, 330–331.

69 Vertical File Information, "The Sciences," Literature Department, Minneapolis Public Library, Minneapolis, Minnesota.

70 *Webster's New World Dictionary of the American Language.* Cleveland and New York, World, College Edition.

71 Wicks, Robert J., and Josephs, Ernest H., Jr.: *Techniques in Interviewing for Law Enforcement and Corrections Personnel.* Springfield, Charles C Thomas, 1972.

72 Woody, Robert H., and Woody, Jane D. (Eds.): *Clinical Assessment in Counseling and Psychotherapy.* New York, Appleton, Century, Crofts, 1972.

73 *The World Book Encyclopedia,* Field Enterprises Educational Corp., 1972, Vol. 15, p. 350.

74 Zuckerman, Harriet: *Scientific Elite.* London, The Free Press, Collier MacMillan, 1977, 211–212.

Articles and Periodicals

75 Eden, D., and Kinnar, J.: Modeling Galatea: Boosting Self-Efficacy to Increase Volunteering. *Journal of Applied Psychology, 76,* No. 6, 770–780, 1991.
76 Fischer, Frank E.: A new look at management communications. *Personnel, 31:*495, 1955.
77 Freeman, G. L., et al: The Stress Interview. *Journal of Abnormal and Social Psychology, 37.* 427, 1942.
78 Gist, M. E.: Self-Efficacy: Implications for Organizational Behavior and Human Resource Management. *Academy of Management Review, 12.* No. 3. 472–485, 1987.
79 Interviewing and counseling. *U.S. Dept. of Health, Education and Welfare, Social Security Administration,* 20, 1964.
80 Phillips, D. L., and Clancy, K.: Modeling effects in survey research. *Public opinion Quarterly,* Summer: 246, 1972.

Films, Tapes and Speeches

81 *Communication: The Nonverbal Agenda.* New York, McGraw-Hill Films, 1975.
82 *Empathy in Police Work.* A Film. L. Craig Parker, Jr., Producer, Madison, Connecticut, 1972.
83 Harris, Thomas A., M.D.: Instruction Tape. *I'm Okay — You're Okay: A Practical Guide to Transactional Analysis.* Distributed by Success Motivation Institute, Inc., New York with special arrangement with R. M. Karen, and Harper & Row, 1973.
84 *I Understand, You Understand.* A Film. Des Moines, Creative Media, 1975.
85 Kellihan, S.J.: "Searching for the Meaning of the Truth and the Ethic of Its Use," Speech presented at the Annual Seminar of the American Polygraph Association, 1982.
86 *Nonverbal Communication.* A Film. New York, Harper & Row, 1976
87 *Officer Stress Awareness.* A Film. New York, Harper & Row, 1976.
88 *Productivity and The Self-Fulfilling Prophecy: The Pygmalion Effect.* New York, McGraw-Hill Films, 1975.
89 *Selling to Tough Customers.* Del Mar, McGraw-Hill Films, 1981.
90 *The Effective Uses of Power and Authority.* New York, McGraw-Hill Films, 1980.
91 *The Empowerment Series.* A Tape. CRM Films, Carlsbad, CA, 1992.

ABOUT THE AUTHOR
Charles L. Yeschke

5200 West 73rd Street

Minneapolis, Minnesota 55439

Telephone 612-831-2606
United States Marine Corps 1955–1958
Bachelor of Science Law Enforcement/Police Administration

Michigan State University 1962
Staff Polygraphist and Instructor,

John E. Reid and Associates, Chicago, Illinois 1962–1968
Polygraphist and Security Officer, Central Intelligence Agency 1966–1968
Special Agent, Federal Bureau of Investigation 1968–1978
Licensed Private Investigator, State of Minnesota since 1978
Licensed Polygraphist, States of Illinois, Iowa, Nebraska and North Dakota
Law Enforcement Instructor: States of North Dakota, Minnesota and Iowa
Member, Membership Chairman, Central Minnesota Chapter,

American Society for Industrial Security
Instructor, Open U, Inc., University Center, Minneapolis, Minnesota
Member, Minnesota Chapter,

Society of Former Special Agents of the Federal Bureau of Investigation, Inc.
Applied Scientist
Instructor, Minneapolis Community College
Charter Member, American Polygraph Association

INDEX

interviewee need, 26
interviewee needs, deeper understanding of, 149
interviewee nervousness, 99
interviewee opposition, 138
interviewee personality traits, 100
interviewee power, 45
interviewee powers of observation, 83
interviewee psychological set, 114
interviewee rejection, 137
interviewee reluctance, 49, 98, 110, 135
interviewee replies regarding polygraph examination, 97
interviewee resentment, 49
interviewee response, 55
interviewee response or reaction, 107
interviewee response patterns of possible deception, 92
interviewee responses, 63
interviewee responses, pattern of, 94
interviewee revenge and retaliation, 137
interviewee secrets, 49
interviewee self-esteem, 51, 78
interviewee signals, 107
interviewee signals of disapproval, 133
interviewee silence, 125, 126
interviewee social status, 133
interviewee tension, 17
interviewee tensions, 126
interviewee thinking, 142
interviewee to comply, 105
interviewee type, 75
interviewee uneasiness, 93
interviewee uniqueness, 77
interviewee veracity, 104
interviewee veracity, assessment of, 94
interviewee veracity, behavior signals regarding, 104
interviewee veracity, conclusion regarding, 92
interviewee who needs consoling, comforting, 73
interviewee words, supplements or belies, tension, 152
interviewee's calm, anticipatory look, 126
interviewee's chair, 120
interviewee's defense mechanisms, 144
interviewee's focus, 127
interviewee's formula, 78

interviewee's lot in life, 39
interviewee's objections, 142
interviewee's personality, 72
interviewee's personality, dynamics of, 160
interviewee's response, 213
interviewee's responses, 92
interviewee's sensitive feeling, 212
interviewee's thinking and memory, 143
interviewee's thoughts, 56
interviewee's truthful cooperation, 81
interviewee's veracity, 92, 93
interviewee, evaluation and assessment of, observation, 92
interviewee-projected thoughts, 144
interviewees are keenly aware, 40
interviewees as rational beings, 123
interviewees avoid appearing dumb, foolish, or uninformed, 140
interviewees leak the truth, 29
interviewees may seek assurance, 45
interviewees need to feel accepted, 21
interviewees, 8, 9, 12, 15, 17, 18, 19, 20, 21, 22, 25, 32, 40, 41, 42, 47, 81, 192
interviewees are invited to present views, 86
interviewees as human beings, 56, 154
interviewees become defensive, 19
interviewees can be touched, 121
interviewees desire to preserve reputation, 33
interviewees elaborate more freely, 141
interviewees fear, 46
interviewees in a defensive stance, 46
interviewees intentionally rebel, 138
interviewees lie, 41
interviewees may fabricate, 47
interviewees often rebel, 49
interviewees react to your mood, 19
interviewees save face, 144
interviewees sense, 160
interviewees sense if you are okay, 85
interviewees sense losing control, 33
interviewees sense rejection, 48
interviewees signal, 163
interviewees talk spontaneously, 165
interviewees tension, 47
interviewees think, 138, 167
interviewees to comply, 140
interviewees to wiggle and squirm, 140
interviewees try to rationalize, 33

Schultz, William C., 25, 224
Schutt, Steven R., 224
science, 5, 6, 7, 8, 23, 36, 112
scientific, 183
scientific authority, 27
scientific life, fact of, 7
scientific method, 6, 7
scientific process, 189
scientific research, 27
seasoned interviewers, 72
seating, 193
seating, allow for privacy and comfort in the, 84
secrecy, 135
secret, 38
secret, no mortal can keep a, Freud wrote, 118
secrets, 119
secrets, innermost hidden, 166
secure feeling, 91
security, 47
security, interviewee need for, 127
Sedgowick, Judge, 181
seductive action, 30
selection of effective interviewer, 34
selective inattention, 18
self, 20, 26, 27, 41, 50, 131, 203
self expressed through face, 26
self has subjective characteristics, 27
self, hidden, expression of, 144
self, revealing hidden data about, 140
self-abasing, 36
self-affirmation, 44
self-alienation is a sickness, 20
self-alienation, 20
self-appraisal, 142, 149
self-appraisal questions, 71
self-assertion, 44
self-assessment, 47
self-assurance, 65
self-assured, 28
self-awareness, 151
self-belief, 37, 38, 68, 87, 114, 133, 160
self-beliefs predict motivation, 64
self-blame, 20
self-centered, 131
self-centeredness, 49
self-concept, 33, 63

self-confidence in one's skills, self-efficacy, 66
self-confidence, 65, 77, 118, 125, 132
self-conscious, 107
self-control, 15, 47, 77, 82
self-control faults, 138
self-control, interviewer, 122
self-defeating, 4, 12, 41, 45, 50, 54, 89, 121, 128, 144, 165
self-defeating move, 124
self-defeating to push them into corner, 148
self-defense, 110
self-denial, 47
self-destruction, impulse of, 49
self-destructive, 16
self-determination, 48
self-discipline, 162
self-disclosure avoidance, 17
self-disclosure, 15, 27, 51, 139, 143
self-educated, 75
self-efficacy, 64, 65, 66, 138
self-enhancing, 47
self-esteem, 14, 20, 21, 24, 32, 33, 37, 38, 42, 44, 47, 51, 54, 65, 68, 69, 77, 115, 136, 138, 158, 160, 161
self-evaluation, 33
self-exam, 176
self-expectation, 65, 66
self-expression, 55
self-forgiveness, 21
self-fulfilling prophecy, 23, 38, 58, 59, 61, 63, 65, 68, 70, 77, 143
self-fulfillment, 55
self-image, 14, 15, 25, 32, 37, 49, 50, 69, 77, 133, 158
self-imposed limitations, 36
self-improvement, 12
self-incrimination, 8
self-instructed, 3
self-interest, 33, 142
self-interpreted, 153
self-made emotional shelter, 31
self-monitoring, 65
self-motivated, 130
self-motivation, 36, 136
self-perceived inefficacy, 65
self-preoccupation, 21
self-propelling effect, 54
self-realization, 55, 116

CHARLES C THOMAS • PUBLISHER